life is a verb

is a verb

Patti Digh

37 DAYS TO WAKE UP, BE MINDFUL, AND LIVE INTENTIONALLY

skirt!

Guilford, Connecticut
An imprint of The Globe Pequot Press

skirt!®

skirt!® is an attitude . . . spirited, independent, outspoken, serious, playful and irreverent, sometimes controversial, always passionate.

Due to limitations of space, additional text and art credits appear on pp. 217–20 and constitute an extension of this page.

Design by Diana Nuhn
Fonts used: Filosofia, Coquette, Corporate S, and Elpiedra
Spot art © Shutterstock

Library of Congress Cataloging-in-Publication Data
Digh, Patti.
  Life is a verb : 37 days to wake up, be mindful, and live
intentionally / Patti Digh.
    p. cm.
  Includes bibliographical references.
  ISBN 978-1-59921-295-1
  1. Self-help techniques. 2. Life. I. Title.
  BF632.D54 2009
  158.1—dc22

2008012936

Printed in China

10 9 8 7 6 5 4 3 2 1

As the poet Rainer Maria Rilke inscribed in
a book he wrote:

*My family, I once gave this book into your hands, and
you cared for it as no one had yet done. So I have grown
accustomed to think that it belongs to you. Suffer me,
therefore, not only in your own book, but in all the books
of this edition to write your names; to write:*

This book belongs to
My brilliant husband, John Ptak,
and our wise and funny daughters,
Emma and Tess Ptak

You are the ones with whom I want to spend my
thirty-seven days, and for whom these words
were written in the first place.
My loves. I keep you in my heart.

Contents

Prologue
WHY 37 DAYS?

Time only seems to matter when it's running out. —**Peter Strup**

At some point in your life, you'll only have thirty-seven days to live. Maybe that day is today. Maybe not.

Such a day arrived on October 24, 2003, for a 6-foot, 5-inch-tall man with a southern accent, a golfer's tan, five World War II Bronze Stars, and a forest-green Lincoln Town Car. On that beautiful autumn day, he was diagnosed with lung cancer. He died just thirty-seven days later.

That man was my stepfather, Boyce. I helped him live—and die—in those brief days between diagnosis and death, a process that prompted me to ask, What would I be doing today if I only had thirty-seven days to live?

My mother and I cared for him at home, since he wanted to die there. Never having been around someone dying, I didn't know what to do. When my father died more than two decades before, I was just twenty and in the intensive care waiting room, not beside him. No one asked if I wanted to be with him as he died; they just asked if I wanted to see him dead after it was all over. It was the beginning of a long realization of how intensively we avoid death in this culture.

Helping Boyce die was at once profound and awkward, as if visiting a place I ought not to be, hearing things I ought not hear, dispensing morphine as if I knew how. He very soon lost the ability to speak, which made it both easier and harder for me. I was scared and anxious all the time, never knowing what was coming next. There was no manual I could find, no prescription for what he was feeling and doing, for how his insides were eating him up. I couldn't tell, and he couldn't tell me, either.

Everything I could think to talk to him about was so petty it was painful. Would he like to watch a movie? I'd pantomime the question—then think, What, and chance Hugh Grant being the last thing he sees on earth? The newspaper failed, too, its contents hardly relevant, a mere deflection. But what *was* appropriate in this important, liminal space—the gap between life and death?

At night I could hear the oxygen machine's pistons moving in and out, and I waited for it to stop. Finally it did, after his feet started turning blue and that blueness marched all the way up him, thirty-seven days after the awful diagnosis.

The time frame of thirty-seven days made an impression on me. We often live as if we have all the time in the world, but the definite-ness of thirty-seven days was striking. So short a time, as if all the regrets and joys of a life would barely have time to register before it was up.

If I had thirty-seven days left, would I spend my time cleaning the attic, purging computer files, or attending committee meetings? Would I have passed on my stories to my children and friends, or would I spend those days regretting not having time to do so? Am I living fully now, or am I waiting until after the kids leave for college or my annuity matures or the Colts move back to Baltimore? It will be too late then.

I tried to reconcile the fact that this fearful death was happening with the understanding that I needed to make something good out of it. What emerged was a commitment to ask myself this question every morning: **What would I be doing today if I only had thirty-seven days to live?**

Some days it's a hard question.

Ten years before, one of my favorite college professors died when he was only forty-six. A brilliant physicist, Sheridan Simon was a man with considerable charm and humor; we had stayed in touch since my graduation more than a decade earlier. Sheridan's doctors told him he had a year to live. "Do whatever you want in that year," they said. And so he did.

His friend and fellow professor Jonathan Malino eulogized Sheridan at his death: "He continued to live the very life he had been leading before his illness. This was his life. His account of his days, his heart of wisdom, lay in the very passions and commitments which he embodied daily. Day by day, this determination not to run away from his life took more and more courage. The pain increased. The exhaustion mounted. And yet, just three nights before his death, Sheridan was still in the classroom, still reaching out to others, still using every bit of his energy to make the lives of others better."

I got a last letter from Sheridan just eight days before he died; he closed it with these words: "Be in touch, OK? Love, Sheridan."

Journalist Marjorie Williams died of liver cancer three days after turning forty-seven. As an "act of mourning," her husband compiled her final essays in a book titled *The Woman at the Washington Zoo:* "Having found myself faced with that old bull-session question (What would you do if you found out you had a year to live?), I learned that a woman with children has the privilege or duty of bypassing the existential. What you do, if you have little kids, is lead as normal a life as possible, only with more pancakes."

Like Sheridan Simon and Marjorie Williams, my answer to that bull-session question wasn't about uprooting my family to take a world tour. It wasn't about climbing Mount Everest or learning Urdu once and for all or seeking enlightenment in a faraway land. **Instead it was about living each individual, glorious day with more intention.** It was simply about saying yes, being generous, speaking up, loving more, trusting myself, and slowing down. It was about more fully inhabiting the life I have, not creating a new one. It was about leading my everyday life with a lot more (chocolate chip) pancakes.

One thing did become clear as I pondered my last thirty-seven days: I needed to leave some greater part of myself behind for my two young daughters. I knew if today were day one of my last thirty-seven days, I would write like hell and leave as much of myself behind for Emma and Tess as I could. I would let them know and see me as a real person, not just a mother. I'd leave with them for safekeeping my thoughts and memories, fears and dreams, the histories of what I am and who my people are.

I would explore what living really means and leave them with a notebook of challenges, an instruction manual to guide them as they live their lives without me. Not where to get their hair cut or how to steam artichokes or combat static cling or change a tire or book the cheapest airfare, but the deeper things—how to know what to care about, how to treat others around them (and themselves), what to question, how to love, what to stand up for, and why they should tell stories and listen to the stories of others. This book is that guidebook.

Writing my stories for them, teaching my daughters to live fully—and learning how to live fully myself in the process—that's what I'd do with my thirty-seven days.

I'm beginning here.

[
Your time is limited, so don't waste it living someone else's life.
—Steve Jobs
]

Introduction

Always Carry a Pencil; or, How to Read This Book

Reading without reflecting is like eating without digestion.—Edmund Burke

When writer Vladimir Nabokov was asked, "Who is your ideal reader?" he said, "My ideal reader is someone who reads with a dictionary and a pencil." In a similar way, poet Billy Collins suggests our pencil acts as a kind of seismograph to register the mental tremors we're feeling as we read. "Such jottings are a sign of our presence, and the book we hold in our hands becomes not just *The Heart of Darkness,* but *my* reading of *The Heart of Darkness*—the silent communication and conversation that took place between me and Joseph Conrad," Collins said in a recent commencement address.

Marginalia is a way of carrying on a larger, broader conversation. It's a physical record of our encounter with a text, scrawled or jotted in margins and on endpapers and flyleaves. And so, too, with this book. I hope you will find yourself in the margins, between and beneath the words and perhaps if I've done my job, in them.

One of Darwin's most famous notations was handwritten in the margins where a rudimentary drawing of his evolutionary tree from 1870 rests under two simple words: "I think." And history's most famous marginal note is probably Fermat's last theorem: In 1637 this seventeenth-century mathematician wrote in his copy of Diophantus's *Arithmetica,* "I have a truly marvelous proof of this proposition which this margin is too narrow to contain." Pity the narrow margin: It took mathematicians 357 years to find that proof.

Instead of a *book,* what if we're actually writing (or not writing) in the margins of our *lives*? **What if our lives are books?** What is the sign of our presence? Are we pressing into the margins our interpretations and questions? Are we circling offending verbs and drawing furious arrows to the margin where we scrawl "irony," "frustration," "voiceless," "unfair!" Or do we simply turn the pages, passively receiving what's given, furiously disagreeing but remaining silent about it?

I read Tennyson's *In Memoriam* while at Guilford College, shortly after my father's death in 1980. Notes upon notes live in those margins, some embarrassing, some naive, some illustrative of my own state of mind, the river of sorrow I was then on: "love/grief are one," "cycle moves on," "he's gone," and, of course, like every good undergrad, "man vs. nature." All in a goofy, loopy, messy hand, a record of a young woman reading her *own* life, too, missing her *own* Hallam. At "He is not here; but far away / The noise of life begins again," I've penned in the margin: "A vanish'd life, it will forever rain . . . me too."

Taking pen or pencil to our books isn't mutilation, it is conversation. As British author Hester Thrale Piozzi put it in 1790, "I have a Trick of writing in the Margins of my Books, it is not a good Trick, but one longs to say something." *One longs to say something.*

I've come to realize that this book is my marginalia, the seismograph of my life, my longing to say something, to catch a ride into the future on a vessel more lasting than myself. Perhaps you, too, long to say something. These wide margins are here just for that reason.

The Design of This Book

I can't read those small paperbacks in airport shops—the thick, stubby ones that buckle when you open them, the texture pebbly, the typography unremarkable and running straight to the edge of the page, clamoring into tiny margins hardly big enough to justify the name. I need a page that doesn't catch my fingers, typefaces that draw me to them, and blank space—a generosity of breathing room, a place to reflect and interact and just "be"—when I'm reading a book. We've tried to create that experience in these pages, for you.

My hope is that you will engage with this book as you engage with life. When I meet you in Des Moines or Ojai or Copenhagen or Stellenbosch, my greatest wish is that you'll show me your dog-eared copy, pages turned down, furious scribblings in the margins to show agreement, disagreement, engagement, those mental tremors you're feeling. Inhabit this book. Put something of yourself into the blank spaces by way of understanding.

Six Practices for Intentional Living

As I wrote these stories for my daughters, patterns and through-lines started appearing, one after another. Finally I stepped back to see the whole: Six practices for living more intentionally emerged from my three-year exploration. This "guidebook for living" outlines those six practices—intensity, inclusion, integrity, intimacy, intuition, and intention—challenging us to live them now, before it's too late.

You'll find more detail about those practices in the coming chapters; first, let me explain the structure of the book. Each practice is illustrated by six stories because, as chapter 1 reveals, we make sense of our lives through story. Writer Flannery O'Connor said, "A story is a way to say something that can't be said any other way, and it takes every word in the story to say what the meaning is. You tell a story because a statement would be inadequate."

From Story to Challenge

Each story is followed by two challenges: One that can be done immediately (Action) and one to do over time (Movement). Both are described below.

Ernest Hemingway warned: "Never confuse action with movement." The more immediate Action Challenges may start the process of change, but without an ongoing practice they can't create enough momentum for real movement—that only happens *over time.* As you approach the Movement Challenges, think of movement as in a watch or clock—a mechanism that produces or transmits action—those tick-tocks that make up our thirty-seven days, a change over time.

A note about altering the challenges: The challenges I've suggested are just that—suggestions. Each reader will have a different take on what the story means to them and, therefore, a different way of incorporating that meaning into their life. Also, to my friends who have disabilities: You are in a far more informed position to know what changes to these challenges are needed for you to participate fully. My hope is that each challenge is doable in some form—using a voice recorder instead of typing, for example—and I would welcome hearing ways in which you've adapted and changed the challenges to fit your needs, whether because of a disability, or simply because of a preference.

✍ *Action Challenges—Do It Now*

These are designed as quick, immediate reinforcements of the story preceding them. Many, but not all, of the Action Challenges are ten-minute writing exercises for which you'll need a few pieces of simple equipment: A notebook, a pen you enjoy holding (or a computer with the screen turned off—I'll explain why in a moment), and a timer with a bell. I recommend buying an eighty-nine-cent notebook at the Piggly Wiggly for these exercises, not a twenty-dollar embossed and gold-edged one—you'll just worry about messing that one up and feel pressured to fill it only with Great Thoughts. No, go for the eighty-nine-cent version in which you can be achingly boring and dull and human. You'll also want something like an inexpensive egg timer with a bell so you don't have to interrupt your flow of thought by looking at a watch or clock. And I can't imagine living life without a big wad of 3-by-5-inch index cards for capturing ideas, so pick up a pack of those, too.

What is a focused free-write?

Each writing prompt is for a "focused free-write" session. Focused free-writes involve writing quickly off the top of your head with no judgment. They tap into a deeper well than the place we usually stay—that nice and tidy place where we punctuate correctly, always abide by grammar rules, and spell *accommodation* with the proper numbers of *m*'s. None of that matters in a focused free-write and, in fact, is a deflection rather than a help. **Stop thinking and write.** Time your free-writing session. A time limit pushes your right brain to produce. If you are really engaged, you can always ignore your timer, but strive for a minimum of a ten-minute session.

TO PRACTICE MEANS TO PERFORM, IN THE FACE OF ALL OBSTACLES, SOME ACT OF VISION, OF FAITH, OF DESIRE. PRACTICE IS A MEANS OF INVITING THE PERFECTION DESIRED.

—Martha Graham

Write in longhand (preferred) or on the computer *with the screen turned off* if you cannot write in longhand (if neither is possible, use a recorder to capture your ideas). Don't correct grammar or punctuation, and don't lift your pen from the page. If you're using a computer, turning the screen off keeps you from stumbling over your mistakes, since you can't see them. Just set a timer for the time specified in the Action Challenge and write whatever comes to mind. If you run out of things to say, just write "stuck" repeatedly until words come back to you. Keep your pen (or fingers on a keyboard) moving. You don't need to speed-write and be physically tense; just don't stop at all. Never stop, make judgments, or correct your writing. The movement of the pen will help. This doesn't need to make sense or be seen by anyone else. At the end of the designated time, read what you have written. Then circle a "hot spot"—a word or phrase that stands out for you. Set the timer again and write about that hot spot for three more minutes. This will take you into a deeper dive. When the timer rings, put your notebook aside for the next writing challenge.

Most, but not all, of the Action Challenges are writing exercises. Some require observation, engagement with others, creating something, or reflection of a different kind. They will be described in detail at the close of each story. Each should only take around ten minutes to complete.

 We create stories and stories create us. It is a rondo.
—Chinua Achebe

⬡ *Movement Challenges—Do It for 37 Days*

At a recent conference, those of us gathered were asked to participate in a movement exercise. "Sit on the ground," we were told. "Now change your position." We moved into odd, awkward, funny positions, trying to outdo the next person. "Now consider whether this position is sustainable and for how long," the speaker said. We laughed, most of us realizing we had contorted into shapes and positions that looked great, but couldn't be sustained. So, too, it is with intentional living. This book isn't about contortions, or awkward, funny positions, or shape-shifting that doesn't feel like you. It isn't about competing with others. It's about sustainable attentiveness.

To live deeper, more meaningful lives, we have to practice. The Movement Challenges are designed to be things you can dip into, come back to later, try out, practice over time.

More specifically, they are things to practice over thirty-seven days. You might choose the one provided, or create one of your own after reading and reflecting on the story. The key is practice.

Doing these challenges all at once would be overwhelming. Choose one or two at a time to focus on, practice them for thirty-seven days, and then dip back into the book for more challenges as you complete the first ones.

FURIOUS ACTIVITY IS NO SUBSTITUTE FOR UNDERSTANDING.—H.H. Williams

just
help
them
get
started

Ruth M. Davis

37 days

PART ONE
Inhabit Your Story

We inhabit ourselves without valuing ourselves,

unable to see that here, now,

this very moment is sacred;

but once it's gone—

its value is incontestable.

—*Joyce Carol Oates*

The first few times
Being lost was frightening
Stark, pregnant
With the drama of change
Then, I didn't know
That everywhere is nowhere
Like the feeling when an ocean wave
Boils you in the sand
But as time goes by
Each occurrence of lostness is quieter
Falling from notice
Like the sound of trains
When you live near the tracks
Until one day
When a friend asks
"How often do you get lost?"
And I strain to recall a single instance
It was then that I realized
Being lost only has meaning
When contrasted with
Knowing where you are
A presumption that slipped out of my life
As quietly as smoke up a chimney
For now I live in a less anchored place
Where being lost is irrelevant
For now, only when there is a need
Do I discover where I am
No alarm, no fear
Just an unconscious check-in
Like glancing in the rear-view mirror.

—David Hollies, "Lost and Found"

CHAPTER ONE
Write to Remember

Every man's memory is his private literature. —**Aldous Huxley**

"Lost and Found," the poem opening this chapter, was written by a man who began losing his grip on memory when he was fifty years old. The author, David Hollies, prefaced the poem with this note: "I must have written this sometime last year. I found it on my desk. Another in a series of writings about my journey with dementia."

I must have written this sometime last year. I found it on my desk. A world of information in fourteen words. As if Mr. Hollies is straddling a chasm between knowing and not knowing, between recognizing and being surprised, between being himself and watching himself. "Being lost," as he wrote, "only has meaning when contrasted with knowing where you are."

"For the last seven years," Mr. Hollies recently e-mailed, "I've been rediscovering who I am again and again, as an unexplained neurological disorder unravels most of the fabric of a life once so rich in doings and connections that I can hardly even imagine it now."

In a family prone to Alzheimer's, I have watched this process of unraveling up close. It is one of the reasons I feel the urgency of writing to remember. We all need mechanisms for storying our lives in order to remember them, learn from them, and leave them behind for others.

My Sissy was a proud woman, always immaculately dressed, coiffed, and with a beautiful coral ring perched high in a golden filigree throne on her right hand. She seemed like royalty to me. My mother's sister, older than Mama by seventeen years, she raised my mother as her own after their mother died too young.

A furniture store owner's wife, Sissy attended to every detail of showroom beauty with the sensibility of a small-town decorator with a subscription to *House Beautiful:* plastic rings of fruit engulfing large candles under glass, and light-imbued pastoral landscapes the exact length of sofas. Henredon and Drexel furniture companies awarded them both a dozen Christian Tours around the world, so Sissy had adventures from which I was the awestruck recipient of treasures like grass skirts and plastic leis, Chinese dolls with intricately embroidered silk dresses, exotic carvings of wild animals—my first introduction to the world outside.

As she slid into Alzheimer's, Sissy tried fearfully to cling to her regal self. It was that middle state that fascinated, frightened, and horrified me—that knowing while sliding. A few years before she fell irretrievably into herself, I visited. Walking into her small kitchen, I was immobilized by dozens of calendars—on the door to the basement, the refrigerator, the painted cabinets above the sink. Every available surface was covered with a calendar—from large pictorial versions to those little tear-off paper ones that insurance agents give away.

On each was a tumbled nest of dark black lines across the squares of days passed, a furious marking, a heavy series of *X*'s across the blocks, the unique and horrible signature of a woman desperately trying to keep track of where she was in time, knowing that she didn't know and couldn't remember, creating strategies for tracking, for knowing, for pretending to know, for convincing herself and others that she did know, for saving face. But she didn't know. As soon as she turned away from each calendar, the day fell from her mind, a problem she solved by ensuring that in every direction her head could turn, there she would find solace, the date, that very one. The person who could help best was gone. When his Alzheimer's turned his generous sweetness mean, her husband and my PaPa had been taken away to play with an Elmo doll at Autumn Care Rest Home.

IN THE DEGREE THAT WE REMEMBER AND RETELL OUR STORIES AND CREATE NEW ONES WE BECOME THE AUTHORS, THE AUTHORITIES, OF OUR OWN LIVES.

—Sam Keen

We took the *Morganton News Herald* to her daily, believing contact with the outside world would help in some way. Puzzled at the untouched piles we found around the house, we finally understood there was one newspaper, next to her bed, that she read and re-read, dozens of times each day, week after week, month after month. And until we took the battery from her car while she slept, she drove slowly each day the three blocks to the Winn-Dixie where she had shopped for decades, and bought her daily Hellman's mayonnaise and toothpicks. Watchful teenage bag boys surreptitiously trailed her slow, queenly processional back home in their own cars, guiding her gently back to her rosebushes and calendars when she got lost.

> To be a person is to have a story to tell.
> —**Isak Dinesen**

In her bedroom were Post-it notes, hundreds of them, many with the same information repeated over and over again. Twenty-three 1-inch by 1-inch yellow Post-its perched precariously on the phone alone, with my mother's phone number and the beautician's. We knew she had lost the battle when she started wearing only sweatpants with elastic waists and—most importantly—when she stopped getting her hair done.

And then, one weekend when my older daughter visited my mother and stepfather, they took her to see sweet Sissy, as Emma called her. It was on that visit they realized Sissy had finally left for good. Sitting proudly in a straight chair in the living room, she had—it quickly became obvious—sat there for days, a phone next to her, not able to move even to go to the bathroom, unable to call for help since it wasn't the phone with the Post-it notes. Covered in her own excrement, she did what she had always done when greeting guests as they entered the room: She briefly touched her now shaky and liver-spotted hand to her hair, as if to adjust the curls. She was lifted gently from the chair, her hair carefully brushed, and then swept away in an ambulance, never to return to her home of more than sixty years with its perfectly matched living room suite, decorative sconces, pewter collection, and one hundred rosebushes in the yard. It is among the worst ways to die, uncoiffed, unremembering, and not yet dead. Ensconced at the Autumn Care Rest Home, she even began forgetting to chew.

Like Sissy, and like David Hollies, **we are all only one step away from losing the stories of our lives.** I write to remember. It is a strategy not unlike the multitude of calendars, a phalanx of Post-its. It is also a strategy for learning. And for determining who and what we are—and who and what we yearn to be.

One morning not too long ago, I heard a plaintive voice near my head. "Mama?" "Mama!" "MAMA!" I reached for my happy red plastic bifocals and looked at the clock: 5:56 a.m.

"Mama?" four-year-old Tess asked, peering at me from her eye level an inch above the mattress on which—until oh so very recently—I had been sweetly dreaming of a small glass house in which to write southern gothic novels and bake honeydew cupcakes topped with white chocolate-cardamom butter cream and chiffonade of mint.

"Yes, honey?" I answered, not knowing where I was, but knowing full-on that it wasn't a small glass house in which to write southern gothic novels and chiffonade some mint.

"Mama? Mama? What makes you *you*?"

Good Lord. I usually need at least one cup of strong, black, free-trade coffee and the corner of an organic spelt scone before we start a conversation about quiddity.

In philosophy, *quiddity* is identity or "whatness," something's "what it is." It comes from the medieval Latin term *quidditas,* "essence," from *quid,* "what." Quiddity describes properties that a particular substance—like a person—shares with others of its kind. Quiddity is also a word that stops looking like itself once you write it a few times. **Such were my thoughts at 5:56 a.m.**

I leaned up on one elbow. "Tessie, do you remember where I keep you when I go away on an airplane?"

"You keep me in your heart," she said, pointing at my chest, smiling.

"And where do you keep me?" I asked.

"Always in my heart." She pointed to her own chest.

"Everything that we keep in our hearts," I said. "That's what makes you *you*."

I walked downstairs with her hand in mine. "Hi, Worldie," she said as we passed the window on the stair landing.

"Let's make a huge big old pot of wonderful, hot coffee when we get to the kitchen," I said. "Want to?"

It is our stories of ourselves and of each other we keep in our hearts. That's what makes us *us*.

"Who are you?" someone asks. "I am the story of my self," comes the answer. —**M. Scott Momaday**

CHAPTER TWO

Start with "I"

No revolution in outer things is possible without prior revolution in one's inner way of being. Whatever change you aspire to . . . must be preceded by a change in heart.
—I Ching Hexagram 49

I recently stepped back from the past three years of writing and, like a passenger on a Boeing 777 in an exit-row window seat, I could suddenly see patterns of colors, lines, contexts, and meaning that never existed while on the ground. Suddenly, silos became orbs punctuating green exclamations of corn, lakes became mirrors for plane shadows, and these stories revealed themselves to have some kind of internal logic that holds them together and explains their proximity to one another.

Perhaps patterns keep emerging because we keep not seeing them, like Bill Murray in *Groundhog Day,* all of us playing that weatherman searching for Punxsutawney Phil and awakening every morning to the sounds of Sonny and Cher on the clock radio. Or perhaps we don't have to keep repeating our mistakes until we get them right, as he did, but can break the pattern so new worlds can emerge. **Perhaps we can recognize our way out of patterns rather than repeat our way out of them.**

Seneca said, "The way is long if one follows precepts, but short if one follows patterns." So, I started following the patterns. What emerged surprised me, and also didn't. What would it take for me to live a more intentional life, one I more intensely inhabited? It turned out there were six main ingredients for that fuller, richer life, all starting with the letter *I,* just as all change starts with *I*, the individual. For each of the six practices that emerged, simple actions stood out:

> Intensity: *Say yes*
>
> Inclusion: *Be generous*
>
> Integrity: *Speak up*
>
> Intimacy: *Love more*
>
> Intuition: *Trust yourself*
>
> Intention: *Slow down*

[
When patterns are broken, new worlds emerge.
—**Tuli Kupferberg**
]

Another pattern also emerged. These words not only start with *I,* but start with *I* followed by *n*: *In.* Involved, inhabiting, intense, integrated. The six practices are explored in greater detail in the chapters to follow; what is important now is the understanding that the *I* (namely, you) is vital to each.

What does it take to fully inhabit your life? It takes realizing how important the *I* that is you is to the equation. This is not about other people, it's not about changing the world in big ways, it's not even about doing great things—rather, it is about doing small things that give you life, bring you joy, help you inhabit the stories of your days—and, by extension, help change the world and the lives of others around you. To fully live, you must be present in the biggest way possible.

I not *They*

It's so tempting to start with *They* instead. If only They would let me. If only They would see my value. If only They would stop expecting so much (or so little) of me.

Stop.

As David Bayles and Ted Orland wrote in *Art and Fear,* "The American Revolution was not financed with matching grants from the Crown." It wasn't in King George III's best interests to fund that uprising. Great change does not come when we present our case to the king and believe he will all of a sudden "get it," or when we leave it to His Majesty to give us what we want or need. It won't happen. Matching grants, permission, change—whatever you want to call it—doesn't come to us when we sit and wait for it, or when we ask for official sanction.

Martin Luther King Jr. didn't wait for a grant before marching from Selma. If Rosa Parks had waited to pull together a National Bipartisan Task Force on Bus Seating or for funding to do a multiyear research study, she'd still be standing at a bus stop, and so would a lot of other people. **Great change doesn't come with official endorsement.** It just never has. Gauguin, Picasso, Van Gogh, and Uccello (and all those revolutionary women artists whose names we sadly don't know) all changed the face of art, for example, and all were ridiculed. Change occurs at the edges, without permission.

The same is as true for individuals changing their lives as it is for societal change.

Many years ago an organization focusing on diversity issues asked me to do some work to find out what was wrong . . . what the diversity issues were with the staff.

I dutifully did just that. People had their share of gripes. Sometimes they directly related to diversity issues—barriers they felt kept them from succeeding in the organization, ways in which they were minimized or held back or disregarded.

HAPPINESS IS NOT SOMETHING READY MADE. IT COMES FROM YOUR OWN ACTIONS.

—the Dalai Lama

In some cases there was more than a little vitriol launched at the people in charge, the *They* we hear so much about: They don't recognize our value; They act like we don't matter; They took away our holiday party; They call us all "kiddo"; They create fires for us to put out; They expect us to work late, but they go out for three-hour lunches; They treat the vice presidents better than us; They promote their friends, not the best people for the job; They don't listen to us; They take the corner offices and give us tiny cubicles; They give themselves big pay raises and give us nothing; They lie to make themselves look good. Roiling waves of resentment. Significant complaints.

And many raised the issue of The Chairs.

Each level in the organization got a different set of accoutrements: If you were an administrative assistant, your cubicle was 6 feet by 6 feet with 34-inch-tall walls (they knew the exact dimensions). Program assistants got a cubicle that was 6 by 8 with 54-inch-tall walls. Managers' cubicles were 8 by 8 with 72-inch walls, and they got a visitor chair. Directors got all that plus a clock. And vice presidents in offices with windows got all that . . . and they got visitor chairs with arms. Those chairs were the straw that broke the camel's back.

Those chairs with arms were only a tangible symptom of a larger, invisible disregard, a deeper disdain, the stuff under the tip of the iceberg, below the water. It wasn't the chairs. It was what the chairs represented.

There were harsh words about lack of leadership, of favoritism, of incompetence rising to the top.

"Well," I would ask in my sad and tiny voice, "can you suggest some ways out of this hellhole?" I didn't ask it in quite that way, but the intent was the same.

"They need to do something about it," I would hear. "They need to make things better." "They need to change how they hire people, promote people, reward people, show people they matter, and involve people."

They need to.

They must.

It occurred to me: We give up our power to the very people who took it away from us in the first place.

Why do I step back from participating in my own life? To whom am I giving over the power about my own life? Why am I waiting for permission? Why am I letting other people measure my worth in cubicle wall height? What story am I telling myself about myself? What stories do They tell about me that I've started believing? What does it mean to be in the shadow of Their story about me?

Stop saying *they*.

Yes, we need to work on the systems, the organizations that measure appreciation in cubicle sizes. There's no doubt work needs to be done there, and there's no doubt we sometimes don't have the power to make those changes ourselves. But many times we can't wait for the systems that created the mess to fix themselves. We can't wait for the conditions to be right for change. It will take too long. It's not in Their best interest; things are just dandy from where They sit in their chairs with arms. The crown fits Them.

We cannot give our power away to the people who took it from us in the first place. Put arms on your own chair. If arms are that important to you, then duct tape them on if you must. Find the change you can make and make it. You'll be funding your own revolution.

Start with *I*.

To understand is to perceive patterns.
—Isaiah Berlin

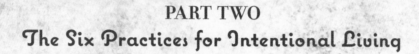

PART TWO
The Six Practices for Intentional Living

Each of us literally chooses,

by his way of attending to things,

what sort of universe

he shall appear to himself to inhabit.

—*William James*

I asked God if it was okay to be melodramatic

and she said yes

I asked her if it was okay to be short

and she said it sure is

I asked her if I could wear nail polish

or not wear nail polish

and she said honey

she calls me that sometimes

she said you can do just exactly

what you want to

Thanks God I said

And is it even okay if I don't paragraph

my letters

Sweetcakes God said

who knows where she picked that up

what I'm telling you is

Yes Yes Yes

—**Kaylin Haught, "God Says Yes to Me,"**
from *The Palm of Your Hand* **(1995)**

CHAPTER THREE
Intensity: Say Yes

Our task is to say a holy yes to the real things of our life. —**Natalie Goldberg**

On August 28, 2007, as I cleaned Cheerios off the kitchen floor for the fifty-ninth time that week, just after the contents of a twelve-and-a-half-ounce glass bottle of maple syrup were ceremoniously unleashed onto that same floor by a 41-inch-tall human tornado named Tess, I happened to look out the window into my backyard. Holding the small of my back, I straightened fully and saw the orange and yellow lilies and happy zinnias and Tessie's bright shoes and swing set and little red plastic chair on the deck outside—all in just the right light, that bold rounded yellow kind of light like the good people of Cadiz so often enjoy. It hit me in a rush of physical sensation: I have everything I need. I don't need anything else, ever.

I don't need to buy heart-shaped Teflon waffle makers with heat-resistant knobs and automatic cutoff valves or bamboo steamers or apple corers or electric bread warmers. I don't need atomic projection clocks that coax me awake in dulcet tones or telescoping Italian bar stools or stacking washers and dryers that look like grounded Calder mobiles or power suits with pizza-slice-pointy shoes or a new car (though, to be honest, if someone would enjoy the pleasure of giving me a car, that VW Beetle convertible is a sweet choice in light teal, green, or orange). The dog doesn't need a little yellow raincoat. No more making lists of things I "need"—I'm done, I'm happy, I'm eschewing materialism once and for all.

Okay, I'm sure there will be momentary lapses—that iPhone looks gorgeous and Tracy Chapman has a new CD out and I'd like to support that nice man downtown named Paul who makes honest-to-God handmade sandals, but you get the point.

When I saw those little-girl shoes in the green grass, one sock nearby and the other one gone to Sock Heaven, the spark of color in those blooms, and the blue, blue sky, what I felt was a sense of satisfaction, even in a toddler-scream-athon syrup-on-the-floor kind of day. It was enough. I simply felt full, satiated, complete, engaged.

> The moment one gives close attention to anything, even a blade of grass, it becomes a mysterious, awesome, indescribably magnificent world in itself.
> —Henry Miller

I was fully attentive in that moment. **I was saying a big yes to my life—to all of it, the zinnias in the sun and the syrup on the floor.**

What keeps us from being fully attentive, from saying yes? I think it's all the stuff we carry around with us.

When I work with a group and invite them to move around and play, the biggest barrier to people participating fully is not their mental inhibitions. Rather, it is all their stuff: They *would* move, but should they take their briefcase with them, and their small plate on which a sticky bun and a cube of pineapple are poised, and what about their legal pad and the pen they love so much from the Graves 601 Hotel in Minneapolis? Should they move that, too? And their newspaper? And that copy of *Blink* they carry around so they'll look hip? Should they cart it all around with them, from seat to seat? Will they be coming back to their home base? Will someone steal their things?

It is Stuff that keeps us from participating fully, from saying yes. Our mobility and sense of fun and playfulness and ability to be directly engaged are muted by our concern for objects, our holding on to. **We cherish our objects and we are hampered by them as well,** unable to move freely around in the world and engage directly for fear of leaving or losing our coffee cup and 8½-by-11 faux leather legal-pad holder with our initials stamped in the lower right corner in faux gold. No, we say, we'll just sit right here with our faux things. Objects distance us from ourselves, from others, from life. Things keep us from saying yes. So, too, do other people. And don't forget us. We most often keep ourselves from saying yes.

Engage with intensity. Say yes. And dance more.

Dance in Your Car

We're fools whether we dance or not,
so we might as well dance. —**Japanese proverb**

While driving downtown last Wednesday, I was pondering the epistemological problems of social cognition and constructivism, the origins of values in transcendent functions, and Kantian categorical imperatives.

Okay. Well. Maybe it was Johnny Depp looking transcendent in *Pirates of the Caribbean* that was actually on my mind as I stopped for a traffic light at the intersection of Montford and Haywood. Suddenly a flash of movement in the car ahead brought me back from the *Black Pearl,* my happy pirate ship.

Caught in the sunlight, a woman's outline swayed back and forth so energetically that her faded Chevette was tipping left and right along with her. I glimpsed a broad face in her rearview mirror, mouth open in some wild song, belting it out like she was on stage at the Apollo, plumb-full of unbridled joy and a force to be reckoned with.

Hers was real movement—not those almost imperceptible toe taps or head shrugs that often harness our responses into mild appropriateness, but wild expressions of feeling and connection.

Thick arms pumping, fingers splayed out like a shock of wheat thrust down, then up, fingers shaking like rain up and down, toward the rearview mirror and back again, like human wipers, in time with music that only she could hear, shoulders heaving up to the right and holding there for a moment before falling back leftward, like a roller

DANCE IN YOUR CAR

Stop judging others, and you free yourself to dance wildly in your car

coaster, an extended pause at the zenith, before falling, falling, then her hands swept up, up, up, and it was at that moment I saw it.

As the woman raised her hands to the heavens, as far as the car top would allow, I saw her shadow's hands, the tiny fingertips rising above the child's car seat behind her, in perfect time with the two hands up front, like Gladys Knight and one Pip. When the light turned green, off they swayed, left hand on the wheel, the other outstretched to the right, a small one echoing from the rear. I followed them; the singing and dancing continued for miles.

Seeing that vehicular tango sadly reminded me of when Greg Alexander, in his tan leisure suit, took me to the junior prom. I never danced once. Why? **And why don't more of us dance in our cars?** Because we're unsure? Because people might laugh? Because we're too fat? Because we don't have rhythm? Because we won't look cool?

My older daughter, Emma, is a teenager now, that hypersensitive time in life when every movement (and particularly those of her parents), however small, is an opportunity for mortification. "Don't scratch your nose!" she hissed at me recently in Malaprop's Bookstore. "Stop moving!" she admonished her dad, who threatened to imitate John Travolta in *Saturday Night Fever* at one of her band concerts. Our breathing in Emma's presence can become a liability.

Her four-year-old sister is at another stage of life, one where that kind of guardedness is unthinkable. "HI!" Tess screams at strangers as she races toward them in bright red sneakers, giving her minuscule peace sign with two stubby fingers, "HI! HI! HI! PEACE!" Dancing and twirling, exhaling deep belly laughs, howling like she cannot help herself, eating cake by diving headfirst into it with no hands, singing E-I-E-I-O at full tilt in grocery

[Next time you're mad,
try dancing out your anger.
—Sweetpea Tyler]

stores—this is her modus operandi. She doesn't know enough to care what other people think; we should all be so ignorant. As American songwriter legend Woody Guthrie once said, "I don't want to see the kids be grown up, I want to see the grown-ups be more like kids."

But when grown-ups are like kids, what happens? We talk about them, ridicule them, divorce them, shun them, send memos to their personnel file, look for needle marks.

Once on a plane en route to Dallas, a young boy in front of me stood up, turned, and stared at me for much of the trip, that unblinking stare of a toddler, uninhibited to look deeply for long periods of time. How cute! I thought, realizing at the same time that if his middle-aged father had done that, I'd be rooting around for the flight attendant call button, hoping Sky Marshals would take him out with a tiny stun gun.

When does this start, this tugging at our clothes to make sure they cover our hips, this loss of dance?

I have come to believe our loss of spontaneity is more about judgment than control: To the extent that I am willing to sit in judgment of other people, I myself am being judged. **If I stop judging other people, I free myself from being judged**, and I can dance! It only took me thirty years after the prom to figure that out.

It is a quote from none other than Mr. Johnny Depp that summarizes the learning: "If there's any message to my work, it is ultimately that it's okay to be different, that it's good to be different, that we should question ourselves before we pass judgment on someone who looks different, behaves different, talks different, is a different color." Or, perhaps, someone who "dances different."

To watch us dance is to hear our hearts speak. **—Hopi saying**

Several years ago on Connecticut Avenue in Washington, DC, I saw a man wearing an outfit unfit for human consumption—there was way too much skin, he was too lumpy, the colors were all wrong. I started to make a snide remark about his getup, and stopped myself, coming to the Big Realization: If I want to be freer and move through the world without caring what other people think, I have to stop participating in the "looking-askance" that makes the whole cycle possible in the first place. Stop yourself from judging others in order not to be judged yourself. Then you'll be free to dance wildly in your car.

✐ *Action:*

Mark Twain has said, "On with the dance, let joy be unconfined is my motto, whether there's any dance to dance or any joy to unconfine." Let's explore joy for a moment.

- Put on some music and dance like a five-year-old for two minutes.

- Then get out your journal and write for three minutes (without pause, without raising your pen from the page or checking for spelling or grammar and all those other things that inhibit the flow of ideas) in response to the following question: What brings me joy?

- After three minutes, read what you have written.

- Now for three minutes, write a description of the dance that would best demonstrate that joy. Be as detailed as you can in describing the physicality of that dance. How would you move in the world to express that joy?

- Then write for two minutes on this question: What keeps me from dancing that dance?

✦ *Movement:*

For the next thirty-seven days, when you find yourself about to proclaim the unworthiness of someone's outfit or way of being in the world, stop. When words that reflect judgment are on the tip of your tongue (How silly! How ugly! How inappropriate!), pause for three seconds. Reframe those words of judgment into positives (How joyful! How unique! How colorful!), and say to yourself: What a wonderful way of being in the world! What an interesting cultural norm! I really must find out more about that! Practice being curious, not judgmental.

Carry a Small Grape

From wonder into wonder existence opens. —Lao-tzu

When my older daughter was just a porcelain-skinned baby with ringlet hair, I told my friends Gay and Rosemary that I loved Emma so deeply and totally, I actually imagined myself eating her sometimes. Literally.

True to form, Gay and Rosemary didn't even so much as blink at the news that I was considering cannibalism; rather, they both said without hesitation, "Oh my, yes, I understand completely. Let's all wear hats and sit in the garden and have some chocolate tortoni."

(As an aside, you really do need a friend or two like that in the world. I do believe I could call them both, reveal that I had robbed twenty-three banks in Fort Dodge last week, taken several dozen Romanian truffle makers hostage, revolutionized butter manufacturing, and was the love child of Johnny Unitas, and they would simply ask if I wanted more hand-cranked lavender ice cream.)

Now, almost fifteen years after that first hint of cannibalism, it's back. Now the taste is for my younger daughter, Tess. Why are my children so irresistible to me? Perhaps it is my attraction to how they live their little lives—open, true, real, flat-out, honest.

For two weeks now Tess's toddler self has been carrying around a small object. It's with her everywhere she goes. She sleeps with it under her pillow, takes it outside, places it on the swing and swings it like a friend or a pet or a charm. When she can't find it, she panics. It is the first thing she

"Lookeee! Awww, it's a teeny, tiny, cute, weeney, bitty, grape!" she said in a little, high voice, her head cocked to one side, smiling, her shoulders pulled up as if to envelope her neck. "Isn't he sweeet?" she asked, holding it gently with two tiny fingers an inch from my nose. "It's very fragile" she informed me.

3 7 D A Y S

3 7 D A Y S

Be thrilled with the small things, the fragile things, the wee tiny things

carry a small grape

reaches for in the morning; it is the last thing she says good night to. It sits next to her in her carriage when we go for walks; it sits on the shelf near the tub when she takes a bath. It is her constant companion. **It is her talisman, her good-luck charm, her grounding.** It is a ziplock bag. Inside, you won't find a cute, fuzzy stuffed animal or favorite blankie or piece of jewelry. You'll find two small pieces of Hampton Inn hotel soap.

One soap piece is rectangular and flat, one is round. Each has edges worn down where Tess has held them. She touches them absentmindedly sometimes, like when we drive to the grocery store; at other times they have her full attention. She plays with them and talks to them as they take rides on her BRIO train set. The soaps are her constant companion—along with her grape.

Last month Tess and I had a snack of grapes (red, seedless, organic, expensive), and she was quite delighted (shriekingly so) when she found a teeny tiny grape, an aberrant grape, a minuscule grape in the bunch. "Lookeeeee!" she screamed, running through the house naked, her teeny tiny grape held high. "Lookeeee! Awwww, it's a teeny tiny cute weency bitty grape!" she said in a little, high voice, her head cocked to the side, smiling, her shoulders pulled up as if to envelop her neck. "Isn't it sweeeeet?" she asked, holding it gently with two tiny fingers an inch from my nose. "It's very fragile."

Like the soap, her grape goes everywhere with her. She took the plastic top off an empty bottle of bubbles and made a grape bed inside the lid with toilet paper, gently placing the little grape on it. Over the weeks, teeny tiny cute weency bitty grape shrank even more. Now microscopic, he still lives on that little bottle-top bed, carried like royalty from room to room with a loyalty rare in this throwaway world.

If we could see the miracle of a single flower clearly, our whole life would change. —**Buddha**

Tess loves tiny boxes, too. She carries her "moneys" around in a hotel shower cap box—dimes and pennies and nickels she deposits around the house, counts repeatedly, and then packs back up into the small box, its flaps wearing thin with the constant opening and closing, opening and closing.

She comes by this fascination with small things honestly. Or perhaps all children do, finding things in their world that fit their wee hands with dimpled joints, things that give them wonder and joy, with which they can create whole worlds. Do we lose that ability or attention as we grow bigger? Tess's big sister Emma, "Sissy" she calls her, started her collection of fragile objects when she was a small girl. It's housed now, years later, on a special "fragile shelf" her dad made her—small china dolls, the entire cast of *The Simpsons* in French porcelain figurines no bigger than a fingernail, a crystal leopard and a tiny glass bird, and more—all small, all fragile, all cherished.

When Emma was Tess's age, we spent our Thanksgivings in Great Barrington, Massachusetts, with John's grandmother, Nana. No matter what time we got there—sometimes in the middle of the night—Nana quietly padded to the front door and welcomed us all with pierogi fried in four sticks of butter. Almost as wide as tall, she was a New Englander through and through—a no-nonsense woman who had lived a long time.

> People usually consider walking on water or in thin air a miracle. But I think the real miracle is to walk on earth. Every day we are engaged in a miracle which we don't even recognize: a blue sky, white clouds, green leaves, the black, curious eyes of a child—our own two eyes. All is a miracle.
> —**Thich Nhat Hanh**

As any mother of a toddler can tell you, it is nerve racking to spend time in a grandmother's house with highly polished coffee tables on which sit beautiful porcelain candy dishes.

Quietly one evening there, I learned an important lesson from Nana. The fragile candy dish on the coffee table in her living room was like a siren song: Emma couldn't keep her inexperienced, chubby little hands off it. I kept moving it away from her, fearful that it was an heirloom—brought over from Poland, perhaps, the last memento of Nana's parents' life there. I was terrified that Emma might break it, so I moved it, watched it, admonished Emma, then moved it, watched it, and admonished her again. And again.

Finally, without a word, Nana leaned toward Emma, put the box directly in front of her, and silently showed her how to slowly lift and replace the lid gently, teaching Emma to respect the beauty, not holding it from her, showing her how to navigate fragility instead of assuming she wasn't capable. Nana recognized which had the most value, a china box or a great-granddaughter, and it was a lovely, quiet moment, a real lesson for this new mother. For anyone, really.

Years later we took Emma to her first auction. John was bidding on Something Important; Emma was intrigued, her ten-year-old mind racing with the possibilities. As her dad surveyed the lots, Emma followed along, her eye falling to a cardboard box with an odd assortment of china and porcelain objects—Fragile Things for her Fragile Shelf! They were beautiful! **Little miniature pitchers and eggs rimmed with flaking gold paint.** She was mesmerized by the glory of it all, the very thought that she could own such a treasure, not knowing they were odds and ends, probably not of interest to others. She saw only possibility and joy, a bonanza of the highest sort.

Wisdom begins with wonder. —Socrates

When the auction started, John got what he had come for. We then waited and waited and waited some more for Emma's box to be auctioned. People left, the crowd thinned. The little box of treasures wasn't brought to the front until the very last, of course. The large man walked to the front with the box, her Holy Grail. Emma froze. There was suddenly so much at stake.

The auctioneer surveyed the meager contents of the box as an assistant subtly pointed out little Emma in the back of the room, a girl now gripped in total fear, a girl who had stood for hours to bid on this small gathering of objects. The bidding started. His voice slowed for her benefit: "Who will give me five dollars for this treasure?" At the hint of Emma raising her tiny arm, he yelled "SOLD TO THE LOVELY YOUNG LADY IN THE BACK FOR FIVE DOLLARS!" She was mortified, proud, delighted in the same instant, and we appreciated his knowing. Even now in the land of her teenage self, those small eggs sit proudly on her Fragile Shelf, a reminder of that wonder, now slipping away with her impending adulthood.

be thrilled by
small things
fragile things
wee tiny things

CARRY A SMALL GRAPE

37 Days: Do It Now Challenge

Let's learn from children who can sense the possibilities inherent in simple things: boxes, bars of Hampton Inn soap, a tiny grape, an egg rimmed in gold. What is your touchstone, talisman, small wonder that you carry with you into the world? Mine is a tiny silver book containing a small brass scruple, given me by my husband, John. Carry your equivalent of a small grape and hold it safe, keep it company, swing it on your tiny swing, sleep with it under your pillow. Let it remind you of finding wonder in the world, share it with others, even those who—like a toddler—need to learn to cherish it, too.

Action:

What's your grape? What creates wonder in you? Take just ten minutes to create a tiny collage or drawing or poem small enough to fit into your wallet using images and words that represent what brings you joy or holds deep meaning in your life. Perhaps it is simply the word *joy,* or a photograph of your partner or pet, or a ticket stub. Slip it into a plastic sleeve or laminate it. Carry it with you.

Movement:

For the next thirty-seven days, when you are sitting in a fascinating three-day strategic planning meeting or waiting in line at the Department of Motor Vehicles to clear up that tiny insurance misunderstanding or standing behind a man with twenty-two items in the express lane at the grocery store, pull out your "grape" and remind yourself of wonder. (And, by the way, unpack your grandmother's china that you've been saving for a special occasion. Use it for everyday meals. Being alive is the special occasion.)

Always Rent the Red Convertible

Be daring, be different, be impractical; be anything that will assert integrity of purpose and imaginative vision against the play-it-safers, the creatures of the commonplace, the slaves of the ordinary. —**Cecil Beaton**

Red Convertible #1

When gun-wielding snipers were busy terrorizing Washington, DC, in October 2002, my family still lived there, feeling hunted like small deer at a salt lick, watching as people who were just living their comfortably boring and insanely precious everyday lives fell irretrievably dead, cheated of that beautifully mundane existence, shot through the head while pumping gas, piling lumber in their car at Home Depot, cutting the grass, walking through a grocery store parking lot with their 2 percent milk, sitting on a bench outside the post office with their new Buckminster Fuller postage stamps, standing in the doorway of a bus on the way to work, crossing the street at a busy intersection to get home to their grandchildren—the salt licks of the modern world. Ten people dead, just like that. Pop. Pop. Pop. Left home one morning to get some stamps, gasoline, a jar of sweet dill pickles, a *People* magazine, and never came home again. So random, so mundane, so vulnerable, so terrorized.

As the siege continued, schools canceled recess. It was too dangerous for kids to be outside. People stopped walking places; we dashed frantically from one set of four walls to another. Gas pumps were a sweet spot for the snipers since people pumping gas aren't typically moving targets. Gas station owners hung dark blue opaque plastic tarps to protect their customers from long-range rifle fire, and people started filling their cars in

Always rent the red convertible

37 Days

two-dollar increments, dancing or hopping while pumping, remembering from *Law and Order* that a zigzagging target is harder to hit.

In the midst of the killing spree, we needed to rent a car because ours had just the tiniest oil pump problem.

I'll never forget the rhapsodic look on my husband's face when he returned in a bright red convertible. "Won't Emma love it?" he said excitedly. "I got a really good deal!"

Let's see.

Snipers.

Red convertible.

Good deal.

Why not just paint a target on our heads and get it over with? I wondered if he had hit his head on the Hertz counter. But John had evidently worked out a delicate algorithm of variables only he understood and that somehow provided irrefutable evidence that his family would not be a target.

John was right. Emma did love it. We didn't get assassinated. And we have a fantastic photo of Emma with her dog, Blue, laughing one of those big-mouthed kid laughs, wind blowing her hair and Blue's ears as they rode like royalty in the back of the convertible. John whistled the last notes of the last work of Mozart in the driver's seat as I sat next to him in my trench coat and big-brimmed hat surreptitiously scoping out gun barrels, looking for all the world like I was taking one last happy drive with my family before they dropped me off at St. Elizabeth's for a long "rest."

So what if renting a convertible was slightly crazy? After weeks of terror, bad dreams, and school lockdowns a mere year after 9/11, Emma felt free that day for a few hours. It was magical. She still talks about that convertible.

> [Anyone who keeps the ability to see beauty never grows old.
> —**Franz Kafka**]

Red Convertible #2

A few years ago several women friends and I went for a long weekend of relaxation at Ten Thousand Waves, a Japanese spa outside Santa Fe. As we prepared to fly there for hot stone massages by large lavender-smelling men with big thumbs, a huge forest fire was raging in New Mexico or in one of those square states nearby. The news reports were full of dire predictions. We wondered if we should even go, but luckily the winds changed and we announced we would be safe. (You'd have thought we all had PhDs in Wind and Raging Firestorm Patterns of the Southwest.)

Our shiny red convertible was ready for us when we touched down in sunny Albuquerque. "How very odd!" we chirped as we drove out of the airport, "such gorgeous weather and no one else rented a convertible!"

We drove with our oversized Liz Taylor sunglasses, scarves flowing behind us like Amelia Earhart or that poor Isadora Duncan. In Albuquerque people kept pointing and smiling, some laughing. "How wonderful!" we gushed, "we must look ravishing and mysterious like so many movie stars! Perhaps they've confused us with Julia Roberts and friends—doesn't she live somewhere around here?"

WHEN YOU HAVE ONLY TWO PENNIES LEFT IN THE WORLD, BUY A LOAF OF BREAD WITH ONE, AND A LILY WITH THE OTHER.

—Chinese proverb

Little did we know the whole time we were tooling around the highways and byways of New Mexico chatting about our imaginary movie careers and favorite leading men (Depp, Duvall, and Hackman, of course), there was a "Red-Alert-Don't-Dare-Breathe-the-Air-Outdoors-Because-of-the-Particulates" warning due to the lingering fires: People statewide were urged to stay indoors *at all costs*. People weren't smiling because we were ravishing in our convertible; they were smiling because we were idiots in our convertible.

Lung damage aside, driving a Taurus wouldn't have made for the amazing memories we have of that time together, nor the fabulous photos of us basking in the sun with ash-covered mountains in the background, not a soul to be seen for miles.

Red Convertible #3

In December 2004 I took my then-twelve-year-old daughter on a surprise cross-country adventure to sleep with manatees at San Diego's Sea World, an overnight camp for kids and their adults to learn the A–Zs of manatees and then sleep straight up against the glass of the manatee aquarium on the cold, hard floor. Those sweet and lumbering giants rolled and played all night long in their seventy-two-degree water bed as we "slept" in frigid nylon sleeping bags on the cold, hard floor. Did I mention the floor was cold and hard? I remember rousing from half sleep, thrilled it must be time to get up. By the dim lights of the manatees' waterworld, I could see that my watch said 1:30 a.m. Imagine my disappointment, my longest night, my achy pilgrimage toward dawn.

When we first landed in San Diego, we headed for the rental car desk. On the way, Emma told me she couldn't wait to see our red convertible! My heart sank. To save money, I had rented something incredibly pedestrian, something cheap and plastic-smelling with hard seats too straight up and down, manual windows that are hard to crank, and no CD player for our Bob Marley tunes. What a terrible disappointment, but I couldn't bear to tell her just yet.

When we got to the Hertz counter, the rental agent first chatted with Emma about why we were there and was charmed by her quiet explanation that **it was a Thelma and Louise road trip but without the drugs, sex, crime, Brad Pitt, and death.** The clerk said we looked like wild women (Emma smiled shyly) and asked if we would like a convertible for the same price. The color? You guessed it—bright cherry red. We were ravishing in our ride; we affectionately named it Rupert.

Here's what all this leads me to believe: Being practical and safe and always logical is way overrated. Sure, I should have saved the manatee trip money to pay for braces, tuba lessons, the college tuitions that are in our future—but at what cost?

What would Emma and I have missed? Just the stories that make up our lives.

We all deserve to have fun, live large, and be ridiculed by less imaginative people existing under the erroneous assumption they get extra credit for being prudent and safe. If I recall correctly, the death rate for people who play it safe and for people who live boldly is the same: 100 percent.

If I were living the thirty-seven days that prompted the launch of these essays, guess which car I would rent for that last month on earth? Okay, maybe not a red convertible. It might be a VW Bug in bright apple green simply because the idea makes me very, very happy.

The good life is a process, not a state of being. It is a direction not a destination. —Carl Rogers

Pick one: good gas mileage in an unremarkable car with scratchy seats or amazing memories and the wind in your hair. It's simple: Life is short. We have choices. Each decision should enhance the journey and be beautiful in some way. It doesn't need to cost money, but it needs to add art and surprise to life. Always rent the red convertible (where convertible is a handy metaphor for what makes you smile, brings you joy). Don't just drive somewhere. Make the journey memorable.

✐ Action:

"I don't want to be a passenger in my own life," said Diane Ackerman.

- Imagine you are in a car, driving down a street near your house.

- Write for five minutes in great detail about what you see and notice as the driver of the car—and about what decisions a driver makes.

- Stop and read what you have written.

- Now imagine you are in the same car, driving down the same street. But this time you are a passenger.

- Write for another five minutes in great detail about what you see and notice as a passenger in the car—and about what decisions a passenger makes.

- Read what you have just written.

- Notice the differences between being a driver and being a passenger. Who ultimately decides where you are going? Who sees more? Ponder the meaning . . .

❍ Movement:

Each day for the next thirty-seven days, find at least one way to incorporate artfulness into your life. For example, make paying bills an art exercise. Each time you send a letter or bill, decorate the envelope with a drawing or picture cut from a magazine—make art of it. Include inside the bill payment a small card with an inspirational quote. Create goofy caricatures of each family member that you can use as a kind of shorthand when you write notes to one another. Arrange your vegetables on your plate in concentric circles, not just a pile, and create smiley faces out of fruit in the mornings. Life is art.

Celebrate Every Orange Flag

The truth is that everything that can be accomplished by showing a person when he's wrong, ten times as much can be accomplished by showing him where he is right. The reason we don't do it so often is that it's more fun to throw a rock through a window than to put in a pane of glass. —Robert T. Allen

One afternoon a few weeks after Emma started first grade, I picked her up from school and drove to my husband's bookshop to say hi. When we pulled up, John ran out to see us, leaning in the car window to give her a kiss. "How was school today, buddy?" he asked.

"I had my first test today!" she exclaimed brightly. (How wonderful, I thought. A whole lifetime of testing has opened up for you!)

What was our first question to her?

"How'd you do?" (Yes, let's get straight to the bottom line.)

"I got 30 percent!" she proudly shouted, a huge grin on her pixie face. The body language between me and John was unmistakable. Oh my Lord, we were both thinking, she's an idiot. She'll never pass first grade, we'll have to hire tutors her whole life, she won't get into college . . .

My first impulse was to say, *You must feel terrible,* but by some miracle I stopped myself. Instead I asked, "How did that make you feel?"

"I got some right!" she burst out without hesitation, so proud of her accomplishment.

Wow. What a fantastic way of looking at the world.

I'm not suggesting we aim for 30 percent, but why don't we stop to celebrate the successes we do have?

The opposite of play is not work. It's depression. —**Brian Sutton-Smith**

I remember a trek-in-the-woods-team-building event years ago with colleagues from work, in the freezing rain, no less. We were on a scavenger hunt in the forest, looking for orange flags and trying to learn these lessons: (1) If we worked together effectively, we would all succeed; (2) what we could accomplish together was more than what we could achieve alone; and (3) et cetera.

I didn't learn what the organizers intended. What I learned instead were six things:

1. I don't like freezing rain. It makes me cranky, itchy, and very cold.

2. Freezing rain appears to make other people passive aggressive.

3. If you would just tell me those lessons rather than make me suffer to discover them, I would believe you. I promise.

4. Some people don't care who is left behind or who falls down in the mud.

5. People don't stop being bullies when they grow up. They just dress differently to fool you.

6. Human beings are lousy at stopping long enough to celebrate those precious moments when we find the small orange flags in the woods.

Every time we found another flag, rather than take ten seconds to say *Aren't we fabulously bright, talented, and frozen scavengers!* our self-proclaimed leader would scream angrily, "We need to move faster! You're slowing us down!"

FLATTER ME, AND I MAY NOT BELIEVE YOU. CRITICIZE ME, AND I MAY NOT LIKE YOU. IGNORE ME, AND I MAY NOT FORGIVE YOU. ENCOURAGE ME, AND I WILL NOT FORGET YOU. LOVE ME, AND I MAY BE FORCED TO LOVE YOU.

—William Arthur Ward

Though there was definitely therapy in his future, he spoke for many in the group—we've got to do it better, faster. Celebrating would take precious time that we could be achieving (or overachieving, as the case may be). Why? I thought to myself. **Why not allow for that momentary glee, just a group yee-haw or even the tiniest round of applause?**

On January 10, 2002, Emma was in the fourth grade at John Eaton Elementary School in Washington, DC, laboring over a timed test on "Pythagorean division." Thank God that special hell is reserved for the young. Her dad found the test paper recently. There were six word problems, the kind that used to drive me insane—why on earth is Mr. Smith driving 15 miles per hour anyway? Isn't the speed limit 55? Why doesn't Mrs. Smith tell him in no uncertain terms to pick up the speed? And why does he eat only 5.25 apples? Why not splurge and eat 6 apples or give the other 0.75 to the long-suffering Mrs. Smith? Who cares which pencil is the sharpest, who gets to town the quickest, who breeds more llamas, or how long the train tracks are?

Looking at Emma's childish, penciled notes, scared and tentative in the margin beside the questions, it broke my heart. I can just imagine her bent over the paper, not quite ten years old, fiercely biting her nails and struggling to make sense of how many chirps a cricket makes as the temperature rises. The question about five- and seven-cent stamps seemed a particularly cruel one, with Emma resorting to creating a circle of numbers to the left of the question, 5¢ shouldered by 7¢, 3 connected to 30¢ to 6 and back to 5¢, a maypole circle of confusion, with small almost invisible question marks above the 5¢ and the 7¢.

When her thirty minutes were up, Emma had only written in three answers, leaving blank the questions about how many acres a large tractor can plow in an hour and what would come ninetieth in a repetitive lineup of thumbtacks, paper clips, and pushpins, and, of course, the horrific and damaging stamp question. Of the three she answered, she got only one right: At eighty degrees Fahrenheit, a cricket would chirp 108 times. If I had only known that years ago, my life would have been so much more complete.

So, after thirty minutes of timed torment, my sweet Emma got only one answer right.

You can just imagine what her teacher wrote in **BIG RED LETTERS** at the bottom of the page.

But no, it wasn't what I expected: "One out of six," Miss Coti wrote, "Great Effort!"

Two words made all the difference in how Emma felt getting that paper back and how hard she tried the next time. It was obvious from her deranged figuring in the margins that she was drowning while testing; Miss Coti chose to celebrate the 108 chirps. It was Emma's finest year in school yet.

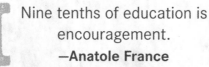

> Nine tenths of education is encouragement.
> —**Anatole France**

37 Days: Do It Now Challenge

In our house, we sometimes run out of vital supplies like toilet paper, lightbulbs, and Purely Decadent Pomegranate Chip soy ice cream, but 365 days a year you can be sure of finding a rather impressive supply of birthday candles on hand for impromptu celebrations. You lived through the swim test? Your pancakes tomorrow morning will come to you in a blaze of glory. Today you're celebrating your half birthday? Get ready for a half cake after dinner. It's the first snow of the season, National Lightbulb Day, new-haircut day, leap year? Lighted cupcakes will no doubt line the floor from your bedroom to the dining table tomorrow morning. You survived your evil fifth-grade teacher who shall remain nameless? How about Cheerios with candles stuck through them for breakfast? You learned to tie your shoes? You fell off your horse and got back on? You read a 1,600-page book? You learned to cover your mouth when you cough? There are candles in your immediate future. Everyday, ordinary, daily life should be a rambunctious celebration, a focus on the positive, a paean to possibility and glee. Slow down, take time, encourage, celebrate your 30 percent.

✐ Action:

A group of fabulous women once created a gold, sparkly, 1-foot-tall Potato Chip Award for me when I joked I had won a blog award but wasn't sure of the prize—perhaps it was a potato chip, I mused. Hence, the award. In *The Art of Innovation,* Tom Kelley describes awards that cleverly capture the heart of someone's contribution: A small shopping cart borne by a Superman figure for someone who worked for four days straight to solve a sticky Web site shopping cart problem, for example. These are awards that symbolize in some way the meaning behind the action that deserves the recognition.

Focused free-write:

- Quick: For three minutes list those people in your life who deserve awards for the little things they do, and note what they have done to deserve an award.

- Read what you have written.

- Then for three more minutes, design awards for them—what would their awards look like? In what fun way could you best symbolize their contributions to your life? The wackier, the better . . .

- Now, for the last four minutes of this focused free-write, list the things you've done—big or small—that deserve an award. Don't be shy. Celebrate yourself. And write a description of the awards you would design for yourself.

Celebrate what you want to see more of. —Tom Peters

I don't deserve this award, but I have arthritis and I don't deserve that either. —**Jack Benny**

Wear Pink Glasses

When you possess light within, you see it externally. —Anaïs Nin

She walked with a pronounced limp, shifting her weight to roll one hip forward; it appeared that one side of her was shorter than the other—and both were quite short to begin with. She wore gray pants with old sweaters, big buttons up the front, a simple style born of quiet necessity. Her body was simply a mode of transportation for her considerable brain. Her shoes were orthopedic, black, square blocks of footwear, as if to prove that point.

People who passed her in airports never took note of her. She was just a small Chinese grandma to them, tiny, old, twisted to one side. When she read—and it was often—she wore old-man glasses from the 1950s, big and bulky and black-framed.

Little would anyone know from a chance encounter that she had gotten her PhD in physics from the Massachusetts Institute of Technology (MIT) in 1951, that she was the first woman on the Central Committee of the Chinese Communist Party, and that she was president of the most prestigious university in China.

One year we traveled together for a month across the United States, just the two of us. She was quiet, reserved, and fiercely smart, with at times a pixie smile. We spent that month bearing together the joys of incessant travel, delays, and the sometimes ill-conceived Chinese meals graciously provided by our hosts in attempts to make her feel at home. What came out of all those days on the road was an unlikely intergenerational, cross-cultural friendship: I was twenty-seven; she was over seventy.

Xie Xide (*SHE-uh she-DUH*) had been invited to the States as one of forty Distinguished Scholars brought here by the Fulbright Program in 1986 to celebrate its fortieth anniversary. Having studied Chinese, I was asked to escort this unassuming powerhouse, a force of nature.

She told me her story, a little at a time. I filled in the gaps with my own research later, those parts she wouldn't tell because of modesty.

WHEN YOU TAKE CHARGE OF YOUR LIFE, THERE IS NO LONGER NEED TO ASK PERMISSION OF OTHER PEOPLE OR SOCIETY AT LARGE. WHEN YOU ASK PERMISSION, YOU GIVE SOMEONE VETO POWER OVER YOUR LIFE.

—Albert F. Geoffrey

In July 1937, when the Japanese occupied Beijing, her family fled south first to Wuhan, then Changsha, and finally ended up in Guiyang, Guizhou province, in the fall of 1938. During their flight she contracted tuberculosis in her hip. Put in a cast, she was hospitalized for three years and spent another year at home recuperating. **While bedridden, she read widely and taught herself English, calculus, and physics.**

By the time I met her, she had become the president of Fudan University in Shanghai, the Harvard of her country. With more than fifteen honorary doctorates from around the world, Madame Xie had played a key role in the development of solid-state physics in China. And, she added quietly with a smile, "I was the first token woman on the Central Committee."

During that month of travel, we rarely stayed in one place very long—she was booked to present lectures across the country—except for New Orleans, where we spent a long weekend. The president of a local university had arranged for us to be hosted by the Fairmont Hotel, a distinguished old landmark. We checked in, the hotel staff evidently alerted to her status—they couldn't do enough for her. Me? Chopped liver. "Call me," I whispered as they whisked her to her suite with one small, old suitcase.

"Patti?" a small voice on the phone said. "Are you unpacked yet?"

"Yes, you?" I asked.

"You must come down here," she said excitedly. "I have never seen anything like this! It is really far too extravagant for me. And there is a large table full of food that I can't possibly eat! Come join me and we'll have a party!"

Her door was slightly ajar. As I pushed it open, I could see her—just barely—ensconced on what looked like a throne away across the gilded room, her legs dangling below her like a character in a Faulkner novel, not able to reach the floor. They had housed her in a 1,300-square-foot rococo suite, dripping with reds and golds and velvets. She sat next to the largest fruit, cheese, and wine spread I had ever seen in my life.

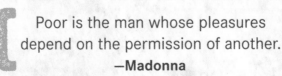

"Look!" she said. "I don't eat cheese, so you'll have to eat all of this!" She also didn't drink, so the burden of sampling the wine on our behalf fell to me. We partied quietly for hours, talking.

In that unlikely setting she told me about her life during the Cultural Revolution. Like many scientists and intellectuals in China, she suffered banishment during that period of political turmoil from 1966 to 1976.

"I was locked inside the low-temperature laboratory for nine months," she said. "My husband was also under house arrest in his own institute, so our son—who was ten at the time—had to take care of himself." After her release from house arrest, she was forced to clean the lavatories of the physics building and sweep the corridors. She also had to work in the university's semiconductor factory, polishing silicon wafers. Xie Xide was finally allowed to do some teaching in 1972.

Five years later she founded the Modern Physics Research Institute, obtaining funding for the establishment of modern research laboratories in surface physics. She revived physics in China by aiding hundreds of young physicists to find opportunities to train abroad; she co-authored a textbook in Chinese, *Semiconductor Physics,* important for the training of solid-state physicists. A member of the Chinese Academy of Sciences, she was also a fellow of the American Physical Society, the Third World Academy of Sciences in Italy, and a Foreign Honorary Member of the American Academy of Arts and Sciences.

We had a glorious few days in New Orleans, playing like children, freed from our responsibility of being important adults presenting speeches (her

[Poor is the man whose pleasures depend on the permission of another. **—Madonna**]

giving, me listening). And of all the things New Orleans brought to us— great garlic mashed potatoes, strolls in the French Quarter, fantastic zydeco music—the thing I most remember is the Woolworth's dime store. She had mentioned that her old-man glasses wouldn't stay up on her nose. "Come on," I said to her, "let's go look at eyeglasses."

We made our way to the reading glasses; I twirled the display rack. "Look at all these glasses!" I exclaimed. "Try some on!" She was shy to do so, but finally reached up for yet another pair of old-man spectacles, with stern and important-looking black frames. "How about these?" I suggested, holding up a pair of faintly pink-colored frames. "They would look wonderful with your hair."

"Oh, no," she protested, smiling. "I couldn't!"

"Just try them—no one is looking," I said.

And so she did, slipping them onto her face and looking up into the mirror. "I'll be back in a minute," I said, heading off to the magazines to give her some space. As I walked away, I could see her looking out of the corner of her eye at herself in those lovely pink frames, touching them gently, turning her head from side to side, and smiling ever so slightly. **She looked beautiful, like a light was shining from inside her.**

"I couldn't!" she said when I returned and asked if she was going to buy them. "I need to look serious! I couldn't look serious in pink glasses!" Instead, she bought the old-man glasses. As we left that twirling stand of lenses, I saw her reach back to touch the pink ones again. Soon after, we left New Orleans and continued our trek. When she was leaving the United States at the end of our journey, I wrote her a letter explaining what the trip had meant to me and enclosed in it a small gift.

I can only imagine her smile when she opened that box to find those pink glasses, a touchstone of our time together.

Give yourself permission to wear pink glasses. Or give someone else the pink glasses they can't give themselves permission to wear. They will wear them, no doubt, when they are alone; perhaps it will make them smile and look at themselves differently.

✐ Action:

Focused free-write:

- Write for three minutes on the following question: In the last twelve months, what have you said no to? Keep in mind that no takes many forms—"I can't," or "I shouldn't," for example.

- Read what you have written. Now write for three minutes on this question: What or who was your "censor," those people (yourself included) or circumstances who keep you from saying yes? From whom do you believe you must ask permission?

- Read what you have written. And, finally, answer this question for three minutes of writing: What would yes look and feel like?

❋ Movement:

In *Improv Wisdom*, author Patricia Madson suggests we practice saying yes to everything for one day. As Madson notes, this comes with a caveat—if you are diabetic and offered pie, for example, you must first protect your health. In that case, though, you can still find a way to say yes: "Yes, I'd love to have this pie to take home to my son who loves cherries," she suggests.

Try it, not for just one day, but for thirty-seven! What happens when you put your own preferences aside and accept the offers that are made to you? What is hard about it? Do you have to relinquish some of that control you like so much? What do you gain from doing so?

Write the word yes in black Sharpie marker on your hand to remind you. It says "permanent marker," but don't let that stop you. Say yes!

Say Wow When You See a Bus

Sell your cleverness and purchase bewilderment. —Rumi

There is a pure and shining glory in the world of my toddler daughter, Tess. It is called a bus, a "big, big bus," to be exact.

For Tess, there is absolutely no greater joy, no surprise more full, no experience more fantastic than that moment of sheer ecstasy and full-body wonder when she sees a bus. Like someone with short-term memory loss, each one is her first: "WOW!!! A BUS!!!" she says with every fiber of her being. "A BIG, BIG BUS!" For someone so small, she has quite the lung power, a voice that carries for some distance, making heads turn in her wake.

There is a close second to Bus Joy when we approach the "TUNNEL, the big, big TUNNEL!" but even that pales in comparison with the bus. Then, of course, there is the penultimate thrill of the TRUCK, THE BIG, BIG, TRUCK or THE BIG RED FIRE TRUCK or the ICE CREAM TRUCK or HAPPY TRUCK or BIG HUGE TRUCK, a very loud announcement made many times each day and complicated only slightly by the fact that every *tr* in her noisy vocabulary is rendered as an *f*. You do the math. We cut quite a figure in the produce aisle or post office when she hears a "great big fire truck" go past, announcing it to the surprised masses.

Being around her is like getting a PhD in exuberance. Hers is a joy we all know—before we divide ourselves and wall off the part we keep to ourselves, the part we hide for fear of ridicule.

I once read of a man who went into a kindergarten class and asked how many of the kids could sing—every hand shot up immediately. How many could dance? Same response. How many could paint? Again, all hands shot up eagerly. He then went into a college classroom and asked the same

37 Days

Say
WOW
When You
See a Bus

Play is hard to maintain as you get older. You get less playful. You shouldn't, of course. —Richard Feynman

questions. Did he get the same response? No. No hands went up. What happens in those years between five and eighteen to our sense of joy and possibility and personal command of the universe?

We learn to mask ourselves, our surprise and our glee, our sense of self-worth and self-loathing: Don't say you can paint, because someone else might paint better than you do and people will judge. Don't say you can sing, because you're no Johnny Cash. Don't say you can write if you're not on the *New York Times* best-seller list. Don't express your sheer wonder at the sight of a bus—that would mark you as unsophisticated and naive.

Pausing to listen to an airplane in the sky, stooping to watch a ladybug on a plant . . . children have their own agendas and timescales. As they find out more about their world and their place in it, they work hard not to let adults hurry them.
—**Cathy Nutbrown**

We don't often allow ourselves to be surprised as adults. Our unwillingness or inability to be wowed is exactly the problem—we equate being surprised with being unprepared and naive.

If I am surprised, I'm weak; if I'm surprised, I'm not ready; if I'm surprised, I'm vulnerable. Therefore, I can't be surprised, I won't let myself be surprised, I will do whatever it takes to not be surprised, not to let other people know I have noticed the big, big bus and am totally floored by the very idea of it. I will not move my head or indicate in any way I am in absolute, ecstatic love with that bus, that seeing it makes me want to shake all over and scream out at the top of my lungs.

Hearing astronaut Story Musgrave speak and show photographs he took of the Earth from space is a lesson in perspective and wonder. He begins and ends his presentation with a slide of a small child on a beach, bent completely double on her haunches as she peers intently at some small thing in the sand, perhaps a shell or seaweed, a bug or just the bubbles of salt water. It is that sense of mystery and wonder and intense focus and fascination we lose as we age, that we need to recover, reclaim, own, cherish, and share.

As I push Tess in her swing ("BIGGER, BIGGER!" she urges, an adrenaline junkie at four), I muse sometimes about what it would be like to approach life as an adult like Tessie does now, boldly marching forward into her days: "Wow! A meeting! Lookie, an insanely long and completely inane meeting! YEE! A huge parking ticket! A 200-page strategic plan! YIPPEE! A report due tomorrow! A mortgage payment! Wow, wow!! A dysfunctional boss in a big, big FIRE TRUCK!"

37 Days: Do It Now Challenge

Give voice to that inner child of astonishment and surprise and sheer joy. Let's all agree to be willing to be surprised by the bus, the fire truck, the shell on the beach, the life.

✐ Action:

Henry Miller said, "The moment one gives close attention to anything, even a blade of grass, it becomes a mysterious, awesome, indescribably magnificent world in itself."

- Go into your yard or a nearby park and find a leaf or rock. The most ordinary, plain leaf or rock you can find.

- Sit and look at your leaf or rock for five minutes, quietly.

- Then put it away so you can't see it and write a description of that object for five minutes without stopping. Describe every detail you recall. What distinguishes your leaf or rock from any other?

- Read what you have written, and look at your leaf or rock again before putting it back in the yard.

- Could you find it again based on your description?

You can apply this kind of "leaf attention" to anything or anyone to increase your sense of wonder, and to enlarge your vision of it, of them.

❂ Movement:

Quick—don't think, just write down the names of five objects you see every day. It could be a spatula, mirror, rug, computer, and coffee mug. For the next thirty-seven days, say this OUT LOUD every time you see one of those things, "WOW! A SPATULA!" (where spatula, of course, is the name of your object). Be delighted by them. Play this role as if you were a five-year-old. Love your spatula. If saying your "wow" out loud is too embarrassing, think it with wild abandon, tap your foot, and in a quiet, private way, feel it to the tips of your toes!

i
you
us
them
those people
wouldn't it be lovely
if one could
live
in a constant state
of we?
some of the most
commonplace
words
can be some of the biggest
dividers
they
what if there was
no they?
what if there
was only
us?
if words could be seen
as they floated out
of our mouths
would we feel no
shame
as they passed beyond
our lips?
if we were to string
our words
on a communal clothesline
would we feel proud
as our thoughts
flapped in the
breeze?

—Marilyn Maciel, "clothesline"

CHAPTER FOUR
Inclusion: Be Generous

Generosity during life is a very different thing from generosity in the hour of death; one proceeds from genuine liberality and benevolence, the other from pride or fear.
—**Horace Mann**

One of the wisest people I know is a man named Eliav Zakay, managing director of a national youth leadership program in Israel, the country of our first meeting in 1995. I spoke at a conference there, and serendipity brought us together in that large crowd—we were both assigned to be part of a small, fictional country during a global simulation at the start of the conference. Neither of us being particularly fond of complicated games that pit imaginary nations against one another, we escaped for a coffee, a tour of the underwater aquarium, and a rather interesting kayak ride that ended with the former tank commander in the drink. Eliav has been a source of wisdom and humor ever since.

He told me a story that made a lasting impression, even though he now protests that it wasn't him. So, to placate him, let's imagine this is a story told me by an Israeli man, a man named . . . oh, I don't know, let's say it was a man named Eliav:

While he was still in the Israel Defense Force, his commander took him to the beach one day. "Eliav," he said, "pick up two handfuls of sand." Eliav did as he was told. "Now," said the commander, "keep one hand open and clench the other into as tight a fist as you can."

Again, Eliav did as he was told.

Polish your mud balls.

"Now open the clenched fist and compare how much sand you have in each hand—the hand you clenched and the one you left open," the commander said. "Which one has the most sand in it?"

"The open hand," said Eliav.

In trying to hold on to the sand, we squeeze it out.

There are people in life who hold their hands open, and there are those whose hands are chronically shut. There are those who use their open hands to help others to their feet. And there are those whose hands are closed to connections, particularly with those they perceive as different from themselves.

What does it take to have a generous nature, to hold your hand open, to live a life in which you give when you don't have, when you gift rather than hold, and when you are generous enough to see the deeply rich humanity in people unlike you?

Generosity, it turns out, is a way of being in the world, not a way of giving in the world. **It has little to do with giving gifts, and everything to do with giving space to others to be who they are.**

We don't see things as they are. We see things as we are. **—Anaïs Nin**

My husband, John, used to exhibit at the Washington Antiquarian Book Fair, where dealers would deal their happy deals and buyers would search for that rare find, that first edition to add to their collection. When Emma was eight, she went with me to the opening reception to say hi to her dad. In addition to the bookshelves in John's booth, he had a lighted display case for the more rare and expensive items: Newton's *Opticks,* Darwin's *Origin of Species,* and Stieglitz's photograph of New York's Central Yard. As she peered into the case, Emma looked troubled. "What's wrong, buddy?" John asked from behind the counter.

"What will the poor people be able to buy?" she asked.

She went home that evening and drew small and elegant pictures of horses that she priced at twenty-five cents in the wavering penciled handwriting of a third-grader, insisting that John include them in his showcase. Hers was a special thoughtfulness, a lifting up, a recognition of the varying levels of financial recourse in the world, a caring for—it was, in the truest sense of the world, an offering. It was a sure example of how to create inclusion—with simple mindfulness that others might have a reality different from our own.

Creating inclusion requires being generous. Most often it consists of simply extending a hand. That's hard to do if you are grasping tightly to *your* sand, *your* rightness, *your* belief system, *your* superiority, *your* assumptions about others, *your* definition of normal.

Perhaps what we believe is "normal" is simply "common" instead. If I place myself at "normal" on the continuum of human experience, then you—by definition—are deviant. And the farther you are from my "normal," the more deviant I believe you to be. I don't really know my "normal" until I meet up with "not normal."

ONE DAY OUR DESCENDANTS WILL THINK IT INCREDIBLE THAT WE PAID SO MUCH ATTENTION TO THINGS LIKE THE AMOUNT OF MELANIN IN OUR SKIN OR THE SHAPE OF OUR EYES OR OUR GENDER INSTEAD OF THE UNIQUE IDENTITIES OF EACH OF US AS COMPLEX HUMAN BEINGS.

—Franklin Thomas

What if I place myself off center on that continuum instead, and place others in the center? What if, instead of my own image, my dictionary illustration of normal is the transgender woman at Whole Foods who gets stared at as she shops for marinara sauce? Or perhaps the young man with dreadlocks and tattoos and big holes in his earlobes at Emma's favorite "goth" store at the mall? With great kindness, he answers all my Uncool Parent Questions ("How do you get your earlobes to do that?" "What does VOTE FOR PEDRO mean?" "How do you eat with that big metal thing in your tongue?"). He and I have moved from difference to similarity, not by ignoring the differences, but by walking straight toward them and talking about them.

Generosity comes from opening ourselves to others. We are often more generous to people we perceive to be like us. We must extend that generosity to those we think are unlike us.

[To receive everything, one must open one's hands and give.
—Taisen Deshimaru]

Squeeze in Next to Someone, Arm-to-Arm

In everyone's life, at some time, our inner fire goes out. It is then burst into flame by an encounter with another human being. We should all be thankful for those people who rekindle the inner spirit. —Albert Schweitzer

Eighty-year-old Jungian analyst and author Marion Woodman captured my imagination with a speech on "Women, Power and Soul." She spoke slowly and quietly and clearly about the loss of the feminine principle in the world; she wasn't talking about gender, but of an energy in the world. "If patriarchy is a power principle that has become a parody of itself," she said, "what we need more of is the feminine principle: the receptive side, the soul, the heart side.

"The feminine is the energy that holds presence, the deeper and slower aspect of ourselves," she went on. The feminine looks for relatedness, asking: Where are we alike? How can we connect? Can you see me? And—perhaps most importantly—do you care whether you see me or not?

When she was a high school music and drama teacher, she experienced for herself the power of being a witness, noticing that when her attention wavered during rehearsals, something went wrong: "The energy became lax, muffled, attenuated, an edge of fear crept in, the courageous spontaneity was lost. I suddenly understood that perceiver and perceived were one."

Quantum physics tells us that the presence watching an experiment changes the experiment; the act of observing affects what is observed. "What an awesome responsibility," Woodman gently noted. How are we changing the people around us by how we respond to them, or don't?

How do we hold presence for others? **How do we hold love for others, with no agenda?** Who was able to hold presence for us as children, without asking us to perform to their standards? Who really saw us and heard us and didn't ask for something in return?

Woodman's message and questions were compelling, and yet they paled compared with what I heard next.

During a stay in India, Marion became sick with dysentery and captive in her hotel room for weeks. Finally, desperate to escape the room, she gingerly made her way to the hotel foyer one afternoon to sit and write a letter to her husband. Sitting near the end of a long, empty couch, she began to write.

Although there were other seats available, a very large brown woman came and squeezed between Marion and the end of the couch, so close that their arms were touching, so close it made it difficult for Marion to write.

Marion scooted away, angry at the invasion of her space. The woman scooted closer, pushing up against her: "Every time I moved, she moved, until we ended up at the other end of the couch."

Once she stopped moving away, Marion realized what a nice, big, warm arm the woman had. **And so they sat, a thin bird of a sickly white woman and a big brown woman, arm-to-arm.** They shared no common language, so they sat in silence. Marion gave in to the broad warm arm, the presence of the other, and relaxed into her.

> SHALL WE MAKE A NEW RULE OF LIFE FROM TONIGHT: ALWAYS TO TRY TO BE A LITTLE KINDER THAN IS NECESSARY?
>
> —Sir James M. Barrie

The next day she went again to the hotel foyer to write. And again, the woman came and silently sat next to her, touching her. And the third day. And the fourth day, and Marion's health improved.

This couch dance continued for a week. One day a man appeared as the two women finished their silent, warm-armed vigil.

"You're all right now. My wife won't come back tomorrow," he said to Marion, nodding toward her couch compatriot. Your wife? she thought to herself, startled. "Why is she here in the first place?" she asked.

Marion was unprepared for his quiet, simple answer. "I saw you were dying and sent her to sit with you. I knew the warmth of her body would bring you back to life," he said.

It took a moment for the magnitude of his message and the enormity of what these two strangers had done for her to sink in.

"She did save my life," Marion said quietly in recounting the story. "That this woman would take the time to sit with me and, most importantly, that I could receive it . . . That is relatedness."

That is what it means to hold presence for others.

I can't help but wonder what the world would be like if we all gave unconditionally and held presence for others, even strangers, just as the warm-armed woman did for Marion Woodman in India. Squeeze in beside someone so you are arm-to-arm. Stop moving away. Be fully present; listen to their story without being tempted to respond by recounting your own. Be there, with words or not. Don't check e-mail, calculate stock gains, or cook dinner as you listen. Recognize and own how your presence "changes the experiment," changes others. Show them that you truly care whether you see them or not. Lend them your strong, warm arm. Let them relax into you.

Or ask yourself: How freely can I accept their gift of an arm?

Show them that you truly care whether you

Squeeze in next to someone, arm to arm

Stop moving away.

Be there, with words or not.

the loss of relatedness recogn

...an energy of the world.

✒ Action:

Grab your journal and go to a coffeehouse, restaurant, or park—someplace where there are other people around you who are talking. Listen to the rhythm of the conversations around you. Hold space for others with your silence and attentiveness. Capture snippets of conversation by writing phrases you hear for at least five minutes. Then spend five minutes creating a poem from the pool of gathered phrases. And help someone while you're there—hold the door open for them, perhaps. Perform one small act of kindness.

✺ Movement:

Pay attention to helpfulness. Be attuned to generous offers. Each day for the next thirty-seven days, move toward someone who might need help (and we all need help in some way, don't we?). If they refuse your presence for them, note how that feels, and move on. It's all free data. For those thirty-seven days, also accept the help that is offered you, even if you know you could do it better yourself. Relinquish control to let someone help you. And note how that feels.

Just Wave

We think sometimes that poverty is only being hungry, naked and homeless.
The poverty of being unwanted, unloved and uncared for is the greatest
poverty. We must start in our own homes to remedy this kind of poverty.
—Mother Teresa

There is a man roaming the streets of my
neighborhood in a very dirty coat and hat.
Perhaps he's scoping out the houses, seeing
who's at home, checking schedules, watching
us. He is always walking. Always dirty. Always
smelly. Let's call him Mr. Walker.

As I drove into town one morning last week,
turning past the woods behind and to the left of
the CITGO gas station, I saw him emerge from his
own house—it turns out he lives in the neighborhood. Who knew?

My house was designed in 1903 by Richard Sharpe
Smith, the supervising architect of the Biltmore
House. Well, designed on a far smaller scale, that is.
And if we just had a Florida room off the back and
one extra bedroom or an office tucked away in the
eaves and could redo the kitchen and make the mud-
room into a little breakfast nook, well, then it would
be perfect. Oh, yes, and a big porch awning, and if we
could get our driveway repaved . . . Well, there's always
something, isn't there?

It turns out that Mr. Walker designed his own house, less than 500 yards
from our place!

My house sits on a triangular point of land.

Mr. Walker's house is surrounded by tall trees and Reed Creek, a beautiful
meandering stream.

My house has a fenced-in backyard full of kids' toys and the promise of a
garden sometime, when in more capable hands.

Mr. Walker's house is in unfettered nature, no fences.

As I saw Mr. Walker come out of his own house, I was stopped cold.

His house is a pile of trash and cardboard in the woods, almost hidden from the road. In that moment, I realized he walks because he has no place to go, sit, eat. He's dirty because he has no place to wash. He sleeps in a trash mound because he has no place to rest.

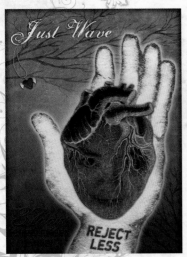

What is my responsibility to this homeless man? How can I help him and save face for him at the same time, and keep myself safe, too? Now that I have seen him stand up and emerge from the trash, how can I ignore that he is there, so close and yet so far away? How can I drive by and not offer a warmer coat, a pair of gloves, a sleeping bag? How can I sleep in a warm bed within shouting distance of him?

There is too much need in the world. I can't hope to keep up with it.

See how easily I have made this a story about me?

How adept we are at dismissing people as less than human. If I can imagine myself in their situation, I pay more attention; if not, no. The wave of horror I feel at the world's pain is often revealed to me as a peculiar form of privilege. There is a sense of fear and relief at the same time: I have not been displaced by hurricanes and tsunamis, so I manage my reaction by keeping these tragedies small, the size of my TV screen. What am I doing about what's happening in the Congo? Nothing. What am I doing about what's happening in the Middle East? Nothing. What am I doing about starving children in the world, about starving children in my own town, about the man with no shoes on Lexington Avenue downtown? Nothing. Nothing. Nothing.

When I first lived in Washington, DC, there was a man who patrolled my neighborhood on Capitol Hill. Fast Walker, we called him, because he walked so quickly, an unlit cigarette always precariously balanced on his bottom lip, hanging like a surfboard on the crest of a wave. I watched him for months, walking, walking, walking, thin and fast.

One spring morning as I made my way to the Union Station Metro stop, Fast Walker and I converged on a small park path, each walking the same way. I stepped up my pace to keep up. "Hi," I said. Fast Walker wheeled around to face me, cutting off my way across the park.

"YOU KNOW ME?" he yelled. "YOU KNOW ME?"

"Well," I replied daintily in my power suit, wishing I had not made the effort to be human, "I've seen you around the neighborhood and just thought I'd say hi."

"YOU DON'T KNOW ME! YOU DON'T KNOW ME!" he yelled back. It was 8:05 a.m. The drivers circling the park were getting an unusual show for this time of the morning, their windows down, turned to face the screams. I continued walking, replying quietly, "No, no, not really—I was just trying to be polite. I'm sorry I bothered you."

"WHERE YOU FROM?" he demanded of me. "WHERE YOU FROM?"

"Originally?" I asked, still parsing the conversation way too small. "I'm originally from a little town in North Carolina; I'm sure you haven't heard of it," I said, plotting my escape, assessing the distance to the 7-Eleven on Massachusetts Avenue.

"MAYBE I HAVE," he screamed, making me think we might have named him erroneously. Perhaps Yelly Man would have been better.

"Well, it was just a little place, called Morganton," I said, just wanting a cup of coffee and a nice anonymous Metro ride where no one speaks or makes eye contact, and perhaps a large chocolate chili truffle just to settle my nerves.

"I'VE BEEN THERE! I'VE BEEN THERE!" he yelled, exciting himself by the prospect of such a connection. Imagine the odds! In the whole big universe of people, here we were in Washington, DC's morning rush hour, evoking our shared history in a small town in North Carolina.

Those odds just seemed too fantastic.

And then it hit me: The North Carolina state mental institution is in my hometown. As he told his story, I realized he had lived there, fulfilling a stereotype I harbor about homeless people—one on which I am challenging myself—that homeless people are mentally unstable. Some are, I know, and some aren't. Is it this fear that keeps me from engaging? And just so I have this straight in my own mind: I would help someone who has cancer, but not someone with a mental illness? Is homelessness just too big a divide to cross? What is the best way to help?

Back in Asheville last Wednesday, I stopped at the CITGO to pick up a Rice Krispie Treat. I could lie and say I stopped for a banana, but I didn't. It was one of those moments when only a Rice Krispie Treat will do.

Beware so long as you live, of judging men by their outward appearance. —**Jean de La Fontaine**

As I sat in front of the CITGO, from the corner of my eye I saw someone approach the parking lot, stopping to slide his finger into the change slot on the pay phone for any coins left there by hurried callers. As I turned to look, I recognized the stained white coat of Mr. Walker. It was the first time I had seen his face. It was like seeing a movie star up close, with a shock of recognition.

He looked a little older than me, a good-looking man with chiseled features and a wind- and sunburned face, tanned against the white of his coat. He always wears a red plaid shirt with that jacket and walks with slightly stooped shoulders, his gaze straight ahead, not looking side-to-side, as if he is so used to people averting their eyes that he doesn't attempt eye contact anymore.

> PEOPLE WHO ARE HOMELESS ARE NOT SOCIAL INADEQUATES. THEY ARE PEOPLE WITHOUT HOMES.
>
> —Sheila McKechnie

He passed my car like a ship of state moving silently through water, straight to the Dumpster to forage for food, looking for pennies you and I have dropped. I watched him navigate the parking lot, back past my car, stooped. Apparently resigned, he bent to slink through a thicket in the woods, branches pushed back by his many trips through it, a path I never see because I don't need to, one created by innumerable trips from his trash pile home to the CITGO.

As Tess and I took John to work downtown one morning recently, she wanted her window rolled down in the backseat of the car. She delights in waving to people with her tiny hand barely visible; in return, she expects nothing less than her own level of enthusiasm from those she greets.

As we stopped at a traffic light, Tess yelled loudly and waved wildly, "HI! HI! HI NICE MAN, HI NICE MAN!" I turned to see the object of her attention and realized it was Mr. Walker making his way slowly up Lexington Avenue, his stained white coat slung over his shoulder this balmy day, his shoulders down. He turned slowly, as if to deflect the notice, and as he saw her little hand and exuberant greeting, Mr. Walker laughed out loud, stood up straight, his eyes smiling at the surprise, saying "HI!" in return and waving a generous wave—a recognition of humanity on both their parts, a connection, however brief.

In that instant Tess had found what I couldn't—his dignity, his right to recognition and greeting, a Self as precious as her own.

This morning we stopped at the CITGO to put air in the tires of our bikes before riding by the river, the weather having warmed, and there he was, picking his way through the brush. When we finished and drove past, Mr. Walker had reached his home and was sitting still, looking straight ahead.

Follow Tess's lead and just wave. Just smile. Acknowledge the humanity of the people around you who don't seem as human as you are—they are. If we turn away to remain safe, we can lose our own humanity. Engaging across these lines is messy sometimes—and sometimes it means being yelled at—but perhaps we need to get dirty once in a while. Just maybe, we should stop complaining about our own lives long enough to remedy our own brand of poverty and help others remedy theirs. As Mother Teresa said, "Hungry not only for bread—but hungry for love. Naked not only for clothing—but naked for human dignity and respect. Homeless not only for want of a room of bricks—but homeless because of rejection."

Action:

Get out your journal for a focused free-write.

- Write for two minutes about your favorite childhood game. What was it, with whom did you play it? After two minutes, stop.

- Then write for two minutes about a secret hiding place, either now or from your childhood. Where is it? When and why do you go there? Stop.

- Write for two minutes about your greatest loss. Where did you feel that loss in your body? Stop.

- Write for two minutes about your first love. What sounds and colors and physical sensations do you associate with that experience? Stop.

- Write for two minutes about your dreams. What do you yearn for? Stop.

Read all you've written in this exercise. Now imagine that every other human being you will ever meet has the same richness and texture of experience and memory and story as do you—whether a ten-year-old boy or a university professor or a person in a homeless shelter or the janitor in your workplace. We are all complex, textured, layered beings—all of us. This is true of every single person we meet.

⚙ Movement:

Starting today and for the next thirty-seven days, make eye contact with people who are living on the streets, homeless. They are people first, then homeless, not homeless people. If they react in a way that shocks or scares you, just remember this isn't about their reaction to you, but about your extending a hand of shared, common humanity to them.

- Don't give money to a homeless person. Instead, provide food to them, or give them coupons to use at local restaurants or grocery stores.

- Get information on resources for the homeless in your area and print contact names and addresses on small cards to offer to them.

- Volunteer at a shelter for people who are homeless.

- Make donations to an organization that helps the homeless in your community.

- If you will host a birthday or anniversary celebration this year, suggest that instead of gifts your guests contribute to an agency that helps the homeless or that they bring canned foods you can donate to a food bank for the hungry.

- Remember the children who are homeless, particularly at the holidays when they may not receive any gifts. Find a way to be their angel.

An individual has not started living until he can rise above the narrow confines of his individualistic concerns to the broader concerns of all humanity. —**Martin Luther King Jr.**

No man can justly censure or condemn another, because indeed no man truly knows another. —**Sir Thomas Brown**

Consider the Flea

And now let us welcome the New Year
Full of things that have never been.

—**Rainer Maria Rilke**

I started writing this on day five of a three-day business trip.

Fog, fate, and freezing rain forced me to endure what felt like decades in airports over those two extra days. Delayed in Chicago, I missed my 11:00 p.m. connection—which, it turns out, was canceled anyway. Somehow the fact that it was canceled seemed lucky, since I would have missed it anyway. When a canceled flight feels like a lottery win, something's wrong.

Desperate for sleep after many false starts (The plane's in the air! It'll be here soon so we can bundle you up in toy seats and get you right home—just sit tight! Aww . . . it was diverted again so we're bringing in a plane from Azerbaijan and a crew from Cape Verde—stay in the gate area because we're sure they'll be here soon!), I bought a book and headed to the Marriott, which practically sits on the runway, a veritable landing strip of a hotel.

The book? Jeffrey Eugenides's novel *Middlesex,* a book I desperately wished I'd written by the time I reached page twelve. The next day, still stranded, I read, then napped, the odd midday, heavy-boned sort of nap that screws you up for the rest of the evening, the sort that sparks dreams of seventeenth-century Dutch microscopist Antoni van Leeuwenhoek.

A mere mention of his name in *Middlesex* brought his flea drawings back to mind.

A minor official in the city of Delft, van Leeuwenhoek had no formal scientific training, but he did have a copy of Robert Hooke's *Micrographia* and a passion for all things tiny.

Using his own homemade single-lens microscope, an instrument so small it fit in the palm of his hand, van Leeuwenhoek observed everything he could imagine and collaborated with artists to produce exquisite illustrations of the marvels he viewed, things that had never before been seen. Although his microscopes used only a single lens, they were capable of magnifications of up to 200X while other microscopes of the time were lucky to achieve 10X magnification.

He could see more deeply, more closely, more fully. And after seeing at such depth, it was impossible to not-know the detail, the intricacy, the complexity. **He couldn't not-know once he knew; he couldn't not-see once he saw.**

When observing pepper (he assumed it had microscopic spikes to produce its effect on the tongue—it doesn't), van Leeuwenhoek made an accidental discovery: the tiny organisms known today as protozoans. He became the first person to see a living microbe. When the Royal Society was able to reproduce his experiment, van Leeuwenhoek became a celebrity, finding little animals everywhere, including "many very little living animacules, very prettily a-moving" in his own dental plaque. He had, in effect, discovered life on another planet—and that planet was us.

In our micro world of iPod nanos and laptops the size of fingernails, I'm unsure if we can appreciate the magnitude (pun intended) of van Leeuwenhoek's work: No one had ever seen what he saw, there was no knowledge of the fine structures of life-forms, no cause for this awe until then. Suddenly different, inward worlds presented themselves, revealing an infinite regress of magnification and complexity and life within life. Thanks to the measuring of infinitesimal things, the whole idea of measurement changed instantly and forever.

When he saw a flea at such magnification, something undoable happened. The minuscule dot of a pesty bug became an undeniably intricate, complex

Look and you will find it—what is unsought will go undetected. —**Sophocles**

creature with its own unique beauty—the flea was complex, not simple; it was worthy of attention, not just an absentminded swat.

How is this true of people? We see two-dimensional categories of people—groupings without definition, big swatches of folks—"Them." What would it take to see more deeply, more closely, more fully, to move from seeing people as a *what* to seeing them as a *who,* more individualized, more beautifully complex, more—well, more human and more like us?

As my friend David watched whales in Alaska recently with his partner, Lora, they were speechless at the enormity of the beauty of the creatures in front of them. Why, David asked afterward, do we reserve such awe for whales and not for other human beings? Why don't we look to other humans (and ourselves) with the same eyes? That man from Cincinnati beside you on the plane in seat 8B? He's miraculous—see it, acknowledge it.

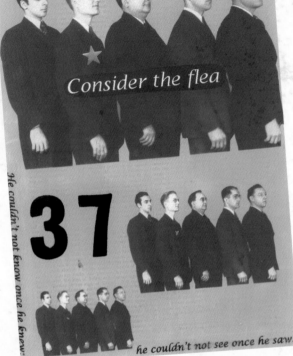

Once, John visited Emma's fourth-grade class to teach about seeing. He used an enlarged poster of a dollar and gave each student a dollar bill and piece of paper with a tiny hole in it. John pointed to places on the poster and instructed the students to find that spot on their dollar, looking only through the tiny hole in the piece of paper. The smallness of the hole focused their attention on the "hidden" objects on a dollar bill (like that tiny owl no bigger than three pinheads—can you find it?). Now that you know those things are there, you can't not-see them, he told the class.

If we learn anything from van Leeuwenhoek, maybe our New Years won't be full of Rilke's things that have never been, but full of things we've just never seen—and after we see them, they will be there all the time; we can no longer not-see. The challenge, then, is to focus, to see more deeply than we have ever seen before, to look for the beauty in the complexity of others.

Van Leeuwenhoek started his miraculous journey by using a magnifying glass to count the threads of sheets in the store where he worked as a linen draper: in the everyday. Where will I begin mine? You and yours?

Consider the flea. Reserve as much awe for the intricate human beings around you as you have for whales and bald eagles and panda babies and Xbox games. Focus your attention. Look more closely. See deeply, inside. Just see. Don't not-know. Stop not-seeing.

✐ *Action:*

You'll need your journal, a pen, and an apple for this focused free-write.

- Sit at your desk with an apple in front of you. Pretend that you have come to this planet from somewhere far away and have never seen an apple before. Examine it by touching it if you'd like.

- Then spend seven minutes writing a detailed description of this object in front of you—what is it? What does it look like? What does one do with it? You might feel that seven minutes is too long—look again. There is plenty of detail in the object to keep you writing for that long. Imagine you are explaining the object (apple) to another alien who also has never seen one.

- When your seven minutes are up, read what you have written.

- Now write for three minutes on these questions: How did the time spent writing about it make you feel toward your apple? Would you be able to pick it out of a basket of apples now? Did those seven minutes of intense scrutiny enlarge your connection to that particular apple? In what ways?

> Be careful how you interpret the world: it is like that.
> **—Erich Heller**

Movement:

⬡ **Movement:**

- Every morning for the next thirty-seven days, look at that apple or re-read your description of it. Then enter your day with the same kind of attention for the people you meet: What are they? What do they look like? What do they love and yearn for? Do they deserve the same kind of attention?

- You can also take a sheet of paper, put a 1/8-inch hole in it with the sharp-ened point of a pencil, and get very close to an object with it. The tiny hole will focus your attention. Try making a larger hole by sticking the whole pencil through the paper. How does that change your ability to focus?

- Explore how to do the same kind of focusing in the world of your everyday life by challenging yourself to do only one thing at a time. For thirty-seven days hone and focus your attention by never doing something else while listening to someone. If a co-worker is talking to you, turn and face them, put down your pen, and listen. If your child wants to tell you something, do nothing else but listen. See what that kind of focus can provide for you—and for them.

. . . WITH AN EYE MADE QUIET BY THE POWER

OF HARMONY, AND THE DEEP POWER OF JOY,

WE SEE INTO THE LIFE OF THINGS.

—William Wordsworth, Tintern Abbey

You become what you think about. —Earl Nightingale

Redefine Normal

The privilege of a lifetime is being who you are. —Joseph Campbell

I sat on the steps of Binford Dorm with my roommate, Anne, to celebrate the first day of spring and the end of our freshman year. We ate Cheese Nips from the box, facing the parking lot. "Look," Anne said, "there's Tane and somebody. Who's that with him?"

Two men walked slowly toward us, laughing, their bodies outlined by the sun behind them as if they were saints. "You know Richard?" Tane asked as they got near, pointing toward the man beside him wearing a black beret and clogs, like me. I shook my head no.

"Hi," I said, looking up at Richard, my right hand over my eyes like a salute, shielding the sun so I could see his face.

"Hi," he answered in a sweet voice. "Nice clogs." When he smiled, I could see deep dimples on either side of his mouth.

"Nice beret," I answered.

"Richard's a DJ at the radio station. He's the guy who plays too much Jethro Tull." Tane laughed, as did Richard.

I looked at Richard again. "I've heard your show! You know how you always try to figure out what the radio voice looks like?" He smiled and nodded. "You don't disappoint . . . but you do look different than I thought you would," I said, looking down quickly.

"Blacker?" he asked.

"Yes." I looked up and held his gaze without blinking. The four of us walked to Huck's for pizza.

That summer, Richard was a roadie for a rock band in Philadelphia. I worked at Joe's Dairy Bar in my small hometown dipping twenty-eight flavors for the Baptists after Sunday-evening services. A letter-writing frenzy connected us: Real letters, since e-mail didn't exist yet, mail flying back and forth with sweet anticipation, a physical representation of thoughts with that satisfying feel of paper folded, unfolded, read and re-read many times.

As the next school year began, so did we, me and Richard. It was 1978. **The world spread out in front of us like a carpet unrolling**, like it had never unrolled for anyone before, a path to some bright and fantastic future. He was funny, caring, strong. There was light in our journey, heady possibility.

> TO BE NOBODY BUT MYSELF—IN A WORLD WHICH IS DOING ITS BEST, NIGHT AND DAY, TO MAKE ME SOMEBODY ELSE—MEANS TO FIGHT THE HARDEST BATTLE ANY HUMAN CAN FIGHT, AND NEVER STOP FIGHTING.
>
> —e. e. cummings

I regaled my parents with stories of Richard, and they were so very happy for me—he was so smart! So thoughtful! So attentive! Finally, they asked to see a picture of Richard. The moment I put the photo on the dining table, I saw a reaction I never expected. The confusion I experienced was physical and immediate, like you feel when you're in another culture and do something you think is witty, only to realize from the reactions of those around you that what you've done is the equivalent of using the F-word with someone's diminutive grandmama.

I quit college for a time, taking the only job I could find—as chief burger maker at the Wendy's on High Point Road. It turns out they hired me not only because of my extensive condiment acumen, but also because my red hair looked suspiciously like that of their mascot. I was called into service as her incarnation at charity events and pep rallies, hair in pigtails, wearing that blue-and-white dress with the puffy sleeves at ice-skating events at Four Seasons Mall to raise money for cancer research. I might add that being a vegetarian chief burger maker was not without its significant ironies.

In the midst of this burger drama and exile, my father died. I was only twenty.

Why did this spiral begin? Because Richard's skin was black. Well, truth-fully, it was honey-and-ginger-colored, but this was not the time to be

We fight for men and women whose poetry is not yet written. **—Robert Gould Shaw**

specific. I was as shocked by my parents' reaction as they were by his skin color. Having been raised in the church and heard messages about "all God's children" my whole life, I was unprepared for the significant loopholes, the escape clauses, the buyouts, the insider trading, the extenuating circumstances and legalistic wranglings, the *yes, but* part of the equality equation that appeared to be at work.

> Common sense is the collection of prejudices acquired by the age of eighteen. —**Albert Einstein**

There's no doubt that my parents were the product of their time and place. There were plenty of "N-lover" epithets hurled our way as Richard and I lived our lives in sunny Greensboro, North Carolina. We were spat at, and worse. After all, this was thirty years ago and there were still Ku Klux Klan rallies downtown, complete with shootings in the streets.

My parents were exercising that particular brand of protectiveness that as a parent myself I now recognize; I know now it was a combination of true and pure and real love and, let's be honest, also not wanting to be talked about in a small town fueled by such talk. I understand that now. I have made my peace with it now. But I know the impact it had on Richard, whom they would never meet. Dehumanized, shunned, judged, erased, disregarded, eliminated, hated, yet never even known.

I was facing out-loud racism for the first time, up close and personal. Up to this point, I guess it was the insidious, invisible, underground, and ultimately more dangerous brand of racism I had lived with. It was formative and transformative to live through this prejudice, ignorance, and fear; it is why I do the work I do now.

Some years later Richard and I decided to part, as do many youthful college couples, our trajectories diverging. Surely things would be easier now for an interracial couple. Or maybe not. Just a decade ago a black man named James Byrd was dragged behind a pickup truck in Jasper, Texas, desperately trying to hold his head up off the pavement until it finally hit a curb and was severed from his body. In such a world where that is still possible, we have not come as far as we would like to believe.

> [Nothing in life is to be feared, it is only to be understood.]
> —**Madame Curie**

Almost thirty years after our first meeting in clogs, Richard wrote to me of a small basket in which he had tucked mementos of our time together, letters, small ephemera of trips we took, photographs of us laughing, and a pair of tiny diamond earrings (so tiny I had forgotten them) left behind when I moved away to graduate school. He now wears those earrings, he wrote, because he is now Amanda, having undergone a transgender transition, recognizing that he was intended to be a woman, not a man. For me, those earrings provide some closure to that circle that was begun with racial fissure thirty years before.

A new set of superficial judgments and indictments await my friend—and a new, complex set of learnings for me. We don't allow too easily for ambiguity in this culture; we see things, pun intended, in black and white. What if someone is physically in a body that doesn't match who they really are, yet for whom society dictates such strong and unambiguous norms—blue blankets for boy babies, pink blankets for girl babies, dolls for girls, swords for boys, tears for girls, silent stoicism for boys? Amanda's journey mirrors Richard's—he, too, was physically in a body for which society dictated strong and unambiguous norms, judged by its surface without looking inside.

My friend's two journeys to self are the hardest trails to traverse in this world, a world in which we constantly ask, around both race and gender, "What are you?"

While deep into my research about transgender issues following Amanda's revelation about finding her true self, my older daughter—then around nine years old—asked what I was doing. As I explained it to her, with all its intricate and confusing focus on "normality," she listened plaintively for a long time, then finally asked the question we should all be asking: "Who gets to say what normal is?"

REDEFINE NORMAL

Coerced conformity has costs. It reduces me and replaces others.

37 DAYS

If G-d had wanted us to be the same, He would have created us that way. —**Koran**

Remember Richard, remember James Byrd trying desperately to save his own life, and remember the many others like them. Fight racism in whatever way you can. Use your voice, hold up your head, step up to the task. Daily. Also, remember Amanda and the many others like her. Read about transgender issues so you'll be informed and supportive when you meet someone who is transgender. Think again about your own definition of normal and the ways that your definition of it subtly (and perhaps not so subtly) excludes others, causing you to judge them. Who does get to decide what normal is? Ignorance breeds fear breeds avoidance breeds misunderstanding breeds stereotypes breeds prejudice breeds hatred breeds violence. Stop the cycle.

Action:

For this focused free-write, pick up your pen in your nondominant hand, not the hand with which you usually write.

- Quick! First one finished wins! Write (in cursive) this sentence, using that nondominant hand: I am writing this with my nondominant hand.

- How was that? Frustrating? What if you were being judged on the merits of that handwriting? What? Not fair, you say?

- Now switch back to your usual writing hand and write for six minutes about a time when you were in the minority: Perhaps you've attended a gathering where you were a racial minority, or were the only woman in a group of men, or the only vegetarian in a sea of carnivores, or the only English speaker in a bus full of Japanese speakers. What was that like? What impact did it have on you? In what ways did you feel you were being judged? Did you change your way of being in the world in that situation? Did you play smaller or quieter as a result?

- If you've never had the experience of being in the minority, that's good information, too. Why not? Write about how you might gain that experience—could you attend services at a Jewish synagogue or a Catholic church, or go to a movie you perceive to be for an African American or other culture's audience? After you finish writing, make plans to do one of those things.

◯ *Movement:*

For the next thirty-seven days, do something every day that takes you out of your "normal."

- If you usually listen to classical music, listen to hip-hop (my favorite is Portland, Oregon—based Mic Crenshaw of Hungry Mob Productions).

- See a movie you don't think is for you.

- Read a magazine you'd never otherwise pick up.

- Read Jennifer Finney Boylan's *She's Not There* or Jamison Green's *Becoming a Visible Man* to learn what it's like to be a transgender person.

- Read Dawn Prince-Hughes's *Songs of the Gorilla Nation* to learn about what it's like to be a person with autism.

- Go to a black barbershop to get your hair cut if you're Caucasian.

- Ask respectful questions about the differences you see around you using the opening phrase, *Help me understand* . . . : Help me understand the headdress you're wearing." Help me understand your beliefs about [pick your topic]. The phrase *help me understand* indicates a desire for something beyond judgment and even beyond curiosity, something at a deeper level.

Experiencing the world of others doesn't imply agreement or adoption of their way of being in the world, but it does require openness. Try respectful curiosity for thirty-seven days.

Polish Your Mud Balls

When you start on a long journey, trees are trees, water is water, and mountains are mountains. After you have gone some distance, trees are no longer trees, water no longer water, mountains no longer mountains. But after you have traveled a great distance, trees are once again trees, water is once again water, mountains are once again mountains. —**Zen teaching**

The book *Art and Fear* brings us the story of a pottery teacher who tells half his class they'll be graded solely on the *quantity* of the work they produce. He'll even use a scale to weigh their output and determine their grade. Fifty pounds of pots would rate an A, for example. The other half would be graded on *quality* and need only produce one pot—a perfect one—to get an A.

"The works of highest quality," the authors reported, "were all produced by the group being graded for quantity . . . while they were busily churning out piles of work—and learning from their mistakes—the quality group had sat theorizing about perfection, and in the end had little more to show for their efforts than grandiose theories and a pile of dead clay."

I see the pottery metaphor play out at conferences. Some speakers are buttoned up, flawless, measured, and practiced, with an expert-focused answer for everything. **They don't risk much or—ultimately—give much.** They are too involved in relentless self-monitoring, creating the perfect pot. Others learn as much from the people they are speaking to—they give and they take, they ride the wave that is in the room at the time, not the one they hoped might be there or the one they planned against as some do; instead, they stumble over new insights and acknowledge the stumble. They co-create meaning with the people in the room, they are subject-focused—they make a lot of pots, taking me along for the ride, letting me see myself in their story.

In the classes I teach, I watch people navigate their fear of looking foolish, their desire not to admit that they don't know, their need to be in control, to know, to have the right answer, to say what teacher wants to hear, to focus on something "out there" and not "in here," to get the A or, at the very least, to leave without being changed in any significant way by their interactions with new knowledge or insight.

What If There Are No Right Answers, Just Mud Balls?

The silt he uses to coat the mud balls is fine; it has been strained through a tiny mesh sieve, like invisible shards of glass, to dust perfection. Holding a handful above its surface, hikaru dorodango (shiny mud ball) master Bruce Gardner showers the orb with dust, building up the surface and polishing it to a fine sheen at the same time. The finished 5-inch spheres have a cool wetness and heft to them that is satisfying, elemental, a beauty born of dirt and patience and care. They can only be completed over time, not at one sitting. Looking like shiny orbs of marble when they are finally finished, he places them on small black wrought-iron stands to display them.

Gardner creates his hikaru dorodango from pure, simple, common dirt and sand lovingly caressed into these desirable and oddly soothing objects. He has perfected the art, but it took a lot of trying. "Even my rough, malformed first attempts grew precious to me as I worked with them," Gardner writes. "This curious attachment is part of what make hikaru dorodango so special. I'm struck by how these objects, created from such humble material, are the nearly perfect expression of process refinement."

FOR A LONG TIME IT HAD SEEMED TO ME THAT LIFE WAS ABOUT TO BEGIN—REAL LIFE. BUT THERE WAS ALWAYS SOME OBSTACLE IN THE WAY, SOMETHING TO BE GOTTEN THROUGH FIRST, SOME UNFINISHED BUSINESS, TIME STILL TO BE SERVED, A DEBT TO BE PAID. THEN LIFE WOULD BEGIN. AT LAST IT DAWNED ON ME THAT THESE OBSTACLES WERE MY LIFE.

—Alfred D'Souza

Children in Japan are fixated on these mud balls—or they were a few years ago when creating hikaru dorodango became a mania there. Professor Fumio Kayo of the Kyoto University of Education, a psychologist who researches children's play, was responsible for the craze. He first encountered hikaru dorodango in a Kyoto nursery school in 1999. Through 200 failed experiments and an analysis using an electron microscope, Kayo devised a method of making

POLISH YOUR MUD BALL

hikaru dorodango that even children can learn. The kids spend hours creating and polishing balls of mud. **They grow attached to and treasure their mud balls even if they are not perfect, even if they do not shine.**

The joy of hikaru dorodango is two-fold: the sheer pleasure that comes with creating, that meditative and wondrous place we go sometimes in the creative moment—coupled with the desire to create the shiniest ball.

And so we polish our own lives, creating landscapes and canyons and peaks with the very silt we try to avoid, the dirt we disavow or hide or deny. It is the dirt of our lives—the depressions, the losses, the inequities, the failing grades in trigonometry, the e-mails sent in fear or hate or haste, the ways in which we encounter people different from us—that shape us, polish us to a heady sheen, make us in fact more beautiful, more elemental, more artful and lasting.

What if we considered our lives hikaru dorodango by showering in the silt and gently turning to let it fall evenly around us, realizing that we need it to complete the work of art that is us? Its granules hold polish and the very possibility of art.

The maxim "Nothing but perfection" may be spelled "Paralysis." —**Winston Churchill**

Don't seek perfection. Make messes. Play. Make a mud ball. Love what you are creating even if it never shines, even if it cracks, like those pounds of clay. Don't fear the showers of silt that make the mud balls of our lives shine. (By the way, you can see Bruce Gardner's beautiful hikaru dorodango at www.dorodango.com.)

✐ Action:

Haiku is a Japanese form of poetry that typically has three lines, the first with five syllables, the second with seven, and the third with five again. For example, I write mini book reviews in haiku. Here's one about the book mentioned in this essay, *Art and Fear*:

> What stops an artist? (five syllables)
> Is it fears about others (seven syllables)
> or about ourselves? (five syllables)

- For the next four minutes, write as many haiku as you can about failure.

- Now write for four more minutes—still in haiku form—about perfection.

- Again, for two minutes—in haiku—write about the beauty of dirt.

- Read what you've written. Is it possible that failure is beautiful, too?

Love absolutely everything that ever happens in your life. —**Paul Cantalupo**

☼ Movement:

Pick an art form and create one item every day for thirty-seven days, whether it be writing a poem or haiku, making a collage, practicing your calligraphy, drawing a 2-inch by 2-inch picture, crocheting a square, painting a small canvas, or arranging flowers. Stick with the same art form for the thirty-seven days—get one done every day without exception. Focus on quantity and not on quality. What emerges from that repetition and habit?

Say Hi to Yaron

Judging is a lonely job in which a man is, as near as may be, an island entire.
—Abe Fortas

A few years ago I boarded a flight that changed my life. As I boarded that plane, I know now I was walking away from one version of myself and into another, but at the time it felt like I was just going to Parsippany.

I was in no mood for idle chitchat on the flight; my seatmate had better shut up and get engrossed in a flight magazine, in all those lovely trinkets in the SkyMall catalog, or in some inane movie about the father of the bride or a wedding planner starring Steve Martin or Jennifer Lopez. I just wanted some peace and quiet. It had been a hell of a trip so far and I was in no mood to go to New Jersey. I just wanted to go home.

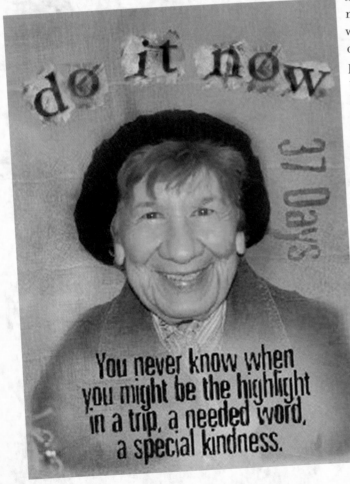

do it now

37 days

You never know when you might be the highlight in a trip, a needed word, a special kindness.

My seatmate was a very large man, a broad-faced wonder, a man whose belly was not to be contained in a too-small T-shirt from the Grand Canyon but poured over into my space instead, over the armrest and into my air, my real estate, my 12B.

Great. That's just great. I put on my Power Suit Mask and opened my book, an erudite volume of poems in their original German by Rainer Maria Rilke; I used to keep it in my carry-on bag for just such emergencies. It stopped people in their tracks, usually.

Not this time.

Grand Canyon Man rifled incessantly through a plastic grocery bag he kept between his feet on the floor, then up in his lap, then down again.

The sound was overwhelming, as if the universe had focused its sound boom on that one piece of plastic, amplifying it beyond all measure: I could hear nothing else. Every movement he made moved me, too. I was irritated.

Suddenly, without any warning, there was a loud explosion from his lap. The large, family-size bag of pretzels he had burst open was thrust before me; I was shocked into silence, only nodding a fierce no and returning to my Rilke.

> Wie soll ich meine Seele halten, daß
> sie nicht an deine rührt? Wie soll ich sie
> hinheben über dich zu andern Dingen?

Yeah, yeah, *your soul is mine,* just keep your extraordinarily large hands and pretzels in 12A.

> Ach gerne möchte ich sie bei irgendetwas
> Verlorenem im Dunkel unterbringen
> an einer fremden stillen Stelle, die
> nicht weiterschwingt, wenn deine Tiefen schwingen.

How shall I hold on to my soul, so that it does not touch yours, indeed? Maybe when he wrote those words, Rilke hadn't been in a plane seat where *everything* touches. *How shall I lift it gently up over you on to other things? I would so very much like to tuck it away among long lost objects in the dark, in some quiet, unknown place, somewhere which remains motionless when your depths resound.*

Yeah, all that, Rainer—and a little space for breathing and leaning back in my very own 12B would be nice, too.

It grew dark as we passed through clouds; suddenly Large Plastic Bag Grand Canyon Pretzel Man reached up and turned on my light for me, still not speaking. Perhaps he is mute. He looks like a larger-than-normal Aleutian. A giant Aleutian mute, that's just great. After the day I've had. I really need to be left alone. I don't want to engage. Can Large Plastic Bag Grand Canyon Mute Aleutian Pretzel Man not understand that?

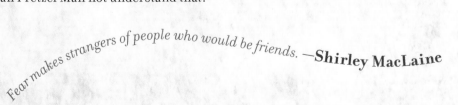

Fear makes strangers of people who would be friends. —**Shirley MacLaine**

I nodded with a forced grin to acknowledge his gentlemanly intrusion. **Then it hit me. I'd just given a speech to 12,000 people about not judging people by how they look.**

I determined, between sips of Bloody Mary mix, to be nicer, to reclaim my humanity, to try—dear sweet God—to restore what little karma I had left. When I saw Large Plastic Bag Grand Canyon Mute Aleutian Pretzel Man taking photos out of the plane window with a disposable Kodak, I made my move.

WE SOMETIMES ENCOUNTER PEOPLE, EVEN PERFECT STRANGERS, WHO BEGIN TO INTEREST US AT FIRST SIGHT, SOMEHOW SUDDENLY, ALL AT ONCE, BEFORE A WORD HAS BEEN SPOKEN.

—Fyodor Dostoevsky

"What are you taking photographs of?" I asked in that slow, loud, excruciatingly enunciated voice sometimes used with non–English speakers.

"We don't have rivers this big in Israel," he answered slowly in halting English, with a beautiful Israeli accent. One of my dearest and wisest friends is from Israel. I turned to face this fabulous voice. "Where are you from in Israel?" I asked. And with that, we began a friendship that endures even now, years later.

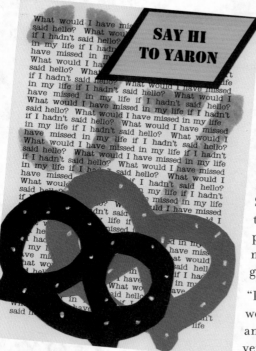

SAY HI TO YARON

Yaron was a policeman in Netanya, an Israeli resort town. He and his police partner saved their money for five years to come to the United States; when her grandmother died the week before the trip, it was clear he would have to come alone. Unsure of his English and here for the first time, he toured the United States by himself, no doubt the constant beneficiary of the kind of cold reaction I had given him. He brought police insignia badges from Israel to trade with policemen in the US; I still barter with policemen I meet to get badges to send him for his collection.

"I have traveled all over the United States in these three weeks," he told me. "I rented a tiny car in Los Angeles and drove to the Grand Canyon." He held his large hands very close together, mimicking how small a steering wheel his budget compact car had. "When you stand at the edge of the Grand Canyon, you want to turn to the person next to you just to say *Look, look at that.*

"I didn't have anybody to turn to," he said.

"I went to Walt Disney World in Florida and my video camera broke. I couldn't help myself; I started crying in the middle of the street. One of the workers saw me and gave me this little paper camera so I could take pictures while I was there. But you know," he said, looking straight at me, "it's not the same. When you see a field of wheat blowing in the breeze, it's so much different than just seeing a still picture of the wheat, isn't it?"

It occurred to me I was in the presence of someone with a poet's soul all wrapped up in a policeman's body.

"Yes," I answered, "it's very different."

We talked the whole way to Newark. It turns out that I had sat beside Yaron on his very last night in the United States; he was taking a city bus from the airport to a distant relative's house somewhere in New Jersey before flying home the next day.

When we landed, the car and driver my client had arranged was nowhere to be found. It was yet another gift. Yaron and I went to an airport coffee shop to talk, emerging hours later. He told me about his fiancée going to the market three days before their wedding and being killed by a truck on the way home, his large sausage fingers moving slowly to just under his eyes where he held them for a moment to serve as logjams for the tears that had collected. He talked about his part-time design business: "You have to see what I got!" he said, digging deeply in one of the bags that surrounded his feet. "It is so beautiful!" His broad face lit up at the very thought of it.

He rooted around for a good while. "I asked the manager if I could please have one because I had never seen anything like it!" he said excitedly. And finally, he sat up again, his large hands dwarfing a Shoney's menu. "Isn't this beautiful?" he asked. "Just look at the color!"

I do desire we be better strangers. —William Shakespeare

Yaron was planning to find a city bus to take him to his final destination. I couldn't have his experience in the States end that way. "Come with me," I said. "We'll get a cab together and I'll take you to your cousin's house."

When we approached the tiny 110-year-old man in the first cab with my efficient, crisp, practiced, I'm-a-business-traveler-leave-me-the-hell-alone rollaboard and Yaron's big suitcases and plastic bags, he balked. "Oh, no, ma'am. You need two cabs. You're going in two opposite directions."

"Well," I answered. "We'll go to where he's going first and then we'll turn around and go where I'm going."

"No, ma'am, that'll cost you over $150; you really need two cabs."

"I appreciate that you're trying to save me money, but we need to go together," I said, insistent on delivering Yaron safely with all his bags and Shoney's menus. I couldn't bear the thought of him lugging those bags onto a city bus, unsure of where he was going, perhaps not being met on the other end by his cousin. It just wouldn't do. It wasn't the image of the United States I wanted to leave him with. The man deserved better.

> I have always depended on the kindness of strangers.
> —**Tennessee Williams**
> *A Streetcar Named Desire*

We got lost many times on that journey to his cousin's house, so the drive gave us even more time to talk. And after I dropped Yaron off, his cousin waving quizzically from her front door, my cab started backtracking to Parsippany.

Yaron called the next morning to wish me well in my speech. He calls from Israel every Christmas Eve and names all of Santa's reindeer even though Santa isn't part of his tradition. He stays up late to call us on New Year's Eve. When he found out that John's grandmother, Nana, was a devout Catholic, he sent holy water from the River Jordan for us to give her.

"And just so you know it isn't water from my bathroom, I made a video of me getting it from the River Jordan," he said.

Sure enough, the water arrived with a videotape of him driving (and filming at the same time) to the River Jordan. He videotaped the RIVER JORDAN sign followed by shaky camera motion while the video camera was set on a rock and Yaron ran in front of the lens, bending down with a Fanta bottle, scooping in holy water.

What would I have missed if I hadn't said hello to him?

37 Days: Do It Now Challenge

Say hi to Yaron. You never know when you might be the highlight in a trip, a needed word, a special kindness. You never know when you might find the friend you've needed, or the learning that changes everything for you. This wasn't Large Plastic Bag Grand Canyon Mute Aleutian Pretzel Man; this was a real person with a name and a history and stories that make him laugh and cry. He was a who, not a what, just like me.

✐ Action:

- For five minutes, just draw a blueprint of your childhood home, the house or living space you most identify with your childhood. Be as detailed as possible.

- Once you are finished drawing the blueprint, take someone on a tour through the house for five minutes. Or, if you're alone, talk aloud as if someone were with you—take them on a tour.

- What stories emerge? What lessons were learned in that house?

The blueprint is simply a catalyst for realizing that we are made up of stories— as is everyone else. The man sitting next to you on the plane? Him, too.

⟳ Movement:

Yaron is everywhere. He is at Starbucks in front of us in line. He's the grocery bagger at the store. He's the man who is chewing too loudly at the table next to us at lunch. For the next thirty-seven days, notice each day what keeps you from engaging with others. Is it that you're afraid of their reaction? Do they scare you in some way? Are you too tired or busy? We are always walking toward or away from others. Make a note of the opportunities you have to meet someone new—and note why you didn't. Patterns may emerge from this investigation. What are you missing? You may never know.

You say that in times like these
You're driven down to your knees
Looking around grieving what peace there was
You promised yourself you would
Work for a world of good
Look at you now wondering what good it does

No lost hope no violent point of view
Can erase all of the good you do

There's nothing as dark as night
But nothing so strong as light
Here is the choice: to let it burn out or bright
In a world where the fear and force
Have buried the silent source
Can you deny the need for a light like yours

No fast pace no jaded attitude
Can erase all of the good you do

If someone has left his wrath
On everything in his path
Taking the wealth and leaving his trash behind
Will you be peace or pride
Can you at last decide
There's no one to fight we are the same inside

So go home and get some rest
There's many more miles and tests
All about love what if it comes to be all that we have left

No dark place no debt and no abuse
Can erase all of the good you do

—Christine Kane, from "The Good You Do"
on her CD *Right Outta Nowhere*

CHAPTER FIVE
Integrity: Speak Up

When we are really honest with ourselves, we must admit our lives are all that really belong to us. So it is how we use our lives that determines the kind of men we are. —**César Chávez**

"How are you doing?" she asked as I entered her office.

"I'm okay," I said.

She sat, quietly, looking at me.

"Okay, I'm a little stressed out, I guess." My acupuncturist, Hannah, invokes truth by silence better than anyone else I know.

I was in a situation at the time that was maddening—and in which I knew I was right. So, I held forth. She listened. And listened some more. "Let's get you on the table and we can continue this conversation," she said.

Then I was prone, under a sheet, and she was holding my hand, taking my pulses. She paused.

"Patti, why do you think you are so attached to being right about this situation?" she asked.

Blink.

Why am I so attached to being right? Oh, I don't know, this is just a wild stab, but *maybe*—

BECAUSE I'M RIGHT?

"Because it's so clear I'm right," I said. "Can't you see I'm right? There's just no way I'm not right!"

"Why is being right about this so important to you?"

Blink.

"And doesn't everyone have their own version of right?" she asked.

Blink.

"I wonder what would happen if you gave up your need to be right?"

Damn. She can do more in four quiet questions than I can do in a lifetime.

After a while she spoke again. "In Buddhism," she said, "attachment is the root of our suffering."

I understand that. I lived with a Buddhist family in Sri Lanka, I studied with Buddhist monks—I get that. I don't feel overly attached to things, to owning new cars and silent trash compactors and Sub-Zero fridges and iPhones (though those iPhones are beautiful).

"And," she said, "maybe you're not so attached to possessions, but attachment to being right is still an attachment. And it is causing you to suffer."

I never knew. It all became clear in that moment in that small room on that table in that sunlight. **My attachment to being right is as much an attachment as lusting after a possession.** I have made being right a palpable thing, like a Chad Alice Hagen felted scarf or a Jane Voorhees watercolor or a Lisa Fidler bracelet or an Ayana Bar necklace from Tel Aviv.

"There is an image of attachment that might be helpful," she explained. "It is said we should imagine a large thornbush in which we are sitting, naked. As you can imagine, every move we make to reach for something"—she moved her arm forward to demonstrate—"causes us to sink our limbs deeper and deeper into the thorns."

I listened, not moving.

"Perhaps it is not the situation that is making you suffer, but your grasping at being right in it," my acupuncturist guru said.

As the poet Rumi wrote, somewhere between right and wrong is a place we can meet and talk. Shouting across the expanse of that field only makes us hoarse—what if we each walk toward the center instead? Even when we are right—when someone is using racial slurs, for example—we need to find better ways of bringing others along rather than alienating them. Most of all, differences of opinion are opportunities for learning.

In a recent class I taught on humor and play as intercultural tools, our conversation turned to humor that ridicules a group—like the Polish jokes my husband endures, or blond or racist or gay jokes. How do we navigate that kind of humor? What are our responsibilities to speak up? What difficulties do we face in doing so?

Class members offered examples of how we are—in effect—participating by not speaking out against such humor. The conversation continued until a woman named Esther Louie offered a tool she uses.

"I learned this technique from a friend," she said, "and it's been helpful when someone makes a joke at the expense of some group.

"When that happens," she continued, "I simply say, 'I don't see the truth in that.' It helps me own my own reaction, honors my desire and responsibility to respond in a way that registers my reaction, and helps me speak my truth." We were struck silent by the beauty of the phrase: *I don't see the truth in that.*

Choosing with integrity means finding ways to speak up that honor your reality, the reality of others, and your willingness to meet in the center of that large field. It's hard sometimes.

Choose with integrity: Speak up, yet detach from "rightness." Stand tall, yet bend to meet others. Move from Why aren't they doing more? to Why aren't we doing more? to Why am I not doing more? Do something. Extend yourself.

Act as if what you do makes a difference. It does. —**William James**

Save Face for Someone Else

Our dignity is not in what we do, but what we understand. —George Santayana

When I was in high school, I had my dream job.

Mrs. Barnett, the head librarian at the Morganton-Burke Public Library, had watched me grow up there. As a child I was in the library every Saturday, and every Saturday I checked out the same book. Year after year.

Up I would walk with that dog-eared book in my arms, and put it in the RETURN BOOKS slot. I would stand very still and wait until Ruth Setzer, the bony-armed librarian, checked it in, taking out its ink-stained due-date card and closing the cover. Without a word, she would extend that impossibly thin, long arm to me, with my treasure at the end of it. I would grab it and run back to the children's section until Mama was ready to go. Then, as we readied to leave, I checked it out again and took it back home where it obviously belonged.

One Saturday, Mrs. Barnett summoned me to the circulation desk, a formidable walnut fortress. The other librarians gathered around as she smiled and handed a package to me. "Now," she said sweetly, "we hope you might leave *The Adventures of Pippi Longstocking* here so other children might read it. Here's your very own copy to take home."

As a wildly redheaded and freckled child myself, Pippi was somewhat of a goddess to me, my alter ego, my she-ro.

When I turned fifteen Mrs. Barnett offered me a job working at the circulation desk, that great ship I had hovered in front of so many Saturdays as a child. **I was ecstatic to be among all those books.** I still hear the sound of the wheels on Book Cart Number Two as I rolled it through the stacks, getting lost in that world in which one tug at a shelf could unravel and reveal so much wonder. It was magical.

Until one day when the quiet magic was shattered as a very angry woman slammed a card catalog drawer shut and stomped up to the desk. This was highly unusual in the Morganton-Burke Public Library. There didn't seem too awfully much to get angry about. There hadn't been this much activity here since a fellow who worked at Hardee's had been caught drinking aftershave in the men's room.

Teach this triple truth to all: A generous heart, kind speech, and a life of service and compassion are the things which renew humanity. —**Buddha**

"I cannot believe," she hissed, "that this library doesn't have any books about psychology! It's an outrage! How dare you call yourselves a library!" Her voice ricocheted off the reserve shelves. Being the only one at the helm at that moment, it was up me to respond.

Timidly, I did.

"I know I've shelved some psychology books before—" I began.

"Really!" she interrupted. "There's none in the card catalog—none, zero! Ridiculous! Aren't there any grown-ups who work here?"

"They're in a meeting right now," I whispered, scared. "But I'll help if I can."

At that, she stomped her way back to the card catalog, with me trailing meekly the way Pippi never would have done. "Where were you looking?" I asked.

"Well, young lady, where on earth do you think I was looking?" she answered as she flung open a card drawer until it nearly fell out.

The drawer she had opened was the S-drawer.

It hit me like a bolt, a heat wave that spread through my face.

Kindness is my religion. —the Dalai Lama

This book is to be returned on or before the last date stamped below.

SAVE FACE FOR SOMEONE ELSE
PERSONAL RECORD.
1920-1972

"Well," I answered very quietly after a moment, "perhaps we should try the alternate spelling. Sometimes that works." And I gently moved her to the P-drawer.

I don't know how I knew to do that, but even now I'm proud I did. Helping her save face and retain her dignity was important, even though (and maybe especially because) she had been berating me.

Decades later, I was in line at the Giant Food supermarket in Washington, DC, when a woman ahead of me in line was buying some basic foods, a very few items, including a package of the cheapest, fattiest meat I had ever seen.

As the cashier got closer to the end of ringing up her eight items, the woman kept asking for the subtotal and digging into her small change purse, realizing as the meat made its sad journey up the conveyer belt that she could never afford it. She lacked $1.07. **With the saddest eyes I had ever seen, she told the cashier to put it back.** I couldn't bear it. "Excuse me, ma'am," I said as I bent down between my cart and the chewing gum display, "you must have dropped this five-dollar bill."

I had read once about a millionaire who gives money to people in need by pretending to find it on the street, as if they dropped it. It is a way for him to give without appearing to be the grand poobah of cash, without taking credit for the gift, without assuming the power that sometimes comes with giving.

It puts the impulse for giving and helping where it should be—on the dignity of the receiver.

If we always helped one another, no one would need luck. —**Sophocles**

Face is an important concept. As Mohammad Al-Sabt wrote in his guide to Arabian culture, "Saving someone's face or dignity involves using maneuvers or holding one's reactions to give the other party a way to exit the situation with minimal discomfort or harm to their dignity. It involves creativity, compromise, patience, and sometimes looking the other way to allow things time to get back to normal." Many cultures around the world encourage people to act humbly and with sensitivity to a person's dignity, especially when that person's dignity and self-respect are endangered. Find ways to help save face for other people.

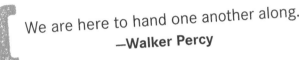

We are here to hand one another along.
—Walker Percy

@ *Action:*

All of us have lost face at one time in our lives, perhaps more. Focused free-write:

- For six minutes, write about a time you felt shamed publicly—whether you fell, flubbed a presentation, or misspoke, or your credit card was declined in a store. What did that feel like, physically? How did it feel in your face, your gut, the back of your neck?

- Read what you have written.

- Then circle a hot spot, a word or phrase that stands out for you.

- Set the timer again and write about that hot spot for three more minutes.

- Sit with the insights that emerged. Did feeling embarrassed keep you from raising your hand the next time, or did it make you lash out at others? These insights tell you something important about the impact of losing face—and how important it is to help others not experience those same feelings of frustration, diminishment, anger, or loneliness.

✿ *Movement:*

Marian Wright Edelman has said, "We must not, in trying to think about how we can make a big difference, ignore the small daily differences we can make which, over time, add up to big differences that we often cannot foresee."

- For the next thirty-seven days, pick someone you see every day and be an angel for them in some way. If picking one person isn't possible, be an angel to different people you encounter.

- For example, if someone's parking meter is about to expire, put money in the meter for them and leave an anonymous note asking them to "pay it forward" to help someone else. If someone makes a faux pas, ignore it rather than call attention to it—doing so not only won't cost you anything, but will give them a way out, too. When your children wait until the last minute to do their homework, help them without berating them.

- As you go through each day, you will have many opportunities to help others—if you are intentional about looking for those opportunities. Can you be an angel each day, using your angel powers to help people? Can you do it without being noticed or wanting praise for it?

- Reflect on how people responded, and on how being a stealth angel felt to you.

When you are kind to others, it not only changes you, it changes the world.
—Harold Kushner

37 DAYS
Saving face for someone else does not mean losing your own.

Don't Sell Your Red Books

Heroes take journeys, confront dragons, and discover the treasure of their true selves. —Carol Pearson

Years ago when John had his fantastic odd little bookshop full of antique science books in the Georgetown neighborhood of Washington, DC, a local Decorator to the Stars of the US Government came in one day looking for books—and lots of them.

Georgetown is a wealthy neighborhood in the nation's capital (think ambassadors and secretaries of state), so the prospect of a Big Sale was in the air, that Electric Moment of Possibility, that Vacation in Tuscany and College Fund and New Heat Pump all wrapped up into one.

"I'm looking for books for an important client who is redoing their house here in Georgetown," the decorator informed John. "And I think you have just what we need!"

"Really? What's their area of interest in the sciences?" John asked.

"Oh, they're not scientists!" the designer replied, laughing at the prospect. "We're looking for books in lovely shades of red to match their new imported silk draperies—burgundy, that nice wine color that old books have, that beautiful, brightish red with gold print—along those lines."

"But I'm wondering what *kind* of book they need for their collection," John responded, quizzically, unable to grasp the full measure of the situation unfolding like the slow opening of a creaking door.

"Oh, the subject doesn't matter at all," the decorator replied. "But they do need to be red or in the red family, old and distinguished looking, leather-bound if at all possible, no bigger than 9 inches tall, and we need 50 yards of them."

Like so much fabric. Like so many carpet remnants or white yard markers on a football field.

"And we're willing to pay top dollar for them. I see some there in the back that would be perfect!" he said, pointing to John's history of science collection, a beautiful sea of dark red on the back wall of the store.

> Not everything that can be counted counts, and not everything that counts can be counted.
> —Albert Einstein

At the time, we were knee-deep into our first pregnancy, expecting Emma to arrive in a few weeks, and what he was offering would buy a lot of baby necessities, like a seafoam-colored Vespa scooter on which she could ride behind me to Montessori school. But John had built his collection over many years. **He loved his books for the history of ideas they represented.** He couldn't bear the thought of them being used as so much ribbon on the package of a nonreader's living room, like so much icing on the cake of an antebellum bookcase, like so much—well, you get the awful idea.

John declined the generous offer, explaining why he couldn't sell books in such a way—that to him, it wasn't just a transaction, but something more. I've always loved that he did that—that he cared too much about his books to sell them short. He wanted people to use and absorb the knowledge in the books, not merely dust them and throw them out when the draperies changed to forest green or ochre. He walked away from The Deal for the integral love of what he had and was offering to the world.

My most important lesson from John's response was this: **We should love what we do—and I mean be truly, deeply passionate about it—enough to protect it, cherish it, and offer it in the most respectful way possible, not by the yard or ton.**

In my earliest consulting days, those scary days when you accept every gig that comes your way because the future seems really uncertain (as opposed to the times when the future just seems plain uncertain), I worked on developing a diversity strategy for a major health care organization, one aspect of which was hearing the stories of people in the organization about their experiences around diversity issues—did they feel welcomed? Included? Valued? (Short answer was no. Long answer was painful.)

The organization represented a disease that perversely affects people of color. The phrase I heard from people all over the country to describe the largely Caucasian organization was *good ol' boy network.* As I fed back the data to the CEO, he stopped me short: "You know why it's called a *good old boy network*?" he sneered. "Because it's *good* and it *works*."

After I regained consciousness, I walked away.

Though I needed the money, having just started my own business, I couldn't see simply marking time, doing work that raised expectations of the people in the organization that change was coming—when I knew it wasn't, when I knew my work was only being checked off a to-do list to satisfy the incoming chairman of the board, an African American man, as if this diversity thing would placate him. I wouldn't be the instrument of that deception. This sneering ol' boy was not someone I could work with, no matter how much the kids needed shoes, no matter how much I still wanted that Vespa or Tuscany was calling my name. It made me feel dirty to participate, the dirtiness no money can erase. I had to bundle up my red books and leave.

Don't get me wrong—I commit to hard work. I often stay where things are difficult because that's where the work needs to get done, isn't it? Like my big beautiful former personal trainer Thor once said as I whined about how difficult those incline sit-ups were, what with him lobbing a twenty-five-pound medicine ball at my head every time I struggled my way to the top: "Listen, Patti, if it were easy, everybody walking around DC would look like me."

Egotistical, perhaps, but true.

As Thor taught me, if diversity work were easy, wouldn't we all be working in fantastically inclusive organizations where everyone's ideas are sought out and valued? We'd be living in a world where the phrase *peace in the Middle East* is redundant; where hate crimes are a historical oddity, not a daily reality. So I understand that doing the hard work is the point. Even so, to save my own sense of worth and worthiness in this world, sometimes I realize that I must walk back to myself and away from Mr. Good Ol' Boy. I must offer my library of red books to people who will embrace and love and learn from them, not merely pay for them in order to show off the color.

John has a new fantastic odd shop now, this one in our beautiful little mountain town. He specializes in old maps and prints and books. Just yesterday evening on the way home from his shop, he rued selling a beautiful copy of Arnheim's *Visual Thinking* to a woman who, he realized later, simply liked the cover.

The magic is still there.

The strongest principle of growth lies in human choice. —**George Eliot**

37 Days: Do It Now Challenge

First, figure out what your red books are. Then hold on to them lovingly because they are you. Cherish them. Honor them. Offer them where the need is great and the willingness greater. Open them to voracious readers, and to people who can't yet read—but first explain why you love those books and what meaning they hold for you. Make your interactions with people transformational, not just transactional. Don't buy, or sell, knowledge by the yard.

Action:

Focused free-write:

- If your work (at home or outside the home) were the answer to a question, what would that question be? Write for six minutes.

- Read what you've written.

- Circle a hot spot, and continue writing on that word or phrase for four more minutes.

After you have finished, think about what this writing reveals about your work— is it the thing for which you have the most passion, the thing you would most protect and cherish? If not, why? And how can you make it so?

Movement:

Life comes down to choices. Daily, incremental, simple choices that accumulate over time.

- For thirty-seven days keep a catalog of all the choices you make each day: Coffee or tea? Bagel or toast? Truth or white lie? New job or old one? You'll soon realize you make innumerable decisions every day—probably many more than you'd estimate. Those decisions, over time, make up our lives.

- At the end of each day, review the ledger and circle the ones that caused you to pause—perhaps those are the ones that tap into what is meaningful to you. What were they?

- Did you choose based on what you thought others expected, or what you needed and wanted? Was there a sacrifice involved that influenced your choice? Did you choose safety over risk?

- Examine your list for any patterns that emerge. What did you learn about choice?

Roll on the Floor

Emma and I watched a show on Animal Planet last Saturday that made me laugh. Then it made me think. Then it made me realize I laughed because I could identify with the people who made me laugh in the first place. I like it when it happens in that order.

The show is called *Who Gets the Dog?* and it is yet another reality show, this one a competition among three sets of people vying to adopt a lucky dog plucked from the jaws of death at an animal shelter (or saved at least from the fingers of small children poking incessantly). The dog in question this week was Rocky, a black Labrador–pointer mix.

During the show, each set of participants talked earnestly about why they would be the best parents for Rocky, what kind of home life they would provide, how they wouldn't mind if Rocky peed all over their Persian rug and chewed up their $468 Coach Beekman black briefcase with its front gusseted pocket made of glove-tanned cowhide. They waxed poetic about what Rocky would mean to them, how Rocky would change their lives forever, and how much they loved their last dog, whom they nonetheless let run loose, seemingly surprised when he got killed by a FedEx truck.

Dog specialists, people who read doggy auras, canine therapists, seers, behaviorists, and others too numerous to mention rated the competitors, who each hosted Rocky overnight, working to specific challenges during the sleepover—teaching Rocky doggy tricks, for example.

One group was asked to teach Rocky to howl; another had to teach him to walk backward. The third couple needed to teach Rocky to pray, putting his front paws up on their outstretched arm and bowing his head.

That last group provided the humor.

Essentially, they failed. They tried to talk Rocky into praying by showing him what it looked like, one fellow pretending to be a dog, his partner with outstretched arms yelling "pray." Rocky looked bemused, thinking, I imagined, Boy, I wish Spot were here to see this. He definitely was not inclined to mimic what he saw, seeing no reason to do it, not understanding what they wanted him to do in the first place. Finally (and here is where I laughed the daintiest of snorts), they actually resorted to conversing quite seriously with little Rocky about the presence of a higher being and what prayer is and means. I could not make this up.

> CREATIVITY INVOLVES BREAKING OUT OF ESTABLISHED PATTERNS IN ORDER TO LOOK AT THINGS IN A DIFFERENT WAY.
>
> —Edward de Bono

What went wrong, pray tell (sorry—I couldn't resist)? What might have been a more effective strategy to get Rocky to pray? The experts told us: First they needed to get Rocky to consistently lower his head by offering a treat and then continuing to lower the location of the treat while saying the word *pray*, praising him when he did it correctly, working diligently and repeatedly to positively reinforce the behavior. Only after that skill was solidly in place should they teach the paws-on-arm part of the trick, then put the two together—an altogether incremental approach that looks at each step, each behavior independently, unlinking the spiritual associations of the concept *pray* from the behaviors that make up the action.

Perhaps the word *pray* gets in the way. Let's look at it differently. Let's suppose I invited you and some of your friends to my house for dinner, and you've never been here before (yes, you can bring something: Joan Armatrading, Tracy Chapman, or Nina Simone CDs, and one or two or ten dark chocolate truffles with wasabi). You get lost on the way and call me on your cell phone, describing where you are. Is it more effective for me to tell you how to get to my house from where I am or from where you are?

It's not a trick question.

Obviously, I need to give you directions from where you are, turn by turn. I need to put myself in your space, see what you see, and move you from that point to where I am. Perhaps, in some instances, it'd be better to just come meet you where you are and hang out there for a while at the corner bar or bookshop, get comfortable, meet the local characters—Floyd the barber, Goober, Andy (or, more recently, Phoebe, Monica, and Rachel)—so I can really understand where you are.

But how often, when we're trying to change someone's thinking or behavior, trying to get them to be where we are, do we stand steadfastly where we are, repeatedly insisting they pray or chant or stand on one leg rather than looking at it from that person's perspective, going where they are to start the conversation? A man I used to work with communicated with visitors from overseas—"foreigners," to use his welcoming terminology—by speaking loudly while moving his mouth in exaggerated ways. He got louder as the conversation continued, not changing vocabulary if his listeners didn't understand, but repeating the same words while increasing the volume and moving his mouth more widely. He never adopted a more effective strategy of—oh, I don't know—speaking different words to help them understand.

How much of my laugh at *Who Gets the Dog?* emerged from my own nervous realization that I, too, have been guilty of talking to people about the meaning of *pray,* say, or just increasing my volume when another approach altogether was required?

I see this in training rooms when talking about difficult issues like diversity: I presume a starting point and a willingness that often isn't there. I get frustrated when They don't get it, and keep going at Them from that position on high where I am, further frustrating me (and Them) and ensuring They will never get it.

What would happen if at those moments I remembered Rocky and the concept of *pray,* and I really explored concepts with the learners in the room unencumbered by all the meaning I've attached to those ideas through the years? **What if I simply went where they are, saw things from their perspective,** and helped them get to the destination bit by bit, breaking it down into small learning objects, discrete turns and navigations, rather than hammering them over the head with a large concept like *pray*?

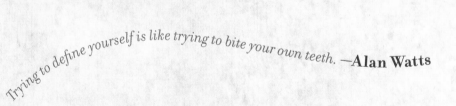

Trying to define yourself is like trying to bite your own teeth. —**Alan Watts**

Rather than show or tell learners what I want them to know—the equivalent of those doggy participants down on hands and knees to demonstrate praying—what would happen if I actually let learners experience what it feels like to be excluded, to be disregarded, or, because of their skin color, to have to adapt to a dominant culture? Showing Rocky what the desired action looked like was ineffective—they needed to engage him in actually doing it.

Here are the nine things I learned from little briefcase-chewing Rocky last Saturday:

1. Language isn't objective, but full of associations created in our own minds. *Pray* doesn't mean the same thing to Rocky as it does to me.

2. There often needs to be a treat associated with learning a new trick, or (to use the happy vernacular of management consultants worldwide) a business case for doing what we're asking Rocky to do. Rocky's business case clearly involves liver treats.

3. I have to motivate Rocky with what matters to him (liver treats), not what matters to me (truffles).

4. To learn a new behavior, people can't just hear about it or see me demonstrate it. They have to do it themselves, try it out, fail sometimes.

5. We need to celebrate success more than we do. Whip out those liver treats and pig ears, let's party!

6. Rocky (and people) needs consistency. We can't send mixed messages and expect results. It's confusing and makes Rocky resort to peeing on the carpet—you figure out the equivalent in humans.

7. It takes time to teach new tricks to a dog. A lot of dedicated, focused, engaged, consistent, and individualized time.

8. We all create different stories about what is happening in the world around us. Rocky's story to his pals Rover and Spot about that event is likely different from the people who were trying to train him, don't you think?

9. I shouldn't pretend I don't care if Rocky pees on my Persian rug and eats my $468 Coach Beekman black briefcase with its front gusseted pocket made of glove-tanned cowhide, if I really do care.

Rocky, by the way, learned best from the group of three goofy guys who got down on the floor and rolled around with him like a dog, shedding their human superiority. They honestly enjoyed him for who he was, not who they wanted him to be. They went where he was.

Those guys won the competition and took Rocky home to howl, walk backward, and maybe pray.

The next time you get frustrated with someone who just isn't "getting it," slow down. Ask yourself if you're giving them directions from where you are, rather than from where they are. Remember Rocky. Roll on the floor and play. Shed your human superiority awhile.

✐ *Action:*

We move on automatic pilot much of the time. In this focused free-write, you'll be asked to turn that switch off for a time.

- For six minutes, list and describe in detail the steps you take to get ready in the morning, starting when you first open your eyes and ending when you walk out the door.

- Pretend you are writing an instruction manual for someone who doesn't have a clue what to do once they wake up in the morning.

- Break your routine into small, clear steps and describe them so others could follow them. Which leg do you fling off the bed first? Do you put your slippers on before you go to brush your teeth? Pretend you are writing a technical manual or the directions to putting together one of those IKEA shelves once you get it home—make it that detailed.

- After six minutes, read what you've written. Would it be possible for someone else to follow your directions, or are you still taking your individual actions for granted?

- For the last four minutes of this free-write, answer this question: In what ways am I on autopilot in my life?

Habits are at first cobwebs, then cables. —Spanish proverb

⟳ *Movement:*

What we do every day is often based on a pattern that we can no longer recognize because it is so ingrained over time—or so unconscious. For the next thirty-seven days, focus on the patterns of your life. Start with this exercise:

- Sit in your kitchen in the dark, as close to your refrigerator as you can get—on the floor next to it, if you can. Turn off the radio or TV. Close your eyes. Listen to the hum of your refrigerator for five minutes. Try to determine if there is a rhythm emanating from your fridge. What is it? Can you pat it out on the floor or table near you?

- When you go out into the world, believe that life is a piece of music that you must memorize. For the next thirty-seven days, find all the rhythms you can—the sound of people's feet on the sidewalk around you produces a pattern, for example, as do turn signals in a car, or the heater coming on and shutting off.

- Listen intently for rhythm for the next thirty-seven days. These are the patterns of our lives.

Open your mind up to things that have no connection with the problem you're trying to solve: Subscribe to an unusual magazine; go to work two hours early; test-drive an exotic car; try an Indonesian recipe. —**Roger von Oech**

Let It Be a Barn

There are hundreds of paths up the mountain,

all leading in the same direction,

so it doesn't matter which path you take.

The only one wasting time is the one

who runs around and around the mountain,

telling everyone that his or her path is wrong.

—Hindu teaching

It doesn't take long to get far away from home. Within twenty minutes up Route 19/23, we turned onto a road that held witness to its soily past—barns falling over, pitched roofs crumbling, whole wooden structures wizened by sun and rain and time tilting at carnival angles.

"LOOK!" Tess screamed from her Britax Marathon baby seat, holding the little Johnny Depp talking doll she carries around. "LOOK! There's a building falling down!"

"That's a barn, honey," John said. "It's a very old structure that was used to—"

"HEY!" She interrupted his fascinating lecture on our agrarian past. "HEY! There's another one! A red one!"

We drove our country drive, past barns by the dozens, each met with a decibel of excitement that increasingly irritated her worldly teenage sister, who scrunched smaller and smaller into the corner where door meets seat, glaring out the window, then glaring at the front seat as if to challenge our very right to have brought this flailing screaming creature into the world. "There's another one! A Barn! A Barn!" Tess screamed, pointing to a small shed housing wheelbarrows and hoes.

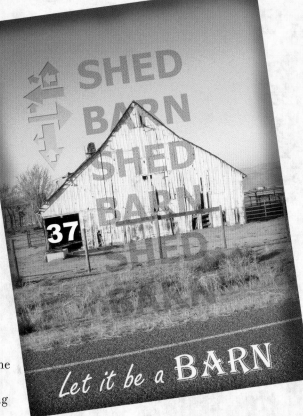

Let it be a BARN

"That's not a barn," Emma growled from her exile. "It is not a barn, Tess."

"YES! IT IS!" Tess wailed. "It's a barn! A little barn! A little teeny weeny barn!" she insisted.

"Not," Emma said. "Not. A. Barn. That's a shed, not a barn."

"A BARN! It is TOO a barn! It's a barn! It's a barn!"

I looked in the glove compartment for a pencil to stick through my eye.

Emma is as close to a fifteen-year-old attorney as you'll find on the planet. "It's time for bed," I inform her each night.

"What time is it?" she'll ask.

"Nine thirty," I'll respond.

"Actually, Mom," comes her rebuttal, "it's only nine twenty-seven."

LET IT BE A BARN

The constancy of certainty is change, I think to myself, looking wistfully out the car window at the barn-shed, diving into my vast internal monologue: *Time brings new eyes, new advances, new theories, new discoveries—it reveals errors of judgment, errors of incomplete observation or faulty equipment, errors due to incomplete experience. The passage of time can speed up or slow down the meter of our understanding, like the meter of a poem. The closer we stand to something—say, a barn—the more different it can look.*

Benoît Mandelbrot's "fractals" came as the result of looking at a seemingly simple question: How long is the coastline of Britain? The answer began a new branch of mathematics, and the next question—How long do you want it to be?—deals with what a barn is or isn't. As it turns out, the coastline of Britain can either be measured exactly, or it can be infinite. It is really a question of perspective, of identifying your parameters, your yardstick. As are most things, I think to myself. *If Einstein's hated quantum mechanics places us here and there at the same time, and there is no such thing as consciousness, and the only thing solid about applying labels is the glue that holds them on, then what does it possibly matter if a barn is a barn, a shed, or barn-like?*

> Barn burned down.
> Now I can see the moon.
> **—Basho**

The litany from the backseat continued, bringing me back to the moment.

"Barn!"

"Not!"

I muttered something under my breath.

John heard. "What?" He leaned in toward me. "What did you say?"

"Let it be a barn," I said quietly, plotting my escape to a small vineyard in New Zealand on Paper Road in Martinborough, where children speak in fancy accents, quietly tend the sheep, and eat corn sandwiches.

"Let. It. Be. A. Barn."

My head slowly rotated like that delightful Linda Blair in *The Exorcist.* "Just let it be a barn, honey," I said to Emma. "Just let it be a barn."

"You mean it's all a matter of perspective?" she asked.

"Yes, peanut," I responded, so very proud of her brilliance, her perception, her ability to rise above the petty quarrel. "Yes, that's it."

"That's so poetic, Mama. What a wonderful, enlightened, broad-minded, and interesting way to see the world!"

I smiled the satisfied smile that mothers smile.

"But it's still not a barn."

A Hindu teaching about paths up a mountain came to mind. And if I hadn't squandered so many brain cells pondering how to leap from a speeding car without anyone noticing, I might have been able to point it out to Emma at the time of The Barn Incident.

Your reality is different from mine. What I see as racism, you see as an overreaction. What I see as dangerous, you see as bold. What I see as precious, you see as disposable. Is it two forty or two fifty? Is it a barn or a shed? Is my reality any more real than yours? How long *is* the coastline of Britain?

The story is told of Picasso that a stranger on a train challenged why his paintings weren't realistic: "Why don't you paint things as they really are?" Picasso responded that he didn't understand exactly what the man meant, and the stranger produced a photograph of his wife from his wallet. "Like that," he said. "That's how she is . . ."

"She's rather small and flat, isn't she?" Picasso answered.

> THE REALLY TOUGH CHOICES . . . DON'T CENTER UPON RIGHT VERSUS WRONG. THEY INVOLVE RIGHT VERSUS RIGHT. THEY ARE GENUINE DILEMMAS PRECISELY BECAUSE EACH SIDE IS FIRMLY ROOTED IN ONE OF OUR BASIC, CORE VALUES.
>
> —**Rushworth Kidder**

> *There is no truth. Only points of view.* —Dame Edith Sitwell

Let it be a barn.

37 DAYS

37 Days: Do It Now Challenge

Buckminster Fuller once wrote: "You were given a right foot and a left foot, not a right foot and a wrong foot." Stop arguing, start listening. When you find yourself insisting on a point, step off it, tango to the left, slide to the right, do-si-do around it, dance with it, speak to it. Your truth will wait, and sometimes grow or change by its proximity to someone else's. Your barn might be my shed; surely both can coexist.

✐ *Action:*

Focused free-write:

- Write for six minutes on this question: How does it feel to be wrong about something?

- After six minutes, stop writing.

- So . . . when we're fighting to be right, we're dooming the other person in the argument to being wrong and experiencing some of the feelings we just wrote about.

- Think of a recent argument you've had.

- Now write for four more minutes framing the other person's perspective as right.

◌ *Movement:*

To a four-year-old child, a chair is a castle, a race car, a secret cave. To an adult it's just a chair. We lose the ability to see things once we name them. Language reduces possibilities, sometimes. This is true of objects, and it's true if we name groups of people, too.

- Write a list of ten everyday, common kitchen tools.

- For the next thirty-seven days, choose one of those tools each morning.

- Your task is to come up with five alternative uses for that tool each time you choose it, to loosen them from the category in which your mind has placed them. Stretch your imagination!

- What's a good way to do this challenge? Ask others to brainstorm with you! They will see possibilities you don't.

Bust Your Toast Rules

Any fool can make a rule and any fool will mind it. —Henry David Thoreau

As my plane touched down in Washington, DC, I could see the heat waving to me from the tarmac, a harbinger of sweat and grumpiness. It was a day in which even your sweat hurts, stings, burns, and people just plain bother you.

"Let's grab a cup of tea and do some planning before dinner," I said to David when we met at the hotel. We sweated our way to a cafe, one where I used to eat when I lived in DC, a cafe that shall remain nameless unless you happen to know of a place near Dupont Circle with a bookstore in the front and restaurant in the back. I'm just saying.

Only four tables were occupied. It was a little after 3:00 p.m., so the lunch crowd was back at work and the dinner crowd was still dreaming of 5:00. "Could I get you something to drink?" the waiter asked.

"Do you have Earl Grey tea?" I asked. He nodded. "Then I'll have that."

"A cup of coffee, black," David added. We talked as the waiter left. I was hungry—hadn't had anything before my flight—but I didn't want to eat a meal because we were meeting Julie for dinner. I just needed a little something to tide me over.

"What can I get you?" the waiter asked when he came back with our drinks, smiling pleasantly.

"Nothing for me," David said.

"What I'd really love," I answered, **"is a piece of toast and this side of avocado slices."** I pointed to the menu.

"Oh, I'm sorry," the waiter said, beginning a statement that would mark The End of Modern Civilization As We Know It. "I'm sorry, but it's past toast time."

Blink.

"Past toast time?"

"Yes, ma'am, it's past toast time."

I slowly turned to look at David, who was smiling the smile of a man who is unsure what will happen next.

"Wow. And here I never actually knew there was an official toast time."

I wonder if it is the same time across all time zones, I thought.

The waiter nodded, now impatient, what with all my incredulous blinking cutting into his smoking break. Evidently it's always cigarette time.

"Well," I said sweetly, "I just never knew you could actually go past toast time. Call me crazy, but it seems to me that if you have bread and a toaster, it's pretty much always toast time."

Blink.

"Well, then," I responded, wondering how this would play out if I let it run its course, thinking in a yelly voice inside my head THERE'S NO ONE HERE! IT'S NOT LIKE RUNNING THE TOASTER WILL SET YOU BACK. I'M NOT ASKING FOR RISOTTO WITH FRESHLY SHELLED SPRING PEAS STIRRED FOR A BLOODY HOUR AND LOVINGLY TOPPED WITH RARE YET PUNGENT PARMESAN FROM A REMOTE PROVINCE OF NORTHERN ITALY WHERE MEN WEAR BERETS! YOU HAVE THE MEANS! YOU HAVE BREAD! YOU HAVE A TOASTER! YOU HAVE ELECTRICITY! YOU HAVE ALL THE TIME IN THE WORLD BECAUSE YOU HAVE NO CUSTOMERS!

That's some toast rule, I thought.

"I'll just have the side of avocado slices then."

He blinked. "Well," he said slowly, "I'll ask. I don't believe that's possible." He left.

"What's to ask?" I asked David. "What's to believe? This isn't a religion we're talking about—it's avocado slices. They are on the menu," I said plaintively.

Suddenly, on that humid Washington day, I had been transported to a Denny's in Eugene, Oregon. My name was Jack Nicholson, I was playing the role of piano prodigy Bobby Dupea, and I was starring in a movie called *Five Easy Pieces*, just trying to get a plain omelet, tomatoes instead of potatoes, and some wheat toast. "No substitutions," his waitress said. "Only what's on the menu." I'm sure he was as incredulous as I was: "You've got bread. And a toaster of some kind?" he asked. "I'll make it as easy for you as I can. I'd like an omelet, plain, and a chicken salad sandwich on wheat toast, no mayonnaise, no butter, no lettuce. And a cup of coffee. Now all you have to do is hold the chicken, bring me the toast, give me a check for the chicken salad sandwich, and you haven't broken any rules."

Rules are not necessarily sacred, principles are. —**Franklin D. Roosevelt**

The waiter arrived back at our table. "I'm sorry," he said with a smile, "but They told me that giving you avocado would break every rule known to man."

Every Rule Known To Man. I couldn't make this up. David is my witness. Forget my irritation at the invocation of They. Every rule? Every single rule? That's some exciting avocado. I want me some of that avocado.

I was Yossarian trying to save a bombardier and facing Catch-22: "Orr was crazy and could be grounded. All he had to do was ask, but as soon as he did, he would no longer be crazy and would have to fly more missions . . . If he flew them he was crazy and didn't have to; but if he didn't want to he was sane and had to. Yossarian was moved by the absolute simplicity of Catch-22. 'That's some catch, that Catch-22,' he observed. 'It's the best there is,' Doc Daneeka agreed."

"But it's on the menu," I said. I pointed to the menu. "Right here, see?"

"Yes," he answered, "but sides only come with entrees. We can't serve sides without entrees."

My Lord, there is so much I don't know. I am sometimes just plain overwhelmed by the fact that not only can I not remember more than three places of pi, don't really know how to change a tire or speak Urdu, and keep losing my calendar, but somehow—oh how is this possible?—I have gotten to this advanced age without ever knowing sides depend on entrees.

"Well, then," I said simply. "We wouldn't want to break every rule known to man." He left for his Cigarette Time, which evidently extends far past Toast Time and isn't subject to the vast vagaries of Customer Time. I quietly reached into my bag, pulled out The Camera, and started making photographs of the menu, knowing that the Toast Rule and Side Rule would be a source of great inspiration to me much later in life, like now.

That's some rule, that Toast Rule. It's the best there is. It's one thing to acknowledge the absurdity of other people's rules; it's another thing altogether to recognize and own the absurdity of the rules that we've made up (helpful hint: They're all made up, some so ingrained that we can no longer see they are Toast Rules). So when a rule pops to the surface, see it for the Toast Rule it is, made up to serve some social norm that is itself made up—or to serve the convenience of a waiter, where waiter stands for "person" or "group." Toast Rules. Girls don't become backhoe operators, you can't eat dessert before dinner, never wear white shoes after Labor Day, boys don't cry, girls don't play tuba, never whistle in the dark, don't take wooden nickels, or marriage is the sole right of heterosexual couples. Made up, made up, made up. Bust your toast rules. Because in my little universe, it's always toast time.

✐ Action:

Quick—cross your arms. Now cross them the other way. Hard to do? Feel awkward? Our lives are full of patterns, preferences, and habits, most of them unconscious. Some of those patterns serve us well. And some do not.

- Do a five-minute focused free-write on this question: What are all the sayings you've grown up with? Things like *Children should be seen, not heard,* or *Always wear clean underwear because you never know when you might be in an accident,* or *Never buy dented cans.* List as many as you can in five minutes. Don't censor yourself—just write them all down.

- Stop and read what you have written.

- Spend two minutes circling the ones you actually do live by—there might be more than you imagined! Some might even reflect your deepest values—but others might not. For instance, even though it might not be rational, I never buy a can that has a dent in it . . .

- Spend the last three minutes underlining those that are Toast Rules, rules we've embedded into our lives, but that aren't necessary or real.

We have to concentrate on surfacing our patterns (Toast Rules) in order to change them.

For the next thirty-seven days, use your list to notice and then break the Toast Rules. You might start in this way:

- Do the equivalent of crossing your arms the other way: If you usually sit in the back of a movie theater, sit in the front. If you attend church or synagogue and you're a side sitter, sit in the middle. If you always have coffee with breakfast, drink tea instead. If you always sit with the same group at lunch, sit with another group for a change.

- How does it feel to make those kinds of changes?

- When Toast Rules emerge during that time, make note of them. For example, if you find yourself saying, "I can't do that," or "I'm supposed to . . . ," stop and question if this is a rule deeply rooted in your values or if, in fact, it is simply a Toast Rule, borne of habit and not intent.

I am free, no matter what rules surround me. If I find them tolerable, I tolerate them; if I find them too obnoxious, I break them. I am free because I know that I alone am morally responsible for everything I do. —**Robert A. Heinlein**

If you obey all the rules, you miss all the fun. —**Katharine Hepburn**

Don't Stop to Wave, You'll Drown

Why are women immobile? Because so many feel like they're waiting for someone to say, "You're good, you're pretty, I give you permission." —**Eve Ensler**

I recently watched a videotape of Eve Ensler speaking at the 2004 Omega Institute "Women in Power" conference. Ensler is a playwright most famous for *The Vagina Monologues*, which has played in seventy-six countries, with thirty-five translations, in places like Karachi and New Delhi and Cairo.

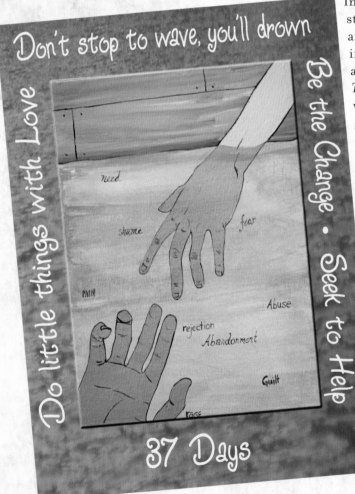

Don't stop to wave, you'll drown

Do little things with Love

Be the Change • Seek to Help

need

shame

fear

pain

rejection

Abandonment

Abuse

Guilt

rage

37 Days

In it, Ensler gives us real women's stories of intimacy, vulnerability, and sexual self-discovery. Based on interviews with more than 200 women about their experiences of sexuality, *The Vagina Monologues* gives voice to women's deepest fantasies and fears, guaranteeing that no one who reads or sees it will ever look at a woman's body, or think of sex, in quite the same way again.

Ensler was overwhelmed by the numbers of women who lined up after performances of the play to tell her their experiences of abuse at the hands of others. She herself was a victim of childhood sexual abuse from her father. She knew she had to do more and founded V-Day, a global movement to stop violence against women and girls.

Ensler's new work is called *The Good Body.* "Whether undergoing Botox or living under burkhas, women of all cultures and back-grounds feel compelled to change the way they look in order to fit in with their particular culture, to be accepted, to be good," she said. "Just imagine what we could accomplish if we harnessed all the energy we spend hating and changing our bodies in order to be 'beautiful' or 'good enough.'"

In a recent interview with *Mother Jones,* Ensler said: "There's the violence that comes toward us, and there's violence we do to ourselves—we're picking up the magazines, we're dieting, we're getting the lipo. Why are women immobile? Because so many feel like they're waiting for someone to say, 'You're good, you're pretty, I give you permission.'"

I want to be Eve Ensler when I grow up.

I'm going to Kim's Wig Shop downtown tomorrow to get her black, shiny pageboy hair in wig form. I'm going to speak out and be energetic and articulate and have something important to say. I'm going to pay attention to what's going on in the world as if the fate of the earth depends on me paying attention. I'm going to have a point of view and an opinion without waiting for other people to tell me what it is. I'm going to do the work that I know I need to do, that I must do, that I've been waiting my whole life to do, without waiting for an audience. I'm going to sit up straighter and I'm going to make people hear me. I'm going to ask a lot more questions, and I'm going to pay attention to the answers as if they really matter. I'm going to really, really *listen* to people when they tell me their stories. I'm going to raise my voice when it needs to be raised. I'm going to lend my voice to people who have none. I'm going to figure out how to be an effective advocate for others. I'm not going to care anymore whether people like me when I speak my truth. I'm never going to ask for permission again. As Ensler said, "I am going to hold who I am in the face of anything."

> DO NOT CARRY THE BURDEN OF THE PAST; DO NOT LIVE IN THE FUTURE. THE ONLY IMPORTANT THING IS THAT ONE LIVES IN THE PRESENT AUTHENTICALLY AND FULLY. WHATEVER YOUR CURRENT LIFE IS, BE THE MOST YOU CAN BE BY LIVING IN THE MOMENT.
>
> —Chan Chih

Don't stop to wave, you'll drown.

37 days

keep moving,
keep seeing,
keep knowing,
and keep saying
what you know
to be your truth

[Be who you are and say what you feel because those who mind don't matter and those who matter don't mind.]
—Dr. Seuss

"Know what you know," she said, "see what you see, say what you say wherever you can say it."

Women, she told us, have to overcome their fear of not being liked. "It's a choice we have to make between being good—quiet enough, thin enough, pretty enough, pleasant enough, good enough—and being great."

When she wrote *The Vagina Monologues,* Ensler said she was a way-off-Broadway playwright who had created her persona around being marginal, being outside the power structure. When the play became successful, she feared losing who she was by becoming part of the mainstream. Then she realized that she didn't have to lose herself. She spoke of being drawn toward a fast-moving and powerful river, being part of that river, and of creating in and of the river.

Don't stop to wave,
you'll drown.
—37days

"The only time I got into trouble in the river," she said slowly, "was when I wanted people to look at me in the boat in the river, when I wanted to stop and wave and make sure people saw me in the boat."

At those moments when we try to wave and be seen and praised, we are actually drowning.

Give in to the river. Fully embrace it and flow with it because it knows what you should be doing with your life. Move with it without trying to stop the boat so people can admire you and like you, so they can say "You're good, you're smart, you're pretty, I give you permission." Keep moving, keep seeing, keep knowing, and keep saying what you know to be your truth, without needing or looking for the admiration of others.

You *are* good. You *are* beautiful. You *are* smart. Give *yourself* permission.

Seek out that particular mental attribute which makes you feel most deeply and vitally alive, along with which comes the inner voice which says, "This is the real me," and when you have found that attitude, follow it. —**William James**

37 Days: Do It Now Challenge

What's your river? Find it and jump in. There will be times, as Ensler said, when you have to paddle a little, sometimes a lot. And there will be other times when you are swept into a maelstrom of white water. Be there; don't stop to wave, to have your picture taken, or to have your boat admired. Just go as if your life depended on it. Know what you know, see what you see, say what you say wherever you can say it. Chance being great, not good.

✐ Action:

Emil M. Cioran said: "It is because we are all imposters that we endure each other."

Focused free-write:

- There are times in all our lives when we feel like an imposter, like someone who will be "found out." Write for five minutes in response to this question: When do you feel like an imposter? What do you fear people will find out about you?

- Stop. Read what you have written.

- Circle a word or phrase that stands out as a hot spot and write for five more minutes on that topic.

◎ Movement:

In her book *Turning to One Another*, Margaret Wheatley asks a compelling question: "Am I becoming someone I respect?" At lunch each day for the next thirty-seven days, ask yourself that question. If the answer is no, you still have the rest of that day to change it to yes by the actions that you take or don't take. This daily questioning is how change really occurs in our lives. Use it to become someone you respect, lunch by lunch.

Fourteen thousand pounds
Shift silently
Over ruts worn deep
By the lure of water.
A behemoth link
In the tail to trunk chain,
Slinking under night's cover
Toward the wide, gentle sea.
Each massive foot,
Distinct as a thumbprint,
Hints at treetops and weather,
Speaks of dry and cracked earth.
Using sub-human decibels,
He sounds out over miles,
Summoning kin to the water,
To its cool and its drinking,
To its diving and bathing,
To its feasting and mating.
His way there is slow,
Just five miles in an hour.
Imagine the courage.
One hundred thousand muscles
And nerves all bundled together,
Trumpeting the call
To elephant love.

—Liz Granfort, "Elephant Love"

CHAPTER SIX
Intimacy: Love More

Your task is not to seek for love, but merely to seek and find all the barriers within yourself that you have built against it. —**Rumi**

"Our property taxes—just property taxes—were $30,000! Can you imagine! Of course, it was a three-story house on the biggest lake in Texas, and we had two boats and a boat landing, but still!" she exclaimed. I half expected to hear the make, model, and cost of her washer and dryer. "It was a huge amount of upkeep," she continued. "But of course, we hired all that out." Of course.

It was a performance, a tally of worth voiced for my benefit. We were on the deck of the beautiful Pana Sea Ah Bed and Breakfast on the Oregon coast, waves crashing behind us. I didn't know her; she was a guest there, like me. I fantasized about a large wave splashing over her, muffling the sound of her accounting.

Why do we measure our worth in such ways? We all do it—either by our bank account or pant size, our IQ or length of our bio, the number of visitors to our Web site or the number of people in our Rolodex. What is that magic yardstick against which we measure our worth in the world? Is it the square footage in our home, the make of our cars, the number of countries we have visited, the number of links we have? **Do we love ourselves for who we are or only what we have?** Do we love others for who they are, not what they have?

I squelched the perverse urge to ask how large her boats were. It wouldn't do to encourage her.

"We go on two long cruises a year. We've done Alaska, Europe, China." It reminded me, oddly, of Emma trading her Pokémon cards when she was twelve, each trade more of a sacrifice. What if, instead of acquiring country notches on my belt, I measured the depth of my engagement with different cultures. Not how much expensive cut glass I owned, but the way the light shines through it at dawn? Not the number of cruises, but what I learn about and from the characters I meet on board? Not the property taxes and square footage, but the sound of crickets on the lake at sunset?

> IN MANY WAYS WE WERE DRUGGED WHEN WE WERE YOUNG. WE WERE BROUGHT UP TO NEED PEOPLE. FOR WHAT? FOR ACCEPTANCE, APPROVAL, APPRECIATION, APPLAUSE.
>
> —Anthony de Mello

When Emma was younger—at the very beginning of measurement in her life—she stood in the bathroom one day, looking at herself in the mirror. It was a new moment for her. Those young days of carefree movement in the world were ending; soon she would begin tugging on her clothes like all women do, gauging whether those pants made her look fat. As she modeled in the mirror, she called out to me: "Mama! Mama!" I went to the bathroom door, waiting for the truest sign that she was lost to the Beauty Cult. "Mama," she said. "Do you think . . . ? Do you think I look . . . ?" Here it comes, I thought.

> Let me listen to me, and not to them. —Gertrude Stein

"Do you think I look interesting?" she finally asked.

My heart burst open. What a wonderful measure of worth—not "beautiful," but "interesting." It was a better yardstick, a richer and more human one, a sustaining and sense-making one, a yardstick to measure by, a true one.

> [Love is an act of courage, not of fear. —Paolo Freire]

Burn Those Jeans

A lot of disappointed people have been left standing on the street corner waiting for the bus marked Perfection. —**Donald Kennedy**

Since leaving Freedom High School on Independence Boulevard, I've carried a certain pair of pants around with me everywhere I've gone, like a pet Chihuahua in a diamond collar, a dangly gold charm, a passport, a ball and chain.

They are Levi's jeans, at that perfect stage of worn-in-ness, that place where the knees know where to go when you put them on, the pockets reveal a pentimento of your hands, and the hems are adequately frayed.

Over the years they've become a symbol, a talisman, an icon of my perfect high school shape, that lean and strong teenage body that ran and hiked and climbed and bicycled everywhere, that simpler shape before broken hearts, sexual harassments, dead parents, business suits, big promotions, missed deadlines, inane meetings, working with mean people, being mean myself, dead friends, terrorist attacks, hydraulic systems failing on planes I happened to be on, and just plain living the overrated adult life.

These jeans are cosmopolitan, accompanying me to college, abroad to live in Germany, to graduate school, to all my jobs, around the world on a ship, to twenty years in Washington, DC, and recently back to North Carolina where they reside in a closet only 54 miles from where I first wore them. Full circle around the globe, that denim, those rivets, that distinctive red tag.

It wasn't a conscious decision to carry them around with me, no. But there they were, everywhere I went, a reminder in denim that I don't have that body anymore, and that I had a Big Goal: Get back into those jeans.

Years passed.

I still couldn't fit into the jeans. I beat myself up for failing to reach that goal. I joined fitness clubs, worked out with a trainer named Thor in DC who nearly killed me, drank Master Cleanser Lemonade, joined Weight Watchers, and studied before-and-after pictures in *Shape* magazine as if I were consulting the hieroglyphic special edition of *Man's Search for Meaning.* Even with all those starts and stops and high expectations, and the few successes, **the jeans still hung in my closet, unworn and taunting me.**

No matter how well I did in eating right (occasionally) and exercising (sometimes), and no matter my other successes in life—my brilliant husband, amazing children, slightly insane and terribly fascinating friends, the published books and impressive-sounding job titles—I still couldn't fit into those jeans, and so felt a failure all these years, a mostly unconscious feeling that raised its ugly head each time I came across the Levi's in my closet, ridiculing me with their utter hiplessness and unwearability.

When Emma was in the sixth grade, she complained one morning that she had no pants to wear to school. I resisted Parental Lecturette Number Seventeen on Household Laundry Procedures. When I heard her plea for help, I was standing at my closet door and saw in front of me The Jeans. Why not, I thought. It might be awhile before I can get back into these again.

"Try these," I said. "They're kind of retro and too big for you, but you can wear a belt to gather up the extra. And remember, I want them back so I can wear them!"

"Awesome!" she said.

I remember many carefree days in those jeans—marching-band practice with my bass clarinet, hanging out with Meg in Hardee's parking lot, watching *Tora! Tora! Tora!* at the Mimosa Theatre, driving Daddy's blue-and-white Oldsmobile 88—and I just knew through all those years that those jeans were still a worthy goal, a beacon of a thinhood worthy of bony Calista Flockhart and all those despicable, heartless women who give birth then look like Kate Moss the following day. In my heart of hearts, I knew I was right to hold those jeans up as my Mount Everest, my Oscar, my Gold Medal, my dark journey to the heart of the Nile, my People's Choice Award, my Pulitzer, my Nobel for Thinness.

Emma took the jeans to her room, then brought them back. "Thanks, but they're too small," she said, throwing them in my general direction.

Too small?

For thirty years I've tried to get back into a pair of blue jeans that are too small for my thin, strong, athletic twelve-year-old daughter?

Everything is a metaphor, isn't it? Replace the word *jeans* with that albatross hanging around your neck, following you around through life, diverting your attention from the real goal, setting you up for failure. **Is it the wrong goal?** Is it an unworthy goal, unreachable and unreasonable, one that can only make you feel bad, instead of good and right and strong?

Why do we punish ourselves with unreasonable expectations, putting life on hold until we reach them? What is the real danger of such pressures? They delay living, the real life right in front of us. "I'll do that when," we say to ourselves. "I can't do that now because I haven't yet done this." It's like having an incomplete in your graduate Milton class that just keeps hanging over you, making it impossible for you to do anything else because your comprehensive exegesis of the two parallel falls of *Paradise Lost* looms ahead of you at every turn. Not that I have personal experience of this phenomenon.

Are the jeans even the real goal?

Enough!

Do those jeans represent a carefree, simpler more active life, a less stressful way of living, a life less encumbered? Perhaps those are goals I should reach for, not the jeans.

BURN THOSE JEANS
A LOT OF DISAPPOINTED PEOPLE HAVE BEEN LEFT STANDING ON THE STREET CORNER WAITING FOR THE BUS MARKED PERFECTION.
Donald Kennedy

37 Days: Do It Now Challenge

One evening this week, pour yourself a glass of a 2002 Pinot Noir from New Zealand's Mount Difficulty vineyard or a nice bubbly apple cider, brush pollen off a chair in your manicured backyard, put some sweet Eva Cassidy tunes on the CD player, grab the safety matches from the kitchen and a delicate bottle of lighter fluid, and go outside and burn those old jeans. Torch that goal that limits and minimizes rather than frees you. Make your goals challenging, not destructive. Look behind that goal to see The Real Goal: Is it the jeans or is it something else you're longing for?

Have I torched those jeans yet? Not quite yet.

✐ Action:

Focused free-write:

- For five minutes, write a description of yourself.

- Stop. Cross that one out.

- Set the timer for three more minutes and describe yourself again without using anything from the first description.

- Stop. Cross that one out.

- Set the timer for three more minutes and describe yourself again without using anything from the first two descriptions.

Now you're finally getting to the you beneath all that other stuff. In this last description, you might find the real you, the one beneath all those titles and awards and achievements. Getting to that you might help you set different, more real goals.

You got to be careful if you don't know where you're going, because you might not get there. —**Yogi Berra**

BURN THOSE JEANS

⟳ **Movement:**

Write a list of ten major goals you have.

- For each one, ask yourself: When I achieve that goal, what's behind it? What more will I need or want once I achieve it?

- Keep this list handy and review it each morning for thirty-seven days.

- The actions you take each day are either moving you toward achieving those goals, or not. If you habitually aren't taking action that leads you closer to those goals, perhaps it isn't that you are lazy . . . perhaps, instead, those aren't the real goals.

- At the end of the thirty-seven days, revisit the list of goals. Recommit to those you still want, and change those you don't.

Also, for five minutes a day for those thirty-seven days, search out clothing you've been saving for when you lose weight. Give it away to someone who needs it now.

First say to yourself what you would be; and then do what you have to do. —**Epictetus**

Put Your Own Mask on First

I cannot live without my life! —Emily Brontë

I fly a lot. Even so, it's a lot less than I used to fly.

Me and my Delta-Ultra-Flying-Too-Much Super Platinum Card, that sad testament to life way too far above terra firma, see a lot of action in any given year. I pray to the gods of upgrades on a weekly basis, hunkered down over Delta.com in vain hopes that the almost-full-adult-size seat in the front with my name on it will become available. It's as close to compulsive gambling as I ever come, except for that sweet moment one evening in 1995 with my Kiwi friend Richard at a casino in Melbourne, but I was younger then.

I've grown so accustomed to the drone of flight attendants telling me how to save my life in the case of a death spiral from 37,000 feet that I hardly listen anymore. Honestly, isn't what they tell you just to keep you occupied while going down? Would that flotation device really help if we hit the water at 500 miles an hour? Could those little life vests with the fakey blowup whistles and flashing lights really save us if we ditch in shark-infested waters? And, by the way, do flight attendants monitor the alcohol consumption of people seated in exit rows, just in case? No, I thought not, given my recent encounter with Heavy Drinker in 18A, just one large inebriated man between me and that forty-pound pull-down door.

Flying just weeks after 9/11, I began a long internal dialogue over whether it's worth it. I've had problems with flying before. It's not natural for so many people to be so far above the earth, winging from New York to Mumbai in a lighted metal tube with microwave ovens, small bottles of booze, and gale-force suction toilets. The counterarguments always rang false: "But you're not in control, the pilot is!" people would say to me cheerfully, as if that should make me more comfortable with the prospect.

"Exxxxactly," I'd counter. "That's my problem with it. I want to be in control if I'm going to be perched on a precipice between cloud and sod." Hence my dear husband's recent birthday gift to me: flying lessons.

What a lovely surprise to finally discover how unlonely being alone can be. —Ellen Burstyn

As my friend Rosemary wrote after learning of this genius gift: "Ye who has more fear of flying than anyone I know, taking flying lessons? Ye whose deepest fear is being sucked out of an airplane at 30,000 feet? Ye who carry a Coke-can-size breathing apparatus so you won't suffocate evacuating the burning plane? What in the world? Are you facing your fears? Trying to harness ultimate control over them? I can see you now, wrestling the wheel from the pilot in an emergency." Yes, she knew immediately that the flying lessons were intended to empower me to save a Boeing 777 from going into a death spiral when the pilot has a massive heart attack or aneurysm or allergic reaction to those damned peanuts and slumps over the controls unconscious.

No, I don't have any control issues, but I thank you for asking.

The flight that slammed into the Pentagon on 9/11 was my flight, the one I always take when going to Los Angeles to see my friends, the Gubes. Since then I have put myself onto that doomed flight many times, imagining my last moments, that surreal realization of ending so quickly, so fruitlessly, so horribly, knowing and being unable to change the course of events, my luck and good living having run out. It would have been a real shock, not only that I was dying but that I had finally met my match. Surprise at the lucklessness of it would wash over

> Language . . . has created the word "loneliness" to express the pain of being alone. And it has created the word "solitude" to express the glory of being alone. —**Paul Tillich**

me, quickly followed by those regrets, plus the horror of what I would leave behind—a legacy of pain for my family, those motherless girls, irreplaceable anguish, all in one moment's time.

I experienced a lesser but still vivid horror of extended and violent turbulence on a flight from Atlanta to Asheville one late night, dropping 1,000 feet in a second, the kind of drop where no one can speak, where you grasp onto the armrest to stay in your chair, too shocked to wildly attempt a goodbye note on an airsick bag or mentally calculate how little you're getting paid per hour to risk your life, especially if you count all the dry cleaning and child care that makes it possible to go on the road. And of course, there was also that near-death landing when the plane's hydraulic system failed a few years back.

[
Everyone is a moon, and has a dark side which he never shows to anybody.
    –Mark Twain
]

But it was during a flight with Emma that I felt compelled as a Parental Unit to pretend the safety instruction was Important and Vital Information (which it is, I know, even in my heart of denial). I followed her lead as she reached for the laminated emergency procedure placard in the seat pocket in front of us to follow along as the nice woman suggested.

Emma was struck by the drawing of people jumping out of the plane onto the emergency chute. "I guess you can't touch the chute," she said, quizzically, and—knowing her—she worriedly wondered how she could achieve this feat.

"What do you mean?" I said, half listening, half focused on finding the audio channel for *Stuck on You,* our mindless in-flight movie.

"Well, there are all these people jumping out of the plane, but none of them is touching the chute."

Indeed, all those small business people without shoes were levitating in a nicely proper seated position over the bright orange slide stuck at a wild angle out of the plane door. Were they all allergic to latex? No wonder she was worried—how do they stay a good 3 feet above the slide, and where are their shoes and all that junk they lug onto planes (and hit me with as they go down the aisles)? Is it possible his precious laptop with those chunky Power-Point slides about market share would be left behind by the loud-talking businessman in 17D? I think not. It all looks so orderly on the laminated card, but somehow I doubt the death slide would be—I've watched people try to get into a Jethro Tull concert.

What I did hear clearly on that flight with Emma was the instruction: "In case the oxygen mask falls from the compartment above your head, put your own oxygen mask on first, and then help others around you."

Put your own mask on first.

It was as if I had never heard that before.

If you don't put your own mask on first, you'll be of no use to others who might need your help. There are only seventeen seconds of consciousness when the oxygen fails on a plane. Seventeen seconds, then you're of no use to anyone.

selfish fairy

Put your own mask on first

How often we ignore that kind of wisdom. Immersed in a life happily spent taking care of others in one form or another, as either parent or child or partner or teacher, **we forget sometimes to take care of our own needs.** We don't put ourselves first for fear of being called selfish. Not to our face, of course, but in those quiet moments when people make infallible pronouncements about others, the kind that allow for no ambiguity: He's selfish, she's self-centered— interpretive words to measure someone else's outside from our own inside, tinged perhaps with our own longing, our own set of insecurities or inadequacies, knowledge of our own faults and fears.

Sometimes I wonder if taking care of others—saving others—isn't simply a diversion from saving ourselves. If I focus on you, I don't have to focus on myself. And maybe saving others deprives them of their own agency. Does repeatedly bailing out a friend from the police station after they've been arrested for driving drunk really save them or does it merely reinforce your own self-image as Savior? As Anne Lamott wrote in *Bird by Bird,* when a wife describes repeatedly picking up her husband from the front yard so neighbors won't see him passed out drunk there, a woman tells her, "Honey, just leave him there where Jesus flang him."

Nurturing my own self first in order to be better able to help others—what would that look like? Would I schedule time at the gym like I schedule taking kids to tuba lessons and birthday parties? My oxygen mask might resemble a solitary trip to the library or a lunch with adults or a bubble bath without animals or children as rambunctious witnesses. Imagine.

I HOLD THIS TO BE THE HIGHEST TASK FOR A BOND BETWEEN TWO PEOPLE: THAT EACH PROTECTS THE SOLITUDE OF THE OTHER.

—Rainer Maria Rilke

37 Days: Do It Now Challenge

If you're constantly saving other people, slow down long enough to put your own oxygen mask on. While you're tightening the straps, ponder the wacky possibility that the people you're trying to save don't need saving. If you lose consciousness, you won't be any help to them anyway. Breathe deeply first. Be selfish in order to be selfless.

✐ *Action:*

Focused free-write:

- For four minutes, write in response to this question: The most selfish people I know are [fill in the blank]. Name them and describe what behaviors they exhibit that make you feel they are selfish.

- Stop and read what you have written. As you read, consider the possibility that perhaps some of their behaviors are not selfish, but self-focused, allowing them to put their own mask on first.

- Go back to your list and for three minutes, reframe your description of their selfishness as being "self-focused" behaviors that allow them to nurture themselves. Do this for each one, even if you really believe they are being selfish instead. Push yourself to reinterpret their behavior in a more positive light—hard to do, I know, but important.

- Then, for the last three minutes, write the things you could do to "put your own mask on first," whether to simply have a cup of lavender earl grey tea with soy creamer in silence each morning before everyone else gets up, have a massage once a month, create a wellness vision and exercise routine for yourself, or just get more sleep. Make your list and start doing those things.

✺ *Movement:*

For thirty-seven days, be completely alone for thirty minutes each day. No exceptions. At the end of each day, make a brief note in your journal about how you spent that time. What does this alone time feel like to you at first? In what ways do you begin to need it and cherish it? What difference does this solitude make in your life over those thirty-seven days? What would it take to continue this practice indefinitely, and what do you believe you would gain from it over time?

Purge Your Portfolio

For many people, an excuse is better than an achievement because an achievement, no matter how great, leaves you having to prove yourself again in the future but an excuse can last for life. —Eric Hoffer

Two friends from high school visited several months ago. I hadn't seen one of them for twenty-nine years, the other for twenty. Let's call them Tom and Steve. A third was expected, but couldn't come. Let's call him Edward. (I'm setting aside for the moment my horror at being out of high school more than thirty years.)

Edward is a well-known hairstylist and image consultant. I dreaded his assessment of my hair, which—now white—looks suspiciously like a bloated Q-tip or, at its finest, an organic cotton ball. I'm growing it out, so it's in that horrible, wicked, growing-out stage, the ugly one, the one where you feel compelled to tell even strangers on the street you're just growing out your hair and otherwise you would never leave the house looking like this.

Tom is an accomplished interior designer. Oh, Lord, look at my house. I need to redo the whole thing before he arrives. We should paint. I need new furniture. If only the rug matched the couch better! Maybe my friend Gay could fly from San Francisco and tell me how to place the furniture since she's been known to rearrange hotel rooms in which she's staying for only one night. Where's the nice, funny bald man from *Surprised by Design* when you need him? The cats have scratched the back of the couch. It looks like Roadside Attraction Feral Cat Land in here.

Steve is a surgeon for goodness' sake, and we used to disco dance together. Hey, it was the 1970s. **I needed to lose about 1,000 pounds, color my hair, and polish my dance steps before he arrived.**

I didn't.

Even with my puffy misshapen growing-out hair, my house of not-designer furniture, and my child-bearing hips, we had fun. My friends have all come into their own, leaving the unsure world of high school far behind, living big lives of travel and success. I kept wanting to say, Well, honestly, I've had some great years since high school; years where I looked fantastic, where I was even briefly hot, where I traveled the world and stayed in the Peninsula in Hong Kong and the Oriental Bangkok where the laundry folds your underwear into tiny boxes. I've dined with sea captains and ambassadors and published a few books and had lunch with the beautiful and talented Carlos Fuentes and interviewed Stevie Wonder while in my pajamas. You just caught me during an off-year.

> THE TRICK IS NOT HOW MUCH PAIN YOU FEEL BUT HOW MUCH JOY YOU FEEL. ANY IDIOT CAN FEEL PAIN. LIFE IS FULL OF EXCUSES TO FEEL PAIN, EXCUSES NOT TO LIVE, EXCUSES, EXCUSES, EXCUSES.
>
> —Erica Jong

Then I realized that I didn't need to make excuses anymore. The hips, house, hair—they just are. They are me. They are my life. This is me!

Our family went to a comics convention recently to support Emma's burgeoning focus on becoming an illustrator and her interest in drawing Japanese manga. At the suggestion of a comics aficionado, she carried her heavy portfolio of drawings with her, slung across her shoulder as we walked for hours in and among the artists. We talked to a few exhibitors, admired artwork, looked at art supplies, watched artists work. Each time I suggested she show her portfolio, she demurred.

We got ready to leave. "Do you think I should show my portfolio?" she asked as we moved toward the door.

"Would you like to?" I asked.

"I don't know . . . no . . . yes . . . maybe."

I recognized the internal battle—too shy to do so, desperate to. We had talked to several young illustrators from the Savannah College of Art and Design who had been nice when we stopped by earlier. "Why don't we stop by their booth again and ask them to take a look at your drawings?" I suggested.

> *I will not take "but" for an answer.* —Langston Hughes

"You think?" she said.

"This is exactly what you should do at a show like this," one of the young artists said. "Bring your work and start showing it. It's tough to do, but it's important." He talked to Emma like an adult, making eye contact, not talking to me and not patronizing her as adults sometimes do with kids. I stepped back to let her own the conversation herself.

The care and attention the young illustrators took with Emma was a real gift. They pored over her drawings, not only praising her efforts but giving her straightforward, constructive feedback, the kind that will create a burning in her for learning and drawing more.

As one of them turned the page in her portfolio, I heard Emma say "That's not really a good one."

I attribute my success to this: I never gave or took an excuse. —**Florence Nightingale**

"Emma," he said, "if you don't like something, take it out of your portfolio. You don't want to have anything in here that you need to make excuses for. **You want to be proud of everything you put in front of people.** When you show your portfolio, the people looking at it will focus on the weak pieces if you have them in there—so take them out."

"I understand," she said. And suddenly, so did I.

As we walked toward the door, Emma was actually glowing. "I want to sit down and draw right now!" she said. "That was *awesome*!"

Those young artists may never know how much their taking time with Emma meant to her—or to me. To have someone engage with your child in such a way is a gift. To really hear their message—*Don't have anything in your portfolio that you need to make excuses for*—was also a gift.

What in my portfolio (where *portfolio* means house, life, brain, relationships) should I keep? What should I sell? What should I toss? What have I been trying desperately to hide? What do I consistently make excuses for?

> He who cannot dance claims the floor is uneven.
> —**Hindu saying**

Alexander Pope said, "An excuse is worse than a lie, for an excuse is a lie, guarded." What lies are my excuses guarding? What weak pieces in my portfolio do I feel compelled to create excuses for? Remember that young illustrator's words: If you don't like something, take it out of your portfolio. You want to be very proud of everything you put in front of people.

✐ **Action:**

Focused free-write:

- Your memory is going to be completely erased in five minutes. You have only that amount of time to write down everything you want or need to remember. Start writing.

- At the end of five minutes, stop.

- What did you write? Did you look to others to define your life by writing down names and phone numbers of people who could remind you of who you are? Did you write your life as it now is, even with all things you don't like about it—or did you describe it as you'd like it to be? Since your memory will be erased, you can create the life you really want!

- Write for five more minutes and create a compelling image of that life, making it very specific: What kind of room do you wake up in? With whom do you eat breakfast? What do you do all day? What is your mode of transportation? What does your place of work look like? How do you dress and move in the world?

What would it take to start creating that life?

Whoever wants to be a judge of human nature should study people's excuses. —**Friedrich Hebbel**

For the next thirty-seven days, when you feel an excuse coming on, rather than verbalize it, stop for a moment:

- What are you making an excuse about?

- Your hair doesn't look right? Change it.

- Your house is a mess when someone stops by unexpectedly? Spend just fifteen minutes a day putting things away so visitors aren't dreaded, but welcomed.

- You didn't have time to finish something? Reprioritize or say no to more things.

- Keep a catalog of your excuses. Then make your life an excuse-free zone.

Ninety-nine percent of all failures come from people who have the habit of making excuses.

—**George Washington Carver**

Give Free Hugs

> We need four hugs a day for survival. We need eight hugs a day for maintenance. We need twelve hugs a day for growth. —**Virginia Satir**

On a black-and-white video, a tall young man named Juan Mann (pronounced *one man,* of course) takes to the streets with a simple white sign

that says FREE HUGS. People pass him by. Like me, they look at him trying to figure out his deal—What's he up to? Is he unbalanced? Is this a joke? What's the story? And so it goes—in black and white—until a small, bent old woman stops for a hug. To reach down to her height, Juan gets on his knees for the embrace. The video blossoms into color. People begin walking toward him instead of away for a series of wonderful, joyful encounters—unexpected connections. Free exuberant hugs. Hugs just for the sake of reaching out to another human to connect, to link.

It is joyous. It gives me hope. It lowers my blood pressure.

My friend Madelyn first told me about this video. "Emma might really like this," she said. "I'm sure you can find it on YouTube."

My daughter, Emma, did like it. She not only liked it, she loved it. "That really makes me happy," she kept saying after watching it. "I just love that." Her face glowed, a rare event in her universe of studied teenage coolness.

The next morning Emma and I left for the National Storytelling Festival in historic Jonesborough, Tennessee, where she was to videotape interviews with Big Deal Storytellers for a school project. In our excitement to see storytellers like Kevin Kling, David Holt, and Andy Offutt Irwin, we forgot to eat all day. Late that night we checked into our hotel and headed to dinner before collapsing.

"You know what I'd really like to do?" Emma asked as we ate grilled cheese sandwiches at Shoney's, our feet hurting from all the walking. "I'd really like to do that free hugs thing at the Storytelling Festival."

We ventured out into the night looking for poster board and markers. An always-open Walgreens provided what we needed. By 1:00 a.m., the large sign was complete: **FREE HUGS.**

Morning came, more interviews with storytellers, and then The Moment. In one of those circular amazements of life, Emma walked into the center of Main Street at exactly the same time as Madelyn, the woman who had first told me about Free Hugs.

"I can't do it," Emma said nervously. She rolled and unrolled her sign, shifting her weight from foot to foot. "I can't do it," she said again, biting the inside of her lip. "I can't."

"You don't have to, honey," I said. "But if you really want to, we'll help."

MILLIONS AND MILLIONS OF YEARS WOULD STILL NOT GIVE ME HALF ENOUGH TIME TO DESCRIBE THAT TINY INSTANT OF ALL ETERNITY WHEN YOU PUT YOUR ARMS AROUND ME AND I PUT MY ARMS AROUND YOU.

—Jacques Prévert

Emma has lived much of her life being shy. This would be a big leap, far beyond her comfort zone. It would be her Apollo mission to the moon, that giant step. In some of the interviews she had done the day before, she couldn't speak. "I forgot my first question," she would say, looking over at me nervously, like a bird anxious to fall. "Mama, can you remind me of my first question?"

"I think you wanted to ask why they believe storytelling is so important," I'd remind her, "or perhaps you wanted to ask if the pursuit of a story ever became the story." Even after being prompted, she often couldn't speak to the storytellers. They all did yeoman's duty to help her find her voice, watching as she struggled to get the words out.

A friend, Marybeth, recently told me about gathering a group of women from around the country to help her celebrate a birthday—and to help her be more herself, to give her feedback, to embrace her. At one point in the weekend, Marybeth said to the group something like: "I am trying to find my voice."

Her friend Pat spoke up, giving the kind of honest feedback Marybeth needed and wanted: "I'm so sick and tired of middle-aged white women saying they need to find their voice. I've heard that a million times. I just have one question for you: If you did have a voice, what would you say?"

If you did have a voice, what would you say?

Perhaps, like Emma, you would announce free hugs with that voice. Perhaps your voice would say—what?

Madelyn walked with Emma to the middle of Main Street. I stood with the tripod and video camera. As Emma tentatively held up her sign, Madelyn walked quietly toward her and hugged her. I was filming from a distance. When Madelyn stepped back, a bright flash appeared in the viewfinder from the left side—a brilliant, fast-moving, purple comet of arms with black dreadlocks swinging behind in wild exuberance. **The woman swept Emma up into her arms and swung her around, lifting her off her feet.** Thus, Emma's free hugs experience began.

Love is much more demanding than law. —Archbishop Desmond Tutu

Some passersby were more tentative, walking past, looking back, wondering. Others walked silently toward her, hugged, and walked away with a smile. There was no way to predict who would hug and who wouldn't—I'll admit that some of the people who stopped surprised me. I don't know why. They didn't look like huggers. How wrong we can be. I wondered as I watched what gifts we don't put out into the world because we are afraid of the response we might get. It's damned hard to walk out into the world with our FREE HUGS sign and be ignored, passed by, laughed at, questioned, isn't it?

Emma ventured farther, her sign held higher. She moved out of my viewfinder, out into the world on Main Street, expanding her way of seeing the world. At first I panicked when I couldn't see her; then I relaxed, understanding how big a metaphor this was for our future when she does leave. She was in direct engagement with the world without my protection, and without—more importantly—my interference. A TV crew interviewed her, people passed her by, others stopped and hugged and smiled. She did it—the thing that was the hardest for her.

We drove home, exhausted. "You did a great job with your interviews, peanut," I said. "I know that was hard. I'm really proud of you. What was your favorite part of the weekend?"

[I felt it shelter to speak to you.
—Emily Dickinson]

"The free hugs," she said without hesitation. "The free hugs were awesome."

Pushing past that envelope of comfort—those edges we impose on ourselves—is where Big Stuff Happens, Stuff the Meaning of Which We Often Don't Even Know at the Time.

Hugging has health benefits. It makes people smile.

37 Days: Do It Now Challenge

It feels as if we have lost some vital part of ourselves in a dense forest of political correctness, that awkward avoidance of others for fear of misunderstanding or offense or sexual harassment charges, the siren song of "appropriate behavior." Why is a hug so fearful, I wonder. Is it that we have given up our need or our capacity for direct engagement? What fear drives our disconnect from one another?

And what does free *really mean? It means without condition, without expectation, freely given without determination of worthiness, without ulterior motive. How often do I really give freely? Are my gifts instead some odd expression of power or need on my own part?*

The reason Juan Mann moved me so, I think, was that the free hugs were, in fact, free. Give free hugs. Try four a day to survive. Aim for twelve. Err on the side of the hug.

✍ Action:

Focused free-write: Imagine you are standing in the center of your town with a free hugs sign.

- Write for five minutes about how that makes you feel, both physically and emotionally. How does it feel when people stare and point or walk past without acknowledging you? How does it feel when they swoop you up in their arms to hug you?

- Stop writing. Circle a hot spot, a word or phrase that stands out from what you've written.

- Now write for five more minutes about that word or phrase.

♻ Movement:

Some of us aren't comfortable with hugging, but can show openness to human connection in other ways. In addition to hugging, what are five simple ways you could connect with the people around you? Perhaps with a smile, or saying "good morning," or paying them a compliment? What about by remembering to ask about their partner's new job, or mentioning their child or pet by name? Create a short list of ways to connect, and then practice those connections for the next thirty-seven days. Notice what is different about the quality of your life by doing so.

Save a Grocery List

The palest ink is better than the sharpest memory. —**Chinese proverb**

A luggage tag is my reminder of the ways in which my father's hands moved, of how he grasped his pen, always that blue plastic one with MODERN BARBER SHOP on one side and his name on the other as OWNER.

He's been dead since 1980—dead longer than he was alive in my life. Surely he's been gone long enough that I am healed from that confusing, awkward, and sickening day, and all those years of lack. Sure. A simple, gray plastic luggage tag—ironically, an accidental icon of a man who never got to travel—surfaced in an attic box recently, unannounced, and pushed the air straight out of my lungs. I even got that little tinny taste you get in your mouth when you accidentally bite into aluminum foil.

What I realized as I remembered to breathe again was this: I need to also write things in my own hand, not just type here at my obsessive machine, but stop and pull out real paper and a nice fountain pen and make note of my passage through this world in my own hand, with curves of letters and angular bits that don't seem distinctive to me, but look like me to others. Just as I recognized my father's handwriting and would have even if he hadn't been writing down his own name—that odd combination of little and big letters, caps and caplets mixed together, that *l* in *Melvin* never capitalized, but that *E* and *N* always uppercase, that turned-back loop at the bottom of his *5*s and the small *g* always hovering above the line of other letters.

That cadence of small *i*'s with tiny dots is all pure Daddy. I'd know it anywhere. I had a grocery list of his for years that I carried in my passport all

The past is never dead, it is not even past. —**William Faulkner**

over the world: **"BrEAD, MilK, grapE jEllY," it simply said.** I lost it on a long trip to Asia, devastated because it was the only shred of him I had left, until this luggage tag emerged.

So I have him back, the part beyond a static photograph, the part where he's actually made something of his own volition—an identification tag for all those trips he and I planned to take someday. (Now if I could only get his voice back.) My daughters have mainly these typed images of me, the ones you see in front of you now. Not swoops and odd dots and strong *T*'s. In this typed text, they have symbols that could be anyone's, not just mine.

Several years ago, just after my first book came out (I gave copies to family and friends with small red plastic magnifying glasses attached to the spine, my name was so small on it), someone asked Emma what her mommy did for a living. Emma was seven at the time. "She's a typer," I heard her say. "She types." I didn't bother to elaborate or qualify it or make it nicer or more impressive. "Yes," I said quietly. "I type. I'm a typer." What happened to being a writer, with a magnificent obsession for paper and pens?

The distinctiveness of a voice, a person, a way of sense-making, is contained not only in the accumulation of words and their meaning, but in their construction as well, those marks and lines and curves. To hold them is as if people are again animated for us—or at least we've the pentimento of their movement.

On this luggage tag, Daddy's handwriting doesn't just contain the information he was leaving, it contains the memory of his hands, those fingers, that cadence with which he moved his 5 feet 8 inches through the world in bright green jackets and the broad ties of the 1970s, with plaid green-and-yellow pants, a pair of perfectly polished and heavy black wing tips grounding him.

We mustn't lose that distinctive identifier in our world of typing. Let's rebel, wear berets at a jaunty angle, sit in cafes that proudly announce NO WIFI, and scratch out our poems and grocery lists on recycled 30 percent post-production wastepaper, perhaps with soy inks.

There is more to language than just its meaning. There is its form. There is sense and rhythm and a kind of recognition that it speaks, too, a handwriting shaped at a young age and continuing in that same frame. Well, save for the rounded circles above the *i*'s we're prone to make in fourth grade and

WHAT WE REMEMBER FROM CHILDHOOD WE REMEMBER FOREVER—PERMANENT GHOSTS, STAMPED, INKED, IMPRINTED, ETERNALLY SEEN.

—Cynthia Ozick

IDENTIFICATION CARD
Name *Melwin Digh*
Address *302 Wilson ST.*
City *Morganton*
State *N.C.* Tel. No. *437-5215*

curlicues at the end of words that reach up and over and form a heart or a flower. Those seasonal idiosyncrasies fall away, but a skeleton of those first big letters made with chunky pencils remains.

There is a beauty in the handwriting of years past I fear we've lost, our speed to communicate in bits and bytes diminishing our swirls to antiseptic serifs, our utilitarian approach erasing the flourish of our ancestors, our instantaneous responses negating moments of pensive thought, that thoughtful pause where the right word will arise from the mist of the mindful before the pen descends to paper. Writing, formerly an art, is now no longer beautiful in the same way. It is just really, really fast. If it's fast enough, shooting into our e-mailbox like pellets, maybe we won't notice the loss of art.

Memory is a child walking along a seashore. You never can tell what small pebble it will pick up and store away among its treasured things. —**Pierce Harris**

I recently received a package from my fourth-grade teacher's daughter, a precious gift she sent after cleaning out her basement and sorting through her mother's belongings. Mrs. Smith was The Most Extraordinary Teacher in the Universe. Sixty-five years old when I was in fourth grade, she retired after that year. We corresponded until her death at ninety-three a few years ago, ending almost thirty years of handmade, off-centered little weavings I would make her, postcards I would send from my travels around the world, and her notes to me through the years, challenging me, praising me, and just staying connected.

The last time we visited her, she was ninety and racing six-year-old Emma down the hall, making tricornered hats out of newspaper with her, and playing a recorder, a beige-and-red plastic instrument from the elementary school she loved so much. That energy for life that had made her such a remarkable teacher in the first place was still there, thirty years later.

The package contained two glass birds from Mrs. Smith's house, one for each of my daughters so they can carry forth into their lives the memory of this extraordinary woman. And the most precious gift: a bundle of every letter and holiday card and little scrap of paper I had ever sent Mrs. Smith in those thirty years of our love for each other. Included, of course, were not only samples of my fourth-grade cursive, but her distinctive handwriting, too, the beautiful style that was her signature. Opening the package, it was as if she came back, though, of course, she never left, just as Daddy never did.

There is power in those strokes. Someone someday will cherish your floating G's and loopy 5s, holding on to them as if they were tiny life rafts on which they, too, could float for a moment or two or three. There's meaning in them, and not just the referential, but the embodied, the real sort, the human kind. Hold on to a grocery list, too, for old time's sake. Be a writer, not just a typer.

Action:

Focused free-write:

- Write your answer to this question for five minutes without pause: My grandfather was a man who . . . (If you don't know your grandfather, pick another older figure in your life.)

- After five minutes, stop.

- Now write for five minutes what you would like your grandchildren (or, if you don't have children, a younger friend) to say in answer to that question about you.

Movement:

In the next thirty-seven days, write ten real letters to people you know in longhand. I suggest you make a cup of tea, get a strawberry scone from West End Bakery, pick up a pen that you love (the kind where the ink is satisfying), think pensively with pen poised, then put pen to paper. Decorate an envelope with a caricature of yourself saying their address, and put a stamp on it. That kind of writing. Make it a habit. Surprise people.

Everybody needs his memories. They keep the wolf of insignificance from the door.
—**Saul Bellow**

Love Unlovable People

> Until he extends the circle of his compassion to all living things,
> man will not himself find peace. —**Albert Schweitzer**

It's easy to love people when they're lovable. It's harder when they're not.

In high school I learned intricate details of the battles of the Civil War. I knew my US presidents frontward and backward. I could recite the Gettysburg Address, Martin Luther King Jr.'s "I Have a Dream" speech, and William Faulkner's remarks when he received the Nobel Prize for Literature. I could wax poetic about the drafting of the US Constitution: who was there, who wasn't (women, for example, but don't get me started).

Why did I know so much about history?

Not because I was naturally predisposed to love studying bygone days, but because I had a brilliant young teacher who made the past exciting. Mr. Snow turned the whole school into a history project, with generals and kings and soldiers running through hallways, acne-prone battalions raging across the lunchroom, skirmishes reenacted in the band room and chemistry lab, gangly teens as Napoleon and foot soldiers. We had Patrick Henry's liberty or death, "two if by sea" lanterns, and all that tea in the Boston Harbor.

We knew it all because Mr. Snow made it come alive with never a dull moment, nor a lesson that wasn't experiential and active, with us moving through history, seeing it unfold, acting out our parts with hormonal gusto. He was an inventive and dazzling teacher, fresh from graduate school and bursting with ideas and staggering creativity in teaching a subject that in other, less capable hands is often soulless and pedestrian.

Many of us lose touch with our teachers, even brilliant ones significant to us. I don't know where many of my high school teachers are, but I do know exactly where Mr. Snow is every moment of every day.

He is in prison for the rest of his life.

On December 16, 2002, Mr. Snow was convicted after facing hundreds of counts of first-degree statutory sexual offense, sexual activity with students by a schoolteacher, and first-degree kidnapping of two male students.

Kindness is in our power, even when fondness is not. —Samuel Johnson

What happens to a life?

How could I reconcile this new information, this horrific, awful data even more troubling in its details of decades of abuse, with the Mr. Snow I knew? What utter disconnect! How things fall apart.

My first impulse when he was imprisoned was to reach out to him, but I hesitated. What could I possibly say—how did I feel about all this? Would my writing him be seen as condoning what he did? So I didn't write, though my instinct told me to.

The disquiet I felt as years passed and he continued to pay for his undoable crimes told me that the path of disregard wouldn't work for me. I knew that no matter what he had done, he is a living, breathing human and not simply defined by his crimes. I couldn't bear to leave him there alone.

My first letter to Mr. Snow came after three years of thinking about my own accountability, my writing finally prompted by a column in the local newspaper by a teacher about a former student of hers, a University of Virginia Jefferson Scholar with a genius IQ who has been in prison since 1985 for murdering his girlfriend's parents.

> IF YOU HATE A PERSON, YOU HATE SOMETHING IN HIM THAT IS PART OF YOURSELF. WHAT ISN'T PART OF OURSELVES DOESN'T DISTURB US.
>
> —Herman Hesse

Jens Soering maintains his innocence, and there is compelling evidence to suggest he is telling the truth.

As we corresponded after I read her article, Jean Franklin explained her continued relationship with her student, whom she believes is innocent: "But my decision to visit Jens did not depend on his guilt or innocence. **The teacher–student relationship, for me, is unconditional.** They come to us, warts and all, and we try to influence them for the good. In this case, I taught Jens for two years and knew there was good in him, guilty or innocent. You may also recognize the good in your former teacher, though he wasn't perfect."

I don't condone what Mr. Snow did and am repelled by his actions. I don't doubt he is guilty as charged, nor do I lament his sentence—I believe it is just, given the unutterable anguish he caused many young boys and their families. But I do wish it had never happened—that futile kind of wish, the sad kind we sometimes have when we know it's too late to go back.

I wish his life had taken a different trajectory: He is so talented. But it went in this direction, and now Mr. Snow is Inmate #0787172. Yet he is still under there somewhere, the Mr. Snow I knew. Isn't he?

I am a part of all that I have met. —Lord Alfred Tennyson

I'm not sure what writing to Mr. Snow will mean for either one of us, but I do know that in reaching out to him, I have found an important part of myself. He is providing me a glimpse into a world I would otherwise not know; I am a link to the world out here. Being in relationship with him is providing a lesson about what love really is—not convenient, happy love, but the harder, unconditional sort.

[Wherever there is a human being, there is a chance for a kindness.
—**Seneca**]

37 Days: Do It Now Challenge

Explore and expand your capacity for love and forgiveness. Love people who are unlovable. As G. K. Chesterton said, "Love means to love that which is unlovable, or it is no virtue at all." Who in your life is unlovable? What would loving them look like? How would it change you?

✎ *Action:*

Focused free-write:

- Ask yourself this question: What do I have in common with people in prison? Write without stopping for five minutes, listing as many things as you can that you have in common with people in prison. Write for the whole five minutes, challenging yourself to go deeper to find similarities.

- After five minutes, read what you have written.

- Now answer this question for five minutes: If you were in prison, what might bring you comfort?

✿ *Movement:*

In your journal, list five people who seem unlovable. Perhaps it is a family member who undermines your decisions, or a co-worker who steals your ideas, or a neighbor who is mean to animals, or even a child molester in jail. Each day for thirty-seven days, love them in some way, either in your mind or out in the world. Make a conscious decision each morning to hold those five people in your thoughts. Spend each day examining your reaction to them; reach out to them and show love. This isn't about their reaction—it is about your action.

a bumble bee flies into my apartment
it didn't mean to be there—it panics
and seeing the outside through a glass window
it proceeds to push and push against the glass
trying to get where it wants to go
in its panic never moving from its task long enough
to see the open window just inches away
how like the bumble bee I am in my work or my life
i see where i want to go
and in my panic
i forget to look for the open window
so i push and push and push
thinking i should be rewarded for all this hard work
when, in fact, i am so frantic
like the bee against the glass.

—Marybeth Fidler, "The Bumble Bee"

CHAPTER SEVEN
Intuition: Trust Yourself

It is by logic we prove. It is by intuition we discover. —**Henri Poincaré**

Today—not tomorrow—is the day to jump.

I can feel it, like an old linebacker feels his knees when it looks like rain, like a mother in the Twinkie aisle at the Piggly Wiggly with a child-who-is-screaming-up-a-lung feels it. I can feel the jump coming.

I'm talking *jump,* not "bungee" nor "fall," the latter an accident, the other a deliberate and conscious leap. If you make gravity your friend, falling after a jump is some kind of validation, not failure.

Jumping isn't the same as falling, no. We fall all the time, subject to forces outside us (we think, we rationalize, we blame). Oddly, most times we fall by not jumping.

Today is the day to surprise gravity, let go of the monkey bars, fling, fling. Your wings may burn in the heat of the sun like those of Icarus, but perhaps, as poet Jack Gilbert has written, "Icarus was not failing as he fell, but just coming to the end of his triumph." And your triumph? Perhaps you have to jump to get there: Icarus couldn't have fallen without first flying, could he?

How did Icarus know when to jump, I wonder. How do we know? Is it through careful study of Excel spreadsheets or exploding pie charts in ambitious though misguided PowerPoint presentations? Or is it actually our gut that tells us?

We get in our own way sometimes by not trusting that ineffable impulse. Henry Ward Beecher said, "Most of the shadows of this life are caused by standing in our own sunshine." The other shadows are caused by columns of data, tall and imposing, not really getting to the truth. We ignore our own truths, the ones deep inside of us, seeking affirmation outside instead.

We cast our own shadows in that way. As the Zen proverb reminds us, "Man stands in his own shadow and wonders why it's dark."

When you and I meet, dear reader, as I think we may someday, it is more than likely I will want to take a photograph with my beautiful little Canon to mark the moment.

BE PATIENT TOWARDS ALL THAT IS UNRESOLVED IN YOU AND TRY TO LOVE THE QUESTIONS THEM-SELVES, LIKE LOCKED ROOMS, LIKE BOOKS THAT ARE WRITTEN IN A VERY FOREIGN TONGUE. LIVE THE QUESTIONS NOW.

—Rainer Maria Rilke

Others will no doubt swoop in to say: "Here, let me help. I'll take it for you." And I'll wave them off, preferring to take the picture myself, my own way. I'll imagine myself an Artiste as I do it.

I'll position myself at your left shoulder, and hold the camera in my left hand, index finger on the shutter button on top, the wee strap around my wrist. I'll straighten my left arm to its full length and raise it up, a foot or so above shoulder level. Our heads will move closer together—as if we've known each other for years—we'll laugh or smile knowingly or make a funny face, and I'll shoot the photograph.

Sometimes, if we're lucky, my arm makes it into the photo, a transparency of form I love, as in a recent photograph of me and Emma aboard a trolley bound for Tijuana. A foreshortened arm in the margin of the photograph tells the story: We are two women alone, making our way in the world. We are self-contained, an island unto ourselves, just as you and I will be when we finally meet. I have hundreds of these photographs of meetings with others. It has become an art form, a practice, a meditation on relationship.

In some cases our heads are cut off (my arm misjudged). Then there are the ones in which the sun is too bright and we're squinty. Or blurred, our laughter causing me to shake my pointing arm. All of those are remembrances flawed beautifully just like life is.

I had my camera on a recent business retreat to the Jemez in New Mexico. The sun there is very bright. And the sky is very large. And there is much light there. "Where there is much light, the shadow is deep," Goethe has written, and so it is. The shadows are very deep over the red soil in New Mexico, a soil almost burgundy when the sun is richly angled, not directly overhead.

There were large red rocks near the Pueblo just before we got to Jemez Springs. "We should come back and make photographs of these," I said, "but the light is too bright now. It would have to be later in the day." And so we did go back, a few days later, hitting the rocks with a slanting sun that allowed for their redness to show. "This is perfect," I said. "Let's stop here."

> You have to be available to the invisible voices that are swirling around you.
> —George C. Wolfe

I wanted the red rocks in the background, to show John back home. "Let's stand here so the rocks are in the background," I told David. He knows the drill. We adopted the pose, me on the left with my left arm straight and up, camera poised. We smiled; I hit the shutter.

As I pulled my arm down, I turned the camera over to check the shot. "Damn it!" I said, "there's a large shadow on our faces." I shook my head, squinting up into the sun to see what had blocked it.

"Let's move to the left," I suggested, trying to determine what had caused the shadow. Was it the light pole in front of us? The small picnic shed? It must be. What else was in the way? We shifted 3 feet to the left. I raised my arm and shot again, pulling the camera toward myself quickly afterward to check the shot. "Damn it!" I said more forcefully. "That's crazy—how can that be? What on earth is causing that? Is it the picnic shed? Let's move again!" We started moving left again. I craned my neck around, searching madly for the culprit—what on earth was in our way? David could tell I was irritated.

Trust yourself. You know more than you think you do. —**Benjamin Spock**

I looked again at the camera viewfinder, searching the ruined photo for clues.

And then I realized that the shadow was shaped like a rectangle.

It was, in fact, shaped just like a camera.

I was causing my own shadow. It was caused by what I was holding. **I was blocking my own sun.**

I laughed a big and long laugh, one of those where you bend double at the waist, not so much at the shadow, but at my reaction to it—blaming the pole, the picnic shelter, the sun, anything. And after I laughed, I realized I had experienced a Big Metaphor. A Very Big One.

I wonder if I am casting my own shadows all the time and don't realize it. Am I constantly shifting to the left to get out of a shadow that I, in fact, have cast? Am I holding up something that blocks my own sun?

We need to jump out of our own shadows. But sometimes we hesitate, believing we need more data—we wait until we know enough about how and where and with whom we will land, until it's too late to jump at all. You can't know. Jump anyway. Perhaps you are jumping away from someone, or jumping into your own truthfulness. Your wings will either unfold or they won't (they, too, our own invention), and either way the view will be simply fantastic as you soar.

I find it helpful to remember you're never more than three minutes from the ground. You will no doubt jump into lands with new wildlife and flowers you've never imagined, your parachute falling softly around you, creating a tiny Christo sculpture with you in it, bright yellow silk on green hills, pointing to your landing zone.

Jump, jump.

Intuit the place out of the shadow. It's there. Somewhere, deep inside, you even know it.

Choose Your Seatmates Wisely

You haven't seen a tree until you've seen its shadow from the sky.
—Amelia Earhart

Some years ago I was asked to keynote a large international conference of about 12,000 people. It would be my largest audience ever. I would share the platform with a man I had been working with for a year or two.

We left Washington, DC, on a blue-sky summer day. Shortly after takeoff it became abundantly clear that something was not right. The flight wasn't following a normal pattern after takeoff; our flight attendants were visibly shaking and leafing hurriedly through an emergency manual.

This is not behavior that inspires confidence.

Finally, a voice from the cockpit announced that we were having a tiny bit of a problem and would be returning to the airport. *Problem* is not a word I like to hear that far from the ground. I was worried. My colleague was shaky.

A few minutes later Cockpit Voice announced that we had experienced a failure of the plane's hydraulic system and would be returning not to Washington, DC, but to Baltimore's airport.

Let me stop for a moment to clarify something: **The hydraulic system of a plane is very important. Crucial, even.** Without it, there is no way to turn, go up and down, land—you might say that without it you're fairly well screwed. As Emma said when she was about to throw up in the car as a child, "This isn't going to be good." In fact, my friend, I knew immediately that it could be very, very bad, that kind of irretrievable badness, the last kind you experience, the so-this-is-how-it-ends-eleven-o'clock-news kind of bad I fear every time I fly.

Sitting up front, we had a clear, close view of the fear on the faces and in the voices of the flight attendants, professional though they were.

Because of our little hydraulic problem, turning the plane was, um, problematic. Our return to Baltimore took a lifetime, the silent, palpable fear rising. Baltimore was chosen, I would learn later, so we could crash far away from other planes.

It's the friends you can call up at 4 a.m. that matter. —**Marlene Dietrich**

To turn, the pilot had to alternately shut off one engine and boost the other, left, then right, left, then right. To descend, we had to glide down. The flight attendants near us talked of dumping fuel, presumably so the explosion on impact wouldn't be as big. Were we in a slow glide to a fireball? Meanwhile, the airport was preparing the runway with foam and a phalanx of emergency vehicles, a sight that as we got closer should have been reassuring, but wasn't.

Our slow-motion descent took place in silence, punctuated only by the voice of our most senior flight attendant instructing us repeatedly in assuming the brace position, arms crossed on the seat in front of us, head on arms, with an admonition that as we neared impact, we should immediately assume that position when we heard her yell "NOW!"

We were instructed to take off and stow any sharp jewelry and all eyeglasses. It was at that moment—sightless without my red Mrs. Beasley bifocals—that I began my very small, very quiet, very personal and lonely good-byes.

It was an odd, weightless feeling, that slow descent. The odds were against us, I feared. I had to quietly will myself to give up to fate. There was nothing I could do but think of my daughters, my husband John, my family, all those things undone, that messy house that my Marshall sisters would need to come clean before the funeral, the letters unanswered, conversations unhad, all that future gone, those people I was supposed to meet in my life, but wouldn't.

I had a moment of heart-ripping panic, then talked myself quickly into a calm, reassuring space. I willed myself into spending my last moments not in terror but in gratitude, a conscious reframing of the story I had suddenly been handed. I was determined to end not in fear, but in peace.

One lasting, overwhelming thought stayed with me during this whole event and told me volumes—I did not want to die sitting next to the colleague beside me. I didn't want him to reach out to me for comfort. I didn't want to be comforted by him.

I'm not proud of those thoughts, but I paid attention; it was my body and heart and gut talking to me.

The anxious, loud scream came: "NOW!" Without a sound, we all braced.

We hit, we lived.

SHE IS A FRIEND OF MIND. SHE GATHER ME, MAN. THE PIECES I AM, SHE GATHER THEM AND GIVE THEM BACK TO ME IN ALL THE RIGHT ORDER. IT'S GOOD, YOU KNOW, WHEN YOU GOT A WOMAN WHO IS A FRIEND OF YOUR MIND.

—Toni Morrison, Beloved

It was the talk of the airport. We lived! We survived! We called home.

Rebooked on a later flight—oh, joy!—we went to an airport coffee shop to regroup. It was a clarifying moment, another chance, a time to assess. It was—as Rilke says—time to change your life. "Well," I said to my colleague who had been visibly shaken at 37,000 feet, "how does this change your life? What does this mean to you? What will you do differently with this second chance?"

"All I know," he said, "is that if I've missed my time at the hotel pool because of this, I'm going to be pissed."

I blinked several times.

My midair gut reaction had been right: This is not the person I want to die with, work with, be with.

We show ourselves in moments of system failure and fear and change and difficulty and crash landings and chaos. Does the true self emerge only (or especially) when tested? Lessons about others come, perhaps, from their response to great fear or significant peril or the opportunity for sacrifice taken or not. My colleague had failed that test before, but it was this final failing grade that made it clear: I could no longer work with him. He got his pool time. We gave our speech. I walked off that stage and never worked with him again. I knew I needed different seatmates for the rest of my flight.

A friend is the one who comes in when the whole world has gone out. —Grace Pulpit

37 Days: Do It Now Challenge

On this flight we call life, choose your seatmates wisely. Sit with people you would embrace while going down, who won't hog the armrest or steal your peanuts or take your in-flight magazine. Sit with people who will comfort you when you're scared, whom you would take off your sharp jewelry and glasses for, whom you would forego your time at the pool for.

✍ Action:

Focused free-write:

- Write for five minutes, creating a list of those people who are your fundamental "human survival units," people who will be there for you when the hydraulic system fails. These are the people you can call at 3:00 a.m. when you need help, those who will walk toward you when you are dying.

- Read what you have written. Notice who is on the list, and who is not.

- For the next five minutes, answer this question: Whose list are you on? Whose list do you want to be on?

As you review what you have written, ask yourself this question: If these really are your human survival units, are they the people you spend quality time with, nurture relationships with, and have as priorities in your life? If not, why not? How can you reprioritize to make them first, not only on your list but in your life as well?

○ Movement:

For the next thirty-seven days, review your list every morning and spend more time—physically, virtually, or emotionally—with those people. Perhaps there are people you usually spend time with who didn't make the cut—do you need to let go of any by putting them in the ejector seat (nicely, of course)?

Let Go of the Monkey Bars

When I let go of what I am, I become what I might be. —Lao-tzu

Sometimes taking flight takes letting go.

Letting go takes faith.

Faith takes letting go.

It all requires wings.

And so it goes.

As Kierkegaard said, "Without risk there is no faith, and the greater the risk, the greater the faith." Flying begins with a leap of faith.

At the end of each year, I ask myself two questions: What do I want to create in this New Year and, perhaps even more importantly, what do I want to let go?

This year, I needed to let go of a project I had been holding on to, one that was lucrative but deflected my attention from my real work. I needed to really let go, not pretend to let go, or hold on to vestiges of it to keep me comfortable.

It was a letting go that sent me flying into that space between the monkey bars, where you've let go but haven't reached the other bar yet, the letting go that has to happen before the next bar is in your hand.

Just after my leap, a friend told me I reminded her of a trapeze artist, flinging myself out into the universe. That moment of release before catching the new bar is called transition. Perhaps it is the only place that real change happens. As humanitarian Danaan Parry said, "I have noticed that, in our culture, this transition zone is looked upon as a 'no-thing,' a no-place between places. I have a sneaking suspicion that the transition zone is the only real thing, and the bars are illusions we dream up to avoid where the real change, the real growth occurs for us."

I am enamored of liminal spaces, those spaces in between. I spend my days thinking about them, exploring them, talking to people who are living in them. Airplanes create odd liminal spaces, and so does any transition, from life to death, from here to there.

As I watched the seagulls, I thought, "That's the road to take; find the absolute rhythm and follow it with absolute trust."
—Niko Kazantzakis

Remember monkey bars? The hot feeling in your palm, that squared-off place where your fingers meet your fleshy palm, the heat generated by the holding on? It was hard for me to navigate monkey bars as a child. I dreaded letting go. I would hold on until any momentum my body had was gone, until I was a deadweight hung straight down from the bar, its metal becoming hotter in my palm. And then I would have to drop, off the bars, not go forward or back, palms smelling metallic the rest of the day to remind me. Marilyn Ferguson wrote, "It's not so much we're afraid of change or so in love with the old ways, but it's that place in between that we fear . . . it's like being between trapezes. It's Linus when his blanket is in the dryer. There's nothing to hold on to."

There's nothing to hold on to.

Sometimes letting go is shedding, like a snake sheds its skin in times of growth. Young snakes, it turns out, shed more frequently than older ones. Healthy snakes have no trouble shedding and tend to shed their skins in one piece. Before snakes shed, they have a period of relative inactivity—are they getting ready? Their underlying new skin is soft and vulnerable to damage.

And so it is with humans.

That moment when there is nothing to hang on to is the moment when we are most present, most alive, most vulnerable, most human.

Jump, and you will find out
how to unfold your wings as you fall.
—Ray Bradbury

Here's some advice from a veteran trapeze performer: Throw your heart over the bars and your body will follow. Learn the fall before the trick. Smile and point your toes. And wait for the right moment, Sam Keen tells us: "Waiting for the right instant— what the Greek philosophers called the kairos or fertile moment—is exactly what is most difficult . . . Anxiety makes us too eager or too reluctant and forces us to act too early or too late. It is difficult to believe that, at times, as T. S. Eliot said, 'The faith, the hope, and the love are all in the waiting.'" Let go of the monkey bars. Be a connoisseur of fear. Enjoy the space between. Fly.

Action:

This challenge comes from the world of improv theater: Go outside. Walk slowly forward. Open your hand and let something fall into it from the sky. It might be an idea, it might be an object. Name it. Set it aside. Walk forward. Open your hand and let something fall into it from the sky. Name it. Set it aside. Repeat this ten times, until you have the experience of opening up to whatever falls from the sky into your hand. Catch it, like a trapeze bar. Name it.

Movement:

- In your journal, make a list of things that you are scared to do. Bungee jumping? Baking a soufflé? Calling a friend you haven't spoken to in a long time? Sending one of your poems to a publication for consideration? Checking your bank account balance? Visiting a friend on their deathbed? Dancing in public? Wearing a bathing suit?

- Write until you have listed at least twenty things—some big and some little.

- For the next thirty-seven days, review your list each morning. Then do one of them each day. Or do two. Or three. You won't fall far.

Everything in life is based on daring. —Martin Buber

Write Some Blues

I merely took the energy it takes to pout and wrote some blues.
—Duke Ellington

I entered a writing contest six months ago with "Laid to Rest in Suit Number Nine," a quirky southern gothic tale about a fastidious man named Nial who numbered all his suits as well as every possible suit/tie/shirt/sock/shoe combination, tracking them on a neatly hand-drawn matrix on the inside of his closet door so he wouldn't go to church two Sundays in a row wearing the same combination. Not that anyone would see them under his ubiquitous beige satin choir robe with its long pointy burgundy sash—of course if they did see his outfit, who'd remember which shirt he was wearing with which tie?

Nial is a real person, and it turns out that when he died, he really was laid to rest in Suit Number Nine. It was announced by the preacher at his funeral. I was there when the story unfolded from the pulpit; it had me hoarsely whispering to my mother for a writing implement. I scoured the hymnal rack for a scrap of paper (where are those Lottie Moon offering envelopes when you really need one?), desperate to capture the details of this beautifully odd story, a tale even more compelling because the preacher telling it didn't realize the ripeness of it. It was a Flannery O'Connor novella of a eulogy.

As James Frey and his million little lies have taught us, there is no such thing as an objective first-person narrator, so the part of the preacher in my story is played by my mother, whose tendency to make her eyes get real big is a plus for almost any tale:

> Nial was fastidious, an engineer who cataloged the leftovers in his fridge in a ledger, measured between his tomato plants, numbered his suits, and lived alone. When he died in his corduroy Barcalounger, a numbered list was found inside his clothes closet, a digit for each of the 110 possible suit combinations with tidy notations detailing which Sunday that particular arrangement was worn.

> "The very idea that anybody would catalog leftover squash casserole," Mama said, shaking her head.

> "The preacher said Nial was laid to rest in Suit Number Nine," she said.

> Ah, I thought, nine lives, nine symphonies, nine planets, the harmony of harmony. I fumbled for something to say, surprising myself with what I did say, nearly a direct quote from Siddarta Gautama, thanks to Books on Tape: "Well, Mama, what is the appropriate behavior for a man or a woman in the midst of this world, where each person is clinging to his piece of debris? What's the proper salutation between people as they pass each other in this flood?" Her eyes got momentarily real big as she adjusted her hearing aid. "Estaleen says I ought to wear a wig because my hair's so thin after all that Prednisone. What do you think?"

[There is no greater burden than having great potential.
—Linus from "Peanuts"]

Anyway, the writing contest wasn't an important one with a big publishing deal or dream home at the end of it. It was sponsored by a local writer's group. The attraction? The judge was none other than Kurt Vonnegut! Imagine!

CONTINUOUS EFFORT, NOT STRENGTH OR INTELLIGENCE, IS THE KEY TO UNLOCKING OUR POTENTIAL.

—Winston Churchill

I was sure this was my big break, my opportunity to be noticed, to be swept into Hollywood where they'd wonder whether to use my talents as a screenwriter for black-and-white Scandinavian films full of heavy foreboding angles and people blowing smoke rings into streetlights, or maybe just go ahead and showcase my talents as a movie star proper, in the manner of Kate Hepburn or Meg Ryan before the lip surgery.

So, I waited. And waited and waited and waited. I was amused that my husband, John, also submitted a story. How sad, I thought to myself, since he didn't even remember to include a self-addressed, stamped envelope to get a response. I wonder how he'll deal with my rise to superstardom while he is relegated to the "incomplete" pile.

And so I waited some more. Perhaps Mr. Vonnegut was savoring my every word, picturing himself writing my page-turner of a tale, envisioning Kevin Spacey playing the role of Nial and Julianne Moore playing me. Surely there will be a role for Hugh Laurie and Johnny Depp in there. And that nice Jodie Foster.

> You will never come up against a greater adversary than your own potential, my young friend.
> —**Michael Piller and Michael Wagner,** *Star Trek*

And then it happened! The letter arrived! It was the moment I had been waiting for. And poor John, he didn't even get a response. Now you know, I could hear myself telling him, they mean it when they say to include a self-addressed, stamped envelope.

I ripped open the envelope, hands shaking, feeling that little odd metal feeling in the back of my throat that you get when about to throw up with excitement or fear.

"BRILLIANT!" it read across the top, scrawled in Kurt Vonnegut's very own handwriting! "BRILLIANT!" in very large letters.

Aha! I thought to myself. *Good Housekeeping* magazine, the *Christian Science Monitor, Woman's World,* the *Asheville Citizen-Times, Fast Company,* the AAA travel magazine, the quarterly periodical of the Butter Manufacturers of America, and the in-flight magazines of every major airline have rejected my essays, but Kurt Vonnegut thinks they are BRILLIANT! BRILLIANT! BRILLIANT! That'll show 'em!

I started designing my Oscar gown—something muted and architectural, the color of steel beams, something like Sandra Bullock would wear. Definitely have to get my eyebrows done by that woman named Anastasia I read about all the time in *People* magazine. And all those years of practicing my autograph as a child are so going to come in handy at last!

And then, I took another look. What else did Mr. Vonnegut have to say? When did he want to meet, to talk about my beautiful career?

Then it hit me.

It wasn't the front page of my manuscript that came back with "BRILLIANT" scrawled excitedly across the top. It was the front page of John's story, "Wiltin and Wantin."

I reached for the torn envelope to see how this horrible error could have occurred. But John didn't even send a self-addressed, stamped envelope. **He didn't follow the rules, I sputtered.** There was John's name and address. In my haste, seeing it was from the writer's group, I had torn into the envelope without realizing it wasn't for me.

I spent that entire afternoon resisting the urge to stuff "BRILLIANT" into my mouth and chew it up or swallow it whole rather than show it to John.

My sad little envelope came the next day. The self-addressed and stamped one, the one that beautifully and dutifully followed the rules.

A sobering thought: what if, at this very moment, I am living up to my full potential. —**Jane Wagner**

It didn't say "brilliant." In fact, it had no handwriting from Mr. Vonnegut whatsoever. My story of poor Nial and his cataloged suits and straight tomatoes didn't even make it to Mr. Vonnegut's desk. It was returned with a declarative, xeroxed form letter in a bad typeface, an anonymous rejection strongly suggesting I might wish to take writing classes before entering any more contests.

Well, my Lord, I thought, after all, Kurt Vonnegut must be a hundred years old by now. I'll bet he can't even see well anymore.

To his absolute credit, Mr. Brilliant has resisted the urge to gloat.

Then, in the midst of a pity parade, I opened a book and the very first line I read was this quote from Duke Ellington: "I merely took the energy it takes to pout and wrote some blues."

I had to laugh. Then I had to clear off my desk and write me some blues.

Simplicity is the key to brilliance. —**Bruce Lee**

Don't eat other people's acceptance letters. Don't worry too much about the damned self-addressed, stamped envelope. If Kurt wants to find you, he'll find you. Detach from outcome. Write (paint, sing, love, bake) because you must, not because you might win. Stop pouting, clear off your desk, and write you some blues. Make art of everything, even rejection.

📎 **Action:**

- Get out a blank sheet of paper or open your journal.

- Your goal in the next two minutes is to design the absolutely best desk lamp in the world. Go.

- After two minutes, reflect on the experience. Was it hard? Was there pressure from the expectation that it be "the best in the world"?

- Start again, with one change—this time, spend two minutes designing the very worst desk lamp in the world. Be outlandish! No socket! No lightbulb! Shaped like an aardvark!

This kind of reverse design often frees up creativity rather than squelching it. You can use this technique every day in some way—whether helping your kids figure out how to do something by reverse-designing it ("How could we really screw up this assignment?") or determining your wellness vision ("How can you continue to feel as bad as possible about your health or weight?"). Sometimes in making that outlandish list of don't's, we discover things we actually are doing to sabotage our efforts . . .

⟡ **Movement:**

What if your goal was to create a beautiful work of art out of rejection every day for thirty-seven days? Your challenge is to create art out of *no*.

- You can use any tools you'd like—crayons, markers, paint, pictures from magazines.

- You can use colors, shapes, and designs, but only one word to create the artwork—and that word is *no*.

- Sometimes it helps to create a "frame"—a structure to hold your creativity. Paradoxically, structure doesn't limit us, but frees us. One way to create structure for your *no* art is to draw the same-size square on a piece of paper (say, 3 inches by 3 inches) for each day you are doing this challenge. Each day, one of those squares gets used to make your *no* art.

Just Help Them Get Started

You can discover what your enemy fears most by observing the means
he uses to frighten you. —Eric Hoffer

There is a moment in every mother's life that's a source of deep, dark dread, a moment so terrible to consider we dare not contemplate its possibility, a moment dreaded far in the depths of our souls, in those deep dark recesses rich like rotting compost—a single awful moment around which our lives wobble, a moment of profound, lasting, intense fear.

The moment I am talking about is that sad and simple instant when our small children announce they no longer need an afternoon nap.

My time arrived exactly three months after Tess turned two and a half. On that day she refused the respite that had eased her entry into afternoons. I responded, predictably, by demonstrating the first stage of change— denial—by refusing to believe The Day had come. In defiance, I marched her to her room against her will, determined I would get my time, my moments of silence, my brief dive into personal adult thought.

"Nothing in life is to be feared.
It is only to be understood."
Marie Curie

Kicking and screaming, Tess bellowed from her little bed, her mouth gone square with anger, tears squirting from her eyes, tiny hands frantically pulling at my clothes. She screamed and screamed and I thought she was being mean—scratching

Only when we are no longer afraid do we begin to live. —Dorothy Thompson

at me in anger, it certainly seemed, trying to hurt me. We struggled. This 5-foot-8 person against that 3-foot-2 person.

Finally, as I turned to go, resolute and ready to pop with frustration and with my need for some quiet time, I heard what was really in her voice.

I'm not afraid of storms, for I'm learning how to sail my ship. —**Louisa May Alcott**

It wasn't anger. It was fear. As I stood at the doorway, my back turned to her, I could finally make out what she was screaming: "Just help me get started," she screamed in that sobbing, catching toddler way, "JUST HELP ME GET STARTED!"

Tess just needed help getting to sleep— a story, a song, a restful word perhaps. It wasn't anger, but fear; it wasn't selfish, but scared; it wasn't to be mean to me, but to be connected to me—she just needed help getting started.

And so she slept, and me with her. We helped each other get started.

I wondered afterward how often anger is really fear.

How often do we demonstrate anger—the screams, that clawing, those accusations and venom and vitriol and passive aggressiveness—when what we really feel inside is *Please don't leave me here to ponder the future alone in this dark room of my life: It's too still, too quiet, and this bed is too small, the room's too dark. It's too scary to do this all alone.*

ANGER IS JUST A COWARDLY EXTENSION OF SADNESS. IT'S A LOT EASIER TO BE ANGRY AT SOMEONE THAN IT IS TO TELL THEM YOU'RE HURT.

—Alanis Morissette

Just help them get started, those people around you who seem hurtful or angry with you. They're just fearful and need help settling down, embracing the darkness, being in that quiet space with only themselves when the shades are drawn. And own your own anger—as Marie Curie has said, "Nothing in life is to be feared. It is only to be understood." Where you are angry, there is fear. What is there to fear?

✐ Action:

Each of us has a "Hall of Fears," things that limit us, that keep us from living our fullest lives.

- For three minutes, write a list of things you are afraid of—mine begins like this: "I'm afraid of heights, of stumbling when walking in front of people, of death, of success, of not living my life fully, of snakes, of tight spaces, of getting cancer, of being sucked out of an airplane at 20,000 feet . . ."

- Read over your list. Some fears keep us safe. Some just keep us small. Which fears keep you from doing things you really want to do? Circle those.

- Fear is a learned behavior: For each of those circled fears, spend three minutes trying to describe where and how you learned it.

- Then pick one and spend four minutes writing a short children's story about unlearning that fear: How would you teach a child not to have that fear?

◌ Movement:

There is a powerful momentum that comes from anger, though it can be destructive as well. For the next thirty-seven days, walk into your anger by recognizing (perhaps in your journal?) what fear it represents. When you feel angry—the meeting is starting late, the babysitter canceled at the last minute, your partner left dirty dishes in the sink—acknowledge the anger and challenge yourself to uncover the fear underneath it (I'm not taken seriously; I don't know how to assert myself and people feel they can walk all over me; I haven't made my needs well known and am afraid I'll look selfish if I do). Patterns will emerge that will help you identify the fears underlying your anger. In that process, you may learn how to recognize the fears that underlie the anger of others, too.

Unpack Your Boxes

Leaving's not the only way to go. —Roger Miller

"We were invited; I'm going" was all he said, unfolding to his full height. He pressed his small, round, gold glasses against the bridge of his nose as he stared down at me, silently, winding his scarf around his neck. He didn't break eye contact as he took off his wedding band, laid it on the windowsill behind the couch, reached for his coat, then turned and walked out without another word.

He hadn't shown much emotion when I told him I was ending our relationship. I thought he would fight to keep me. He didn't. I thought he would be surprised. He wasn't. Instead, he left for a Christmas party.

I felt behind me for the couch as I lowered myself down, sitting silently as the cat wandered through my legs as if they were a maze.

Finally, I walked slowly upstairs. At our bedroom door, I hesitated, then entered, picking up only my pillow and alarm clock, before moving into the spare bedroom. The whole house seemed temporary—no rugs or curtains, full of boxes still packed after living there a year, some moved so often that they were waxy from wear. Why were we so hesitant to commit to bookcases and shelving?

Around ten, I lay down on the futon on the floor, pale, freckled arms by my side, palms up. I lay imagining myself a Pre-Raphaelite painting: Redhead floating down river, dead perhaps, certainly cold, immobilized by both despair and relief, too tired to be fearful yet. I squinted at the ceiling, trying to remember a poem I once knew—Ruskin? Rossetti?

I lay as like a chance shadow
In moving water, floating and not
A brief mention of reflected form;
Not even my own dread strong enough
To keep my form together.

I lay perfectly still, but felt like I was in moving water, rapids taking me somewhere new, where? For two hours my heart sloshed in my chest like it had detached from its walls and was free-floating until I heard his Vespa fall against the porch steps. Then it stopped sloshing.

My pulse clicked like a metronome suddenly running faster. I heard metal hit metal as he fumbled the key in the lock. I hadn't prepared myself for the fear I suddenly felt; I should have left. He was capable of anything now.

What was I thinking, staying there?

Seven years before, I sold the small blue Chevette that Daddy bought me just before he died. "We don't really need a car in the city," I explained to Mama on the phone. "You can't park anywhere, we're near the Metro, cars get broken into—it doesn't make sense to own one here."

> How do geese know when to fly to the sun? Who tells them the seasons? How do we humans know when it is time to move on? As with the migrant birds, so surely with us, there is a voice within if only we would listen to it, that tells us certainly when to go forth into the unknown.
> **—Elisabeth Kübler-Ross**

Those weren't the real reasons. I sold it because I couldn't live through one more call from a police station to pick him up, another arrest for driving while intoxicated. I sold it because I knew one night the call would be worse—not him in a holding cell, but a child walking across Wisconsin Avenue for peppermint ice cream with her daddy, now dead. The Chevette must go.

I heard a stumble on the stairs.

I felt the spare bedroom door open and pretended to be asleep while he looked at me quietly for a long time. I heard him breathe just two words, "Screw you," and lay waiting for him to shoot me, strangle me, something. My eyes fluttered wildly behind closed lids, light hitting veiny skin like riding in a car on a bright day through the woods—dark, light, dark, light, dark-light. I hoped I was approximating the eye movements of sleep, not panic.

I knew he had left the room when I heard his crashing torrent of pee reverberate in the still house. He forgot to flush and stumbled toward the bed we had shared, now one pillow short.

A gunshot from the next room tore open the quiet acquiescence to our new situation. Explosive, then a dampened thud, then nothing. My chest expanded violently. I gasped for air. My face went hot; my mouth filled with the taste of bile.

I knew immediately: He did this to get me back. He probably smiled as he pulled, the drunken bastard. I had tried for so long to save him, I was weary from the effort.

> We consume our tomorrows fretting about our yesterdays.
> —Persius

It seemed such a long time since we had met. I was finishing graduate school and he was the only person I'd encountered who had read *The Recognitions,* the focus of my dissertation.

Three years into our relationship, we set sail aboard the SS *Universe,* living on bunk beds in a small metal room for four months and sailing right around the globe, circling like a wedding ring or life vest, or a straitjacket. We were floating on a river of desire, or was it debris?

We were two islands in that cramped underwater room aboard the ship. I didn't know it then, but he rode out a typhoon lashed to the ship's upper deck to record the sounds of fierce winds and waves. We all nearly died on that ship, but damned if he doesn't have a recording of it, packed away in a box.

In our house that night, I couldn't move. I tried lifting one arm, but my heart exploded. As I bent one knee, I was sure my limbs all fell off.

I LIKE LIVING. I HAVE SOMETIMES BEEN WILDLY, DESPAIRINGLY, ACUTELY MISERABLE, RACKED WITH SORROW, BUT THROUGH IT ALL I STILL KNOW QUITE CERTAINLY THAT JUST TO BE ALIVE IS A GRAND THING.

—Agatha Christie

The pathology of my avoidance was never clearer to me than at that moment, though it had started in the second grade when Mrs. Goins towered over my chair, asking if I had urinated in my seat. I was freckled and orange-haired, sitting in an undeniable pee pool at the time, a hot oasis of yellow, a pool so large it lapped onto the floor and made rivulets inching toward Blake Revis's chair. He wailed in horror at the encroaching urine, undeniably mine. "I don't know what you are talking about, Mrs. Goins," I said. **Avoidance wasn't possible now.** I rolled off the futon, pausing on my knees, forearms on the floor in front of me, hands flat, fingers spread so far they whitened.

His body had fallen across the bed, legs toward the door, head off the other side at the far reaches of our bedroom; there was no way to assess the damage except by entering. I stood still, suppressing vomit.

I took one step in, then another, lifting my foot over a photo album that lay on the floor against one wall, its pages at odd angles as if some had been ripped loose; otherwise—except for his body and my pillow—everything was in its place.

I couldn't see his head from where I stood. I had to walk farther in, around the foot of the bed, my emotions smothering me. I smelled death; it smelled sweet.

He looked oddly intact.

I felt myself lunge toward him in regret.

His glasses were still on, but crooked, like he had been pondering Buber or Kierkegaard and moved the lenses aside to rub at one eye.

The smell wasn't death, but Budweiser.

There was no blood, no gun. I looked frantically around the room, trying to understand, my eyes finally falling to that photo album from our trip around the world askew on the floor, directly below where he had slammed it against the wall. It was that sound I had heard, not gunfire.

He moved out. I moved months later to a less haunted space. Then there was the final matter of clearing out the large storage shed out back—a place I never visited in the year we lived there—full of lawn tools and oil cans, I imagined.

I walked through tall, dewy grass to get there, to be momentarily stunned after I opened the shed's door and my eyes adjusted to the light: The ground inside was carpeted with compacted cans so deep they reached above my knees, no floor showing through the crushed aluminum of thousands of beers he had consumed alone in an unlighted, unheated, outdoor shed. I waded through, as if on a metallic beach combing for shells, and hoping for starfish.

37 Days: Do It Now Challenge

*Leaving is not the only way to go. Piles of boxes are metaphorical architecture—
they tell a story. As Margaret Atwood wrote, "No one knows what causes an outer
landscape to become an inner one." Unpack your boxes, stay awhile. Either commit
to the swim or go.*

@ **Action:**

Focused free-write:

- For five minutes, make a list of all the things you want to do before you
  die—those things you wanted to do as a child, perhaps, but packed away
  for years. This might be your "bucket list," as the movie by that name
  suggested—those things you want to do before you kick the bucket.

- Beside each one, spend two minutes listing why you can't or didn't do it
  yet.

- Then spend three minutes reframing *can't* and *didn't* to *can* and *will*. Each
  one.

Now do those things. It might take years. No worries—we'll wait.

What was it about unpacking?

❀ **Movement:**

Pull out those boxes of photos,
old letters, and ticket stubs you've
meant for years to put into photo
albums. For just ten minutes a
day for the next thirty-seven days,
review your life through these
objects, the you that has gone by.
Make one stack of photos that
identify what you are holding on to
that no longer serves you—people,
things, stories that hold you back
in some way or that symbolize a
you that you no longer want to be.
Create a ritual "burning" of those
things in order to re-story your life
from this moment on.

Dress Up for Ed McMahon

If you really want something in this life you have to work for it.
Now quiet, they're about to announce the lottery numbers.
—**Homer Simpson**, *The Simpsons*

Today's the day! The big day! The day when it all happens! Today, this very one! Today the Home and Garden TV (HGTV) Prize Patrol will announce that I've won their new Dream Home! For a whole month I entered their contest online every day, each day perusing the floor plans and photos of the bunkroom, exercise studio, craft room, game room, and laundry room big enough to host dinner parties. My very favorite room was not a room at all, but an "outdoor living space," a breezeway between two wings of my new 5,000-square-foot home.

I'm dressed and ready. I've been fully attired since 7:00 a.m.

The porch has been swept in anticipation, that messy bush I've never liked has been transplanted to a dark corner, out of sight to do what my plants do (die). The cats have their collars on, Tess's face is washed and her pants match her shirt. Emma has opted for a darling goth punk princess look. I'm wearing a shirt the color of seafoam. I think it will look good on TV (unless it's too washed out by the lights). I've got on my new hemp clogs and mascara. Mr. Brilliant will be home soon and I'm sure he'll wear one of those heavily starched white shirts with the black jeans and the black Doc Martens I like so much. If nothing else, my wearing mascara should tip you off: This is a Big Day.

Dress up for Ed McMahon Today's the day! The big day! The day when it all happens! Today, this very one! 37 days...

I've spent the day tidying the house, putting away 10,000 LEGOs, vacuuming crushed Cheerios and dog hair out of the rugs. I've begun packing. By showtime at 8:00 p.m. US Eastern Time this evening, I should have everything in order. Should I bake some cookies for the camera crew? Squeeze fresh lemonade? Do people really look ten pounds heavier on TV? Does my makeup look natural? Will our dog Blue sniff people in inappropriate places when they arrive? Is our house number legible from the road? Can they find us?

There are special occasions that merit dressing up, aren't there? The prom, Easter Sunday for some, weddings, family reunions, bar mitzvahs, your first piercing at the mall, those awkward high school dates where you have no idea what you should wear but you must look fantastic while not looking like you're Trying Too Hard.

For Mama one of those days was always Super Bowl Sunday. We could tell it was Super Bowl Sunday by the elaborate preparations the day entailed: She was always fully dressed, make-upped, coiffed, with a fresh perm. While Daddy and I were big football fans (Baltimore Colts, #19 Johnny Unitas was my favorite), she wasn't—so why all the fuss?

I recently e-mailed Mama to ask about all those fancy preparations. Did she mind if I wrote about it? Here's what she had to say:

> *No, I don't mind—actually, it's more than once per year—the next drawing is February 28th. I think I have lots of company, waiting to win! I'll be curious to see how you make that inspirational . . . !*

On this shrunken globe, men can no longer live as strangers. —**Adlai E. Stevenson**

Mama was not dressing up for Joe Namath, but for Ed McMahon, for the Publishers Clearing House Prize Patrol. She still does. When I asked for more information, here's what she wrote:

I've been entering Publishers Clearing House contests for thirty-five years and have never won, but for some reason, I always think this will be the time—hope, faith, or ignorance, I don't know. I really want to win, not just for myself, but for my Church and so I can set up trusts for the grandchildren's education. Now, I know a lot of people win huge in the lotteries, but I would not buy a lottery ticket because in my mind that is gambling. I think the Publishers Clearing House motto is "where dreams come true" and I'm using 37-cent stamps to try to "make my dreams come true." Love, Mama

P.S. Remember, be kind and don't make me sound like some kind of nut (even if you think I am)! I read the story you wrote about roast beef doors at the hospital and even I had to laugh at the memory.

[The manner of giving is worth more than the gift. –**Pierre Corneille**]

Never fear, Mama. How could I portray you as a nut for dressing up those thirty-five years in anticipation of Ed McMahon, especially since I'm following in your footsteps, coiffed and perched near the front door, all dressed up for the HGTV Prize Patrol? I'll be watching live, waiting to recognize the Viva Europa coffee shop near our house, a sure sign the Prize Patrol is headed my way. They'll turn onto Cumberland and I'll redo my lipstick. When the cameras show the stone pillars at the front of our walkway, I'll no doubt pass out. I'll be watching my life play out on TV, like that airplane full of people who recently watched their own emergency crash landing on the in-flight TV sets at 37,000 feet, then 20,000, 10,000, then ground.

I've once or twice imagined myself winning twenty million dollars, determining what I would do with the money, whom I would surprise with a gift, how I would finally buy that cute little VW convertible bug in seafoam blue. I'd pay for college tuitions and hot stone massages and cartooning classes for Emma, and that long-chained necklace by David Tishbi that I saw last week in the DC airport, and trips to see my friends Kichom in Tokyo, Eliav and Yaron in Tel Aviv, Tony in Stellenbosch, Hilde in Düsseldorf, and Richard in Martinborough (note to self: I need to make a friend in Paris).

I would make sure Emma and Tess experience life outside the United States in significant ways.

Of course, Mama and my brother would be on the list for a cash infusion, then artists and writers who are creating beauty in the world, and people who are fighting for the human rights of all people, and those who work with underprivileged children, and more.

We all just need to be freed up to do the work we were put here to do, don't we?

But then I'd wonder if money changes too much, trivializes too much, encumbers too much. Of course, the answer is yes, but I promise not to buy more shoes than I can wear or plastic lawn ornaments or a big house with white columns. I'll still recycle and shop at consignment stores and drive a 1990 Ford Bronco II.

So don't forget to turn on HGTV at 8:00 p.m. US Eastern time tonight. I'll be the gray-haired woman in the seafoam blouse acting surprised in a lovely shade of Kiehl's Black Raspberry moisturizing lip gloss.

What? There were only three finalists? I wasn't one of them?

All that mascara for nothing.

> EVERY BLADE OF GRASS HAS ITS ANGEL THAT BENDS OVER IT AND WHISPERS, "GROW, GROW."
>
> —The Talmud

What we do flows from who we are. —Paul Vitale

Dream big. But remember that unhappy people who win the lottery are just unhappy in a bigger and more public way. So enter the contest, but don't gamble the life you're living now. Keep on living that life just the same: Make your own house your dream home because of the people in it, even with that peeling wallpaper in the upstairs bedroom. Let's live a life that doesn't need TV's validation, shall we?

✐ Action:

Focused free-write:

- For five minutes create a list of people who deserve your gifts when you win the lottery. Who are they and why would you surprise them with a gift? What would you give them?

- Read your list.

- For the next five minutes, imagine that you still want to support them, but haven't (yet) won the lottery. How can you support them now in ways that would help them? Perhaps with gifts of time, not money, for example. Perhaps something as simple as dropping off muffins one morning to free up their time for doing other things. Make that list.

Then go ahead and support them now in the ways you can. The gifts you give will be more real, more meaningful, more sincere.

❂ *Movement:*

I did a reading recently at a local bookshop. That morning, my friend Kathleen Osta called to say she would be there. "How can I best support you as you get ready for the reading?" she asked. I stammered, surprised. I realized what a generous, perfect question it was, and how unexpected. Sensing my surprise, she even offered answers: "I'll be there early—can I bring water for you, would you like to talk beforehand or can I help create a quiet place for you to pre-pare?" For the next thirty-seven days, look for opportunities each day to call people and ask, "How can I best support you?" Have some simple suggestions ready in case they are as surprised by the question as I was.

When Sonny Rollins walked onto that bridge
to play his saxophone to the wind
he was stepping off the stage
and into the woodshed.
It wasn't a failure of nerve, of course,
nor was it only a deepening
of his craft. He was breaking
a voice apart
and refashioning it.
He was undressing his muse.

That's what I want now:
less stage, more bridge
(the wind steady and relentless)
and room to go about
the private business of becoming—
nothing more, not a single iota less—
who I am meant to be.

—Sebastian Matthews, "Undressing the Muse"

CHAPTER EIGHT
Intention: Slow Down

In dwelling, live close to the ground. —**Tao Te Ching**

When Emma was two years old, I got some wise advice from a friend. "Get on your knees," he said, "and walk around your house in that position to see the world as Emma sees it. Is it interesting? Boring? Scary? Dangerous?"

Mr. Brilliant and I dutifully navigated through the house on our knees. Door handles were too tall to reach. Extension cords yelled out our names: Trip on me! Wrap me around you! Tie up your cat Sim Sim with me! Photographs and pictures were too high to see. Books weren't accessible. Sharp edges poked out from all sides just at eyebrow level. There was more at that height to maim us than to interest us.

Having seen the world from Emma's perspective, we changed things. John installed little tiny door handles at her height so she could feel big and strong and empowered. We hung pictures down low for her, creating a whole little world down there where she was, not up here where we are. They were simple accommodations, but powerful ones. Her little face broadened in glory when she saw the small bookcase holding her favorite book, *"I Can't" Said the Ant,* low enough that she could reach it all by herself, like a Big Girl.

I was reminded of all this recently when Emma's little sister, Tess, now four years old, discovered a way to document her 45-inch-tall life. A few months ago, when we weren't looking, she began commandeering my beautiful and beloved Canon Digital Elph PowerShot SD600 camera. Soon we were privy to her view of the world—she took photos of tables seen from underneath (with nests of seductively dangerous power cords poised under there like wild Amazonian cobras)—and, in addition to all that, many dozens of photographs of her feet. **First the left foot, then the right foot, then both feet together.** First the left foot, then the right foot, then both feet together again, an unerring sequence, like a soldier marching in step, some tiny Tess rhythm, a rightness not unlike creating Chinese characters, the stroke order of utmost importance. Left foot, then right foot, then feet together.

There were literally tens of dozens of these foot images, some still and some action shots, a fascination with grounding, a connecting with the ground, just a few feet down. She seemed to be setting herself on the earth, documenting her groundedness, validating herself in some interesting way like Binx Bolling in Walker Percy's *The Moviegoer.* Binx does it by seeing references to his life in movies—Look! There's a highway sign pointing to my hometown!—and Tess does it by photographing her little broad, plank-like feet with massive big toes as they dig into the earth. She is hanging on to a whirling planet. She has placed herself, which satisfies her immensely. She is documenting her little march through the world, left, then right, then both.

As adults, we see things from such a sophisticated, disinterested, fast-paced distance that we can barely even register them anymore. A fire hydrant to a 45-inch-tall child is an Event, a Shining Glory, a Sphinx. To us, it's often invisible. Neighborhood dogs become alien invaders when seen from Tess's angle and vantage point.

> I may not know who I am, but I know where I'm from.
> —**Wallace Stegner**

At a recent retreat, we asked everyone to gather at the lake near the lodge one morning. "We're going to take a long walk to China," David told them. "In real terms, that means we're going to walk around this lake in the next ten minutes. But if I see you move at all in those ten minutes, you're moving too fast." It took a moment for these instructions to sink in.

From my vantage point, the group looked like a fantastical, life-size sculpture garden. There was only imperceptible movement for the next ten minutes. Some moved a few inches, others only a quarter of an inch during that time.

When we talked about it afterward, it became clear that everyone had their own unique response and strategy to the exercise. Some focused on a distant point either across the lake or across the world; others were frustrated by their inability to reach the goal; one focused on a pagoda and then wanted to change direction but couldn't decide whether to walk all the way back to where she had started (even though her movement had all taken place inside her head) or just launch into a new direction. Whole journeys took place without moving. Several people marveled at the insights they achieved by focusing on the micro-movements necessary to take a step; by slowing down their movement in the world, they could feel each contraction, each lift, each anticipation of movement. The concentration on their toes, feet, and legs reminded me of Tess's focus. Left, then right, then both.

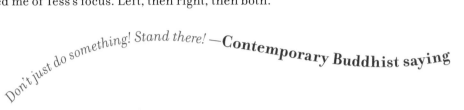

Don't just do something! Stand there! —**Contemporary Buddhist saying**

Lucy Lippard wrote of walking in a straight line to measure rage: "An Eskimo custom offers an angry person release by walking the emotion out of his or her system in a straight line across the landscape, the point at which the anger is conquered is marked with a stick, bearing witness to the strength or length of the rage."

How far would your rage get you? St. Louis? Cheyenne? Taipei? And what if you walked in a straight line to measure your love? Would that take you farther?

Pilgrimages also involve walking, creating straight lines toward faith, toward Adam's Peak, or Mecca, looking for something larger than ourselves: Each step is a thought, and a becoming.

Look at your feet on the ground you call home. Ground yourself, place yourself, literally, and live close to the ground as a four-year-old does. Tear away the frame and be in the scene, near the pavement. Be completely in contact with it all.

Notice your steps, even the anticipation of steps, the way your toes grab hold of the earth beneath you; if you are a wheelchair user, notice the ground moving beneath you as you move through the world. How are you in relationship to it? What shadows do you cast? In what direction are you moving? Slow down.

Do or do not. There is no "try." —**Master Yoda**

Follow Your Desire Lines

Do not go where the path may lead, go instead where there is no path and leave a trail. —**Ralph Waldo Emerson**

In the park where we play, there are nicely laid-out concrete paths leading from the swings to the picnic tables, from the castle to the soccer field, from the water fountain to the bridge, from here to there, from A to B.

And then there are the real paths, the dirt ones, the ones that shoot out from the concrete to connect where people really go, to memorialize the real actions of children playing, to acknowledge the real patterns of living, of human purpose, of some honest destination.

Last year my friend Anita cut an article out of the *LA Times* and sent it to me with a note: "I thought you might like this." Indeed I did. The article, Robert Finch's "Purposefully Straying from the Path," was about those trails people blaze when they cut across the grassy area instead of following the prescribed walkway, the dirt paths that take us where we really want to go.

In the business of landscape architects, these impromptu, unofficial, renegade paths have a poetic, wonderful name. They're called desire lines, the article said: ". . . those well-worn ribbons of dirt that you see cutting across a patch of grass, often with nearby sidewalks ignored—particularly those that offer a less direct route. I love that these paths are never perfectly straight. Instead, like a river, they meander this way and that, as if to prove that desire itself isn't linear and (literally, in this case) straightforward."

Some landscape architects actually design walkways to accommodate these emergent designs, waiting to see where people prefer to go and then building their official paths there. (Would this create more unofficial paths? I wonder. Is the desire to be outside the lines, to forge our own path, so strong?) Desire lines indicate a yearning to go our own way, to push through the brush of life, to make a new path, to ignore the concrete for the feel of our foot on real earth, to see the results of our own agency through space. Some have suggested that desire lines are an ultimate expression of human longing and natural human purpose.

> DOES THIS PATH HAVE A HEART? IF IT DOES, THE PATH IS GOOD; IF IT DOESN'T, IT IS OF NO USE.
>
> —Carlos Castaneda

Natural human purpose. What is mine? Yours? Maybe if I look at the paths I've worn, over and over again, I'll see that purpose show itself, the way cornfields create patterns I see only when I'm flying over them. **Perhaps it takes some distance to see that path.** At the very least, it requires a different vantage point.

It's not where we stand but in what direction we are moving. —**Johann Wolfgang von Goethe**

Several years ago, Peter Merholz, founder of Adaptive Path, wrote about Berkeley's attempt to circumvent rather than accommodate desire lines on campus. Instead of allowing a new desire line to remain and become an established purpose path, they created an oddly out-of-place metal barrier to keep people on the "real" path. People just walked around the barrier. When the official path makes no sense to how we actually live or use a product, we create our own path; we won't be thwarted. (Sometimes, though, it takes most of a lifetime to create that new, real path, our very own, doesn't it?)

When faced with a bird's-eye view of my own desire lines, tracing decisions I've made or not made, do I allow them to become the real path, or do I put up a concrete barrier to redirect myself back to the "official" route?

Plant grass seed in your life and see what the wear patterns tell you about where the path should be. In your mind's eye, take an aerial photograph of your desire lines. Where are they coming from and where are they going? Are these desire lines a representation of your real intention in life, a sturdy setting forth? Or are they merely a shortcut? What landscape are they crisscrossing? Why not make them the real route for your life, since you obviously yearn to go there? Make your own way. Blaze your own sure path. Find the ultimate expression of your human desire or natural purpose. Leave a trail.

Action:

Every story is a *yearning* meeting an *obstacle*, according to writer Robert Olen Butler.

- Think of a yearning you have—you want your children to be better behaved or you want your marriage to work or you want to finish that book you've been writing for thirteen years or you want to lose weight.

- For ten minutes, write a short story about that yearning, using these story prompts to start each paragraph:

  Once upon a time . . .

  Every day . . .

  But one day . . .

  Because of that . . .

  Because of that . . .

  Because of that . . .

  Until finally . . .

  Ever since then . . .

This basic story outline provides a frame in which to explore options. It's amazing what a little structure can do—you might be surprised by the stories (and solutions) you can generate this way. A story prompt is usually a good way to identify more clearly the yearning and the obstacles, whether real or perceived. And don't hate the obstacles—without them, the story never moves forward. "Little Red Riding Hood" needs that big, bad wolf.

> ✿ **Movement:**
> Every evening for thirty-seven days, use the story prompt from the Action Challenge (Once upon a time . . .) to write the mini story of that day. You'll be surprised by the patterns, or "desire lines," that emerge. Perhaps they are patterns that serve you, and perhaps they are patterns that need to be broken, a new path taken, a new story crafted.

[Perhaps, being lost,
one should get loster.
—**Saul Bellow**]

Without deviation, progress is not possible. —**Frank Zappa**

Go See the Tiny Ninjas

There are only two ways to live your life. One is as though nothing is a miracle.
The other is as though everything is a miracle. —**Albert Einstein**

Emma and I both felt a little ill, slightly nauseated, tummies grumbling, and with headaches that make you pay attention and not move too quickly. We both felt the helplessness of victims of food poisoning, facing certain doom.

Perhaps it was the heat, or the Mexican food, or the Indian food, or the Thai food, or the unidentified lunch objects from the conference I had spoken at that day at the Ritz-Carlton where hotel rooms cost $649 a night and where we did not stay. It certainly was not—and I repeat was not—the vegan empanadas from Julia's Empanadas, our first stop when we got to town.

A few days in our Nation's Capital—my home for over twenty years and now not—and Emma and I were exhausted, spent, queasy. After an afternoon at my old stomping ground, the Andre Chreky Salon, our fingernails and toenails looked smashing and I was sporting new, slightly Groucho-reminiscent eyebrows. So we might have been sick, but stylishly so.

We had fallen onto our hotel beds at the end of the day, sweaty. "How're you doing?" I asked a little while later, the air conditioner creating a freezer that held me in some fine molecular stasis.

"Harph . . . ," I heard her groan.

"It's time to go if we're going to get to the Kennedy Center on time," I said. "We've got to catch a cab now if you want to go." What I really wanted to do was sleep or be put into a medically induced coma until the sick wore off, but then again, too much of life is sleeping already and it's not every day you can go see *Macbeth* at the Kennedy Center, and for free.

The show was a production by the Tiny Ninja Theater Company. "I had noticed that there were these tiny plastic ninjas in vending machines all across the city," says founder Dov Weinstein, "but no one was using them to perform classical theater. Something had to be done." When I read that statement on the Kennedy Center Web site, I knew I wanted to go.

Our options at this Moment In Time were narrow and narrowing the longer we remained prone. It was clear that eating dinner was out of the question. We both felt too ill and knew that the next morning our 4:00 a.m. wake-up call for our 6:00

> I embrace emerging experience, I participate in discovery. I am a butterfly. I am not a butterfly collector. I want the experience of the butterfly. —**William Stafford**

a.m. flight would come awfully early. Best not tempt the gods of food poisoning. "I don't know," she said. "I don't feel so good."

"Me neither."

"I don't know, what do you want to do?"

"I don't know, you?" we softly lobbed the decision back and forth, eyeing each other one-eyed to see who would give us the out to stay in our meat locker until morning.

We each suffered in our own silence a few more moments, cool sheets feeling sublime, like a cold bathroom floor feels when you're spending significant fevered time in there, well, you know.

It was 5:25 p.m. If we had any hope of making the 6:00 p.m. show, we'd have to leave now. There's little I hate more than being late. We both stumbled to our feet.

Once outside, the hot air felt like an assault. "I need a ginger ale and some saltines," I said. Instead, we got slowly into a cab—with air-conditioning, blessedly—and made our way at rush hour to the Kennedy Center. **Each lurch of the cab sent us into deep concentrated effort.** "Look at the horizon," I whispered frantically. "Just look at the horizon to keep from getting sick."

The Millennium Stage was completely empty when we got there. "How can that be?" I asked, peering at the chairs cordoned off, struck dumb by their emptiness. "I couldn't have made a mistake—I know it starts at 6:00 p.m." I stood looking at the stage as if staring was a change-agent and Macbeth would suddenly appear. In my weakened state, I was completely befuddled.

"Mom," I finally heard Emma say behind me. "Mo-om!" I slowly turned to look at her, not willing to risk sudden movements. "There's where everybody is going," she said, pointing. I turned farther to peer at the other end of the long overly red hall in the Kennedy Center, past the gigantic gnarly head of John F. Kennedy, to another Millennium Stage, the one with large hordes of people around it. We were too late. There were no more seats, and the crowd kept growing, pinning us against the crowd barrier, the red rope keeping the seatless masses in line.

Everything is something you decide to do, and there is nothing you have to do. —Denis Waitley

"I need a ginger ale," I said again, buying us two Sprites that we both held, reflexively, against our temples and necks.

Get yourself to your life....
Rise above the aches and pains,
the nausea, exhaustion, general malaise.
The show won't run forever.

氣

37 days

Go see the tiny Ninjas

The efficient red-coated ushers looked nervously at the ballooning crowd of us miscreants, latecomers all. One in particular seemed agitated by the size of our army and moved from side to side peering into the crowd. As the show started, the action mercifully projected onto a large screen for the masses, the Efficient and Troubled Usher moved to our side. "I can take six people," she said, looking our way. Suddenly a huge swell of people swallowed us up and pushed me, Emma, and our Sprites aside. The lucky six with the strongest arm muscles were numbered and chosen, like those small children in *Charlie and the Chocolate Factory,* it seemed to me, pushing their way into the chocolate river. Emma, in this moment of insight, was—of course—dear sweet Charlie, quietly standing aside. I played her simple quiet precious Uncle.

We were prepared to stand for the duration. Emma looked particularly beautiful that evening, her dark curls against pale, pale skin and blue, blue eyes. Feverish? Nauseated? Scottish?

Finally, the Very Serious Red-Jacketed Usher appeared just before Emma, locking onto her eyes. "Come, sit," she said, then raising her gaze from Emma to include me. "Come." She opened the red

threshold, pushing back those who surged forward, picking me and Emma out as the chosen ones, shepherding us. "Follow me," she said, and she was gone, lost through a billowing curtain on the far right. We followed, emerging in the very front of the hall. **"You can sit here," she whispered,** pointing to the floor before the front row of seats.

To the left was the performer himself, a man dressed completely in black, with shoulder-length black puppeteer gloves, playing every part in *Macbeth* himself while maneuvering small plastic characters around a small black surface.

We watched Macbeth don a wee plaid strip before he goes into battle, marveled at lighting effects operated by the director's toes, and laughed at his imaginative props. When poor, beleaguered Macbeth cries out, "Is this a dagger I see before me?" a ninja-size dagger appears, hanging by a thread off a long stick. Group scenes are pre-glued; when they need to disappear, Weinstein simply picks them up and throws them offstage.

We laughed from our perch on the floor, looking at each other from time to time in surprise and amusement. We forgot our stomachs and Sprites. It was the delight that was delicious, the delight that only small plastic smiley-faced figurines can bring—even more so surrounded by the auspicious miles of red carpet and curtains of the Kennedy Center.

For a bright shining moment, this little tribe of ninjas made all the world a stage. (Sound effect: Patti laughing Nerdy English Major Snort.)

THE NOTION OF LOOKING ON AT LIFE HAS ALWAYS BEEN HATEFUL TO ME. WHAT AM I IF I AM NOT A PARTICIPANT? IN ORDER TO BE, I MUST PARTICIPATE.

—**Antoine de Saint-Exupéry**

Sometimes, it occurred to me as Macbeth received a standing ovation, life just comes down to showing up, or sitting upright, or at the very least flinging one leg at a time off the bed.

The motto of the Tiny Ninja Theater is "No small parts. Only small actors." Sounds like life. Get yourself there. It's too easy to stay in a darkened hotel room with the air conditioner on high and a Friends marathon turned on low. Pretty soon you wake up and have missed the Tiny Ninja Theater altogether; you've missed Macbeth!

✐ Action:

Henry Miller wrote, "We create our fate every day we live."

- Write for four minutes on this topic: What are the paths not taken in your life?

- Then, for three additional minutes, answer the following: Imagine you are in a forest, walking. You stop and look around. There are three paths to choose from in front of you. Where is each of them going?

- Read what you have written.

- For the final three minutes of your focused free-write, answer this question: What are the creatures in the forest that scare you from walking down one of those paths?

۞ Movement:

Each day for the next thirty-seven days, get yourself there, even those places you dread. Get to the gym, to the hospital to visit a dying friend when you don't know what to say or do, to the Kennedy Center to see a grown man play with tiny plastic dolls attached to pieces of cardboard and duct tape while quoting Shakespeare. Get yourself to your life. Go see the Tiny Ninja Theater. Rise above aches, pains, nausea, exhaustion, general malaise. The show won't run forever. Go now or you'll miss it. And sometimes, tiny ninjas are just the miracle we need.

[
Desire is half of life,
indifference is half of death.
]
—Kahlil Gibran

Get Off the Ship

You gain strength, courage, and confidence by every experience in which you
really stop to look fear in the face. You must do the thing which
you think you cannot do. —**Eleanor Roosevelt**

In the fall of 1988, I circumnavigated the globe on a ship. Actually, that
sounds more romantic and rugged than it was. I was working on a university study-abroad program that stopped in ten ports—from Kobe to Split to
Istanbul and Cadiz—and beyond. The students' experiences in port were
core to their educational program. We arranged in-country programs to
complement their classroom studies aboard
the SS *Universe*.

A month into the voyage, I realized there was
one student who never got off the ship. Lest
we leave someone in Odessa or Taipei, we
carefully tracked students' passports, and it
was clear one young woman never set foot in
any of the ports we had visited.

When we docked in Penang, Malaysia, I
sought her out, and we sat on the promenade
deck near the pool. After watching awhile
as workers brought aboard provisions, I
asked her about staying on the ship all the
time. She admitted she didn't leave the ship
because she was afraid she would get lost—
an answer I wasn't prepared for.

I had to think awhile before I could
respond. Her fear seemed so irrational to
me, but of course it was real and rational to
her, since it literally defined the confines
of her world. "Hmmm . . . ," I finally said.
"How old are you?" She was twenty.

We sat a few minutes. "And what do you
think the life expectancy is for women in
the United States these days?" I asked.

"I guess it's around eighty," she replied.

"Do you think you'll stay lost for sixty years?" I quietly asked. We made a pact to get lost together in our next port, which was Madras, India.

I've thought a lot about that since 1988. How much do we hold back on life because of fear—rational or irrational? **What do we have to gain by getting lost once in a while?** What are we allowing to limit our world? What ship are we staying on?

> DISCOVERY CONSISTS IN SEEING WHAT EVERY-
> ONE ELSE HAS SEEN AND THINKING WHAT NO
> ONE ELSE HAS THOUGHT.
>
> —Albert Szent-Györgyi

With a group of fellow high school students, I once took a hiking trip from Table Rock to Mount Mitchell through the Linville Gorge. The trip was supposed to take five days. It took seven. There were twenty-three of us— eighteen students, two teachers, three guides. Guides provided the training to cross a river, read a map, and find the North Star. They provided the tools to get us to Mount Mitchell. After that "book learning," we teenagers were in charge. Completely.

Being shown how to read a map and actually reading one are two very different things. It was on the third day that we made the wrong decision, leading us 12 miles out of our way. Our guides did nothing to save us from making the mistake; instead, they hiked those extra 12 miles with us. **The mistake was the learning, as it turned out.**

Physicist Hermann von Helmholtz likened knowledge to an alpine climb— when you climb a mountain, you don't go straight from the bottom to the top, you zigzag, you go around and through, eventually getting to the top where you can then see both the top and bottom and the straight line between them. When you're at the top, you can show others what Helmholtz called the "royal road." But being shown the royal road isn't learning, it's only the explanation, just as being taught to read a map isn't the same as reading one.

The learning process is far less exact than the royal road. It is that winding, twisty trail where learning gets done. You make a false start; you backtrack, then go ahead. Sometimes you go 12 miles out of your way. Sometimes getting lost *is* the learning. To do any of that learning, though, you have to first leave the ship.

Far away is only far away if you don't go there. —O. Povo

Many discoveries were accidental and came from being lost: The Big Bang, Post-it notes, Jovian moons, Velcro, X-rays, and even GPS systems that help us get found— all were accidental discoveries. This week, ask yourself what ship you're staying on and what you might be losing out on by not venturing out.

Action:

Muhammad Ali said, "The man who views the world at fifty the same as he did at twenty has wasted thirty years of his life."

- You can use either a camera or your journal for this Action Challenge. Gather your equipment and find an object you'd like to photograph or write about—a flower, piece of fruit, book, coffee cup—anything will work, the simpler the better.

- If you're using a camera, make at least twenty photographs of the object, from very different angles. Play around with changing the light and the context in which you set the object, too.

- If you're using your journal, write a description of the object from at least twenty different angles.

- Where we "stand" changes our perspective and angle of vision. What did changing your point of view do? How might this experience translate into our daily lives? How can we change our perspective to see more sides of the people and events in our lives?

In music, a rondo is a composition with an AB-AC-AD-A pattern. The A motif is constant, but it sounds different as the tune progresses because it is set against different themes—B, C, D. The same is true for what we see around us. By changing the context, we see and hear different things. The object you chose for this challenge might have seemed different, depending on the context. How do you see this play out in your life?

Get off the Ship

A ship in port is safe, but that's not what ships are built for.
—Grace Hopper

⬡ **Movement:**

For thirty-seven days, be a conscious explorer. Pretend you are the A motif in the rondo described earlier. Every day, place yourself against new themes: Get lost, take a wrong turn, veer off the path you always take, walk a different path with your dog, read a magazine you would not normally pick up, connect with someone different from you, eat in a restaurant you've never tried. Break a pattern—how you usually drive to work, what you eat for lunch, with whom you interact, what movies you see. Take the winding trail rather than the royal road. Get off the ship.

How does it feel?

Fear is what prevents the flowering of the mind. —**Krishnamurti**

Close the Boardroom Closet

> The feeling of being hurried is not usually the result of living a full life and having no time. It is on the contrary born of a vague fear that we are wasting our life. When we do not do the one thing we ought to do, we have no time for anything else—we are the busiest people in the world. —**Eric Hoffer**

I don't remember ever being this busy. Not even that time in the fourth grade when I was starring as Johnny Appleseed in our class play, learning to play the autoharp, and simultaneously creating my report on Missouri, the "Show Me" state, in a cardboard box panorama (I believe the Latin term for it is *Cardboardorama*). Remember that fantastic technology? Those stories drawn on long paper rolled between two dowels inside a box decorated to look like a TV set? So you watched the merry history of those stubborn Missourians unfurl before your very eyes? (PowerPoint's got nothing on Cardboardorama 2.0.)

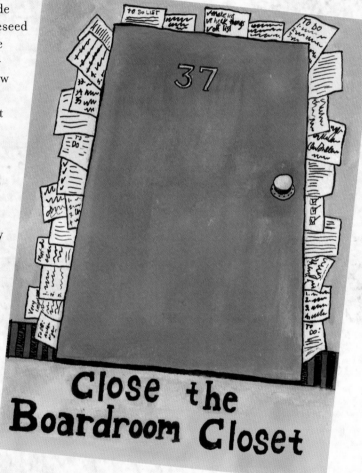

Now, many years later, I'm scaring myself and my small children with my to-do lists. On Saturday my head exploded. Okay, that might be an exaggeration, but my eyes definitely did bulge out a bit at the sheer enormity of all the things I need to do, the things falling through the cracks, things halfway done with no time to finish them because we're off and running to the next happy thing; then there are the things I forgot to do. (Meglet, if you're reading this, I hope you had a fantastic birthday, girlfriend! You too, Lora!) It was bound to happen, this spontaneous

combustion. I knew life was at Orange Alert level when I wasn't sending thank-you notes in a timely fashion.

I could finally stand it no longer, this Angst of Overwhelm.

So I cleared the sidewalk chalk and Poincaré biography off the dining room table and sat down by myself with a nice fountain pen and a legal pad, one with satisfyingly thick sheets where the ink says "ahhhhh" as it glides on. And I sat and wrote and wrote and wrote, like writer Malcolm Lowry on a drunken binge under a volcano but without the worm at the bottom of the tequila bottle and without all the sweat he used to sweat. But I didn't stand up to write like he did (before he inevitably fell down), so maybe it isn't the best comparison.

I wasn't writing the Great American Novel, no. I was just writing my to-do list. Not in any theme or priority, just listing page after page of all I needed to do.

There were big things, like paint the house, raise two children, figure out how much I'm paying per minute for long distance once and for all, and provide what I'm sure would be invaluable input to the human genome project. There were also smaller items: Find the missing sandal, get stamps, sharpen the knives, drink more water, and get my parking sticker at the university. There were literally hundreds of them, yellow brick legal-pad roads of things that need to be done, all rolling around in my head and causing not-so-unconscious anxiety, what with their not being done and my teetering on the precipice of forgetting to do them.

To do two things at once is to do neither. —Publilius Syrus

As I wrote to move them out of my head to clear space for things like Social Security numbers, customer ID numbers, account numbers, and the square root of 389,302, I felt like I was sliding farther and faster into the morass of undone things, paralyzed by the enormity of it all. Then I looked at the pile of writing in front of me and remembered a story I once heard novelist Toni Morrison tell.

Early in her career Morrison worked at Random House publishers. One day her head exploded just as mine had, and she started her list of to-do items.

She wrote pages and pages of things that she must do. Faced with the long list, she sat and looked at it for a long while, finally asking herself one question: **What is it I must do or I shall die?**

After answering that question, there were only two things left on her to-do list: (1) Be a mother to her children. (2) Write.

I used to work for a big national association, with about 600 chapters around the United States. Every year the leaders of those chapters would come to Washington, DC, to a ~~big pep rally~~ leadership development program, and every year we would host them for a reception at our national headquarters building, which meant we had to clean up, as if Grandma (who starched and ironed her bed linens) was coming to dinner.

It's not so much how busy you are, but why you are busy. The bee is praised. The mosquito is swatted. —**Mary O'Connor**

One year my office was particularly messy and I was late in preparing for the Big Event. Very Important Papers and Files covered my desk and every horizontal surface, all demanding immediate attention. To give my office a hip Zen minimalist organized vibe for the onslaught of chapter presidents, I just swept all those Do-It-or-Die action files into a big box and wrestled it into the boardroom closet.

Our life is frittered away by detail . . . Simplify, Simplify. —**Henry Thoreau**

My office was immaculate! I was the self-proclaimed winner of the office decorating contest! I looked über-organized! What a great solution! I patted myself on the back as the reception began. This boardroom strategy actually worked so well that the next year I did exactly the same thing. And that time, when I opened the boardroom closet with the box perched on my hip, there sat proudly the unopened and forgotten box of Vital, Time-Sensitive, Ultra-Important files from the year before.

I guess doing all that stuff wasn't really so vital, after all. None of it got done. Nobody died. Life went on, less frenetic, less fractured, more focused, more full.

[What is the use of running when we are not on the right road?
—**German proverb**]

the boardroom closet

37 Days: Do It Now Challenge

Like my Cardboardorama in the fourth grade, my to-do lists seem to just loop around and around and around without end. The scene moves in front of me, but perhaps I've confused movement with action? Make a Cardboardorama of your to-do list. Watch it scroll past—what catches your eye? What looks interesting? What is merely there to catch people's attention? What do you really need or want to do? Stop the scroll-by.

✐ Action:

This action challenge will take a little more time than usual.

- Today, for one hour, imagine that you can only do one thing at a time. If you are drinking coffee, you can't check e-mail. If you are talking to your neighbor, you can't be folding laundry. If you are walking to get your mail, you can't be talking on your cell phone. If you are eating, you can't be reading. One. Thing. At. A. Time. Try it.

- Then get out your journal for a brief focused free-write.

- For three minutes, write about your experience of doing one thing at a time: How did it feel? Was it difficult? Easy? Frustrating?

- For the next three minutes, answer this question: What do I lose or miss out on when I multitask, doing many things at one time?

✺ Movement:

This challenge starts with a focused free-write:

- Write for five minutes without stopping in answer to this question: What is on my to-do list today? List every single thing you need to do today, those things that are past due, and those things that are coming up.

- Stop. Now write for five minutes on this question: What must I do or I shall die?

- Using your answer to the question, What must I do or I shall die?, practice different ways to say no.

- Over the next thirty-seven days, when you are asked to add something to your to-do list, if it doesn't match your do-or-die list, say no.

Eat Slowly and Thank the Chef

I prefer Hostess fruit pies to pop-up toaster tarts
because they don't require as much cooking. —**Carrie Snow**

My friend Lucy, who creates amazing works of art in food and everyday life
and who might be compared to Martha Stewart (except for the unfortunate
prison part), used to live in Chicago. So naturally, when I was planning a
business trip to Chicago, I asked her where I should eat there. Her breath-
less one-word answer: "Topolobampo."

When my colleague Angela and I made our way to
Topolobampo and our too-beautiful-to-eat salads
arrived, I realized Lucy wasn't kidding—this was seriously good food delivered by seriously skilled waitstaff.

Two weeks later, work in Chicago beckoned again,
another chance to visit the tall white-haired maître d'
at Topolobampo, a gentleman's gentleman if ever there
was one, with a manner so kind and caring that when
he held out his hand and asked for my friend's jacket,
David gave it to him without even knowing who he was.

Before the trip, when I had e-mailed David to tell him
I had made a reservation for us, he remarked that he
just enjoyed saying the name—*To-po-lo-***bam***-po*, **To-**
po-lo-bam-po, *To-po-lo-bam-***po**—and that eating there
could only be secondary to that auditory, symphonic,
percussive pleasure.

> **Recipe:** Do It Now Challenge
>
> **Ingredients:** Love, Friendship,
> Magic, Celebration, Desire,
> Thoughtfulness about Flav
> Beauty
>
> **Directions:** Eat Slowly and
> Thank the Chef
>
> **Cooking time:** 1–37 Days

It was a three-hour sensory experience, that meal,
from the moment we sat until the moment we reluc-
tantly left: a salad so pretty it made me weep, soup
made and poured for David at the table, a vegetarian
mushroom-and-bean ragout baked in parchment and served with homemade tortillas to cut its spice, and—just to be polite—dessert and a sweet coffee that haunts me still.

Each dish a piece of art—both visual and aural. It was the dessert that slowed
us down, that made us dream of a land where tree trunks were stacks of
crisp, thin chocolate wafers rolled around chocolate mousse like clouds in
your mouth; rivers full of warm, rich bread pudding so full of love it felt like

pillows, its rum-soaked raisins like small island nations or at the very least life rafts, floating in a pomegranate sauce.

This, said David, is what eating should be. This, I responded, is where I'm coming to celebrate my fiftieth birthday. In fact, let's all meet there on August 16, 2009; I'll make the reservation for 7:00 p.m. I'll be the one sitting in the left back corner as you enter (now my favorite table) holding my fork up expectantly and muttering something unintelligible about the evils of counting carbs while tapping out the word *Topolo* in Morse code. I can call it Topolo now that I'm a regular.

> The whole idea is to earn the flavor. No one gives it to you.
> —Jamie Oliver

Many moons ago I had another meal in another place that also stopped me. It was the food, yes, but the place, too—and, of course, the company, a newly minted love, John (now my husband, Mr. Brilliant). The place was called La Lunchonette in New York's Chelsea.

Then there was the evening in Helsinki's Alexander Nevski, a Russian restaurant with a menu as tall as a building; or the hot chips and meaningful salsa at the M&J Sanitary Tortilla Factory in Albuquerque; Nana's pierogi fried in a vat of butter; the sticky toffee pudding at Betty's Café Tea Room in Harrogate; lavender ice cream in Waterford; Steve Clyburn's stone-ground grits at the farm, and Mama's brownstone front cake; nightly forays to Meskerem Ethiopian restaurant in Washington, DC, while wild-craving-pregnant with my first child, Emma; that saag paneer at DC's Heritage India; those freshly made pitas and every single thing that Chagit Zakay cooks in Hod Ha-sharon, Israel; that curry lunch wrapped in a banana leaf aboard a train from Colombo bound for Kandy in Sri Lanka.

"I had a perfect hot dog and a Coke in Central Park in 1970," my now vegetarian husband John adds quietly to my litany of memorable food.

Who are the people making these touchstone meals, those wafts of aroma that drove Proust to memory?

They are life's chefs, mixing magic on a plate like my friend Rosemary, who can make a tomato-and-olive torte into a life-altering experience. They cook up much more than sustenance, creating memories, conjuring sights and sounds and conversations with the very memory of a pomegranate sauce, a banana leaf, a perfect bowl of salsa, a hot knish. It is a true calling, cooking like this. And one among their number is John's cousin Philip, a chef in San Francisco.

When John's youngest brother got married in New York years ago, we traveled there to join the celebration. Largely pregnant with Emma, with John tucked into a tuxedo up front in the wedding party, I sat with his cousin, Philip, whom I was meeting for the first time. We talked for hours amid the dancing. Just four years older than John, Philip is his favorite cousin.

Philip has spent his whole life making memories for people at restaurant tables where love is proclaimed, where friendships are forged, where anniversaries and birthdays get celebrated with a toast and a satisfied smile at the merging of tastes (like his ravioli with orange-saffron sauce), where families mark milestones, deals are inked, careers are changed and arguments ended and children named and books inspired and negotiations conducted and jobs offered (and sometimes refused), where lists are penned and lost, where decisions—big and small—are made. Being a chef is a calling. There is desire in that kitchen heat.

COOKING IS A GREAT WAY TO GET BACK IN TOUCH WITH THINGS THAT BROUGHT US COMFORT.

—Liz Scott

Last year John's parents planned a visit to see Philip in San Francisco. I was put in charge of finding a special hotel room that overlooks water, a beautiful place where, when Philip visited, he could look out and see beauty at every turn. I was responsible for booking flights and hotels, and I was desperate for a place with a nice view for Philip: It was the only thing I could do. He was undergoing chemotherapy. It was cancer; it is always cancer. John's parents were going to help their nephew, sit with him, bathe him, watch the little boy they knew and loved as he moved quickly to an end.

Philip Sheremeta provided many memories to people over the years through his art, his food. He died on a Thursday while I sat in Des Moines. Awaiting my flight home. Kvetching about air travel. While he died. Fifty-four years was all, then gone.

Somehow, we eat this life way too fast, just way too fast. In a whirling dervish of a world in which our decisions are between Hostess fruit pies and Raspberry Frosted Pop-Tarts, we need to slow it down, savor each bite, eat dessert, and draw life out a bit.

Anything made with love, bam!—it's a beautiful meal. —**Emeril Lagasse**

Eat your bread pudding slowly, savor it, swim awhile in that pomegranate sauce, reach out for a raisin island and rest. Eat well, eat slowly, appreciate the artistry of your food, make your life's meal last a long time; give up Pop-Tarts and be sure to thank the real chefs.

🖋 Action:

- Spend ten minutes cleaning out your pantry today.

- Start fresh.

- Consider yourself a chef, a kitchen artist, even if your meals are plain, simple, and just for one.

- Make something for dinner tonight that you've never made before. Create art on your plate.

- Even if you're a hardcore carnivore, cook your way though this fantastic tome: *Veganomicon: The Ultimate Vegan Cookbook* by Isa Chandra Moskowitz and Terry Hope Romero.

- Subscribe to a blog that introduces you to real food:

  The Perfect Pantry (www.theperfectpantry.com)

  FatFree Vegan Kitchen (http://blog.fatfreevegan.com)

  I Heart Farms (http://smallfarms.typepad.com/small_farms)

  Gluten-Free Girl (http://glutenfreegirl.blogspot.com)

⚙ Movement:

For the next thirty-seven days, you are a restaurant critic.

- Either at a restaurant or at home, eat all your meals as if you have to describe them to others. What are the tastes evocative of? What colors surround you? What textures delight you?

- Keep a simple list of everything you eat for those thirty-seven days.

- And write a mental review of one meal each day to practice slowing down and paying attention.

Signal Your Turns

People change and forget to tell each other. —**Lillian Hellman**

My sweet old Ford Bronco II has 172,000 miles of history in it, a broken driver's-side door that has to be opened from the outside, a passenger window stuck in one position not quite all the way up to the top (exciting when it's snowing), no air-conditioning, and a busted driver's seat that has to be bolstered up with a very large pillow unless you prefer driving in the blessed horizontal. Add the effluvia of a tod-

dler (Cheerios) and a teenager (Napoleon Dynamite temporary tattoos) and you might approximate my Hot Ride. A Lamborghini Murcielago it ain't.

But this Jethro-mobile is a dear, old friend, transporting me through many, many transitions, like the big one during which I bought it used sixteen years ago while pregnant with my older daughter, Emma.

Until then, I rode my blue 1968 Schwinn three-speed bicycle everywhere, with the brrriing-brrriing of my ladybug bell and two wire baskets on the back, the perfect size and shape for paper grocery bags, one each side, balanced. It was the kind of bike on which you sit up real straight, like the Wicked Witch of the West toting Toto along in that Big Wind, a bike you could imagine Kitty from *Gunsmoke* riding in her long skirts.

When I got good and big and pregnant, people started veering away when they saw me wobble their way on that bike, my balance affected by the addition in my middle front, their faces betraying fears I might give birth in second gear.

Finally my lovely, soft-spoken ob-gyn laid down the law: Stay off the bike and she would reward me with an epidural when the time came. Seemed like a reasonable bribe. Later, in the throes of labor, it was one I'm quite happy

I took. So I asked my stepfather to find me a little used car. Within days he had found me a pristine Ford Bronco for sale by a friend of his who evidently vacuumed it daily and wiped down the engine with Q-tips after every use. **And the love affair began.**

As my little truck has started failing, I've grown embarrassed over her rather than thankful for her gifts. Do I fear others may make assumptions about me based solely on the aged car I'm driving? Probably. Does it color people's impressions of me when I reach outside the driver's-side door to open it? Probably. Should it? No, but it does. Do we have another car I could be driving? Yes, but I like this one.

Lately I've gotten increasingly irritated looks from drivers as I toodle my way around town in little Bronky. Road rage is really out of control, I think to myself as people gesture harshly. Maybe they're irritated because I'm not able to accelerate from 0 to 60 in two seconds. Perhaps they are good Samaritans

trying to warn me that my poncho is hanging out the door, and in danger of wrapping around a wheel and strangling me to death like that nice ballerina Isadora Duncan.

Finally a friend saw me downtown. "By the way," she said. "Did you know that you don't have any turn signals on your car?"

All that time I thought I was signaling my turns, but I wasn't. The people around me couldn't tell what I was going to do next and got angry as they realized I was turning (or not). They didn't know—and yet I thought I was clearly telling them, dutifully shifting my turn signal lever up and down, hearing a click, click, click, and not knowing that it didn't translate into the outside world. They thought I was withholding information from them. I thought they were just cranky.

It reminded me of a bright fall day years ago when I realized for the first time (and too late and with a hot rush to my cheeks) that people couldn't see my intentions, they could only see my actions. So, for example, while I knew about your birthday for weeks, with a smile at the very thought of it and a mental note to myself to send you a card, you couldn't know that when the day came and went and you never heard from me.

You can just imagine how much the stakes increase with different, more complex, more important scenarios.

As in cars, human beings "change lanes" all the time. We shift our direction, slow and accelerate, taking detours and turns. It helps the people around us to know our intention so they can shift, make room, slow down, yield.

Like this traffic conundrum (and metaphor), there's also a gap sometimes between what I intended and what you received. **There's a gap sometimes between what I think I'm indicating to the world and what is really being put out there by me.**

> I think what makes us human is our interconnectedness among people. It's our ability to form and maintain relationships. It's the barometer by which we call ourselves human.
> —**Thomas Jane**

You're at the traffic light, waiting to turn. I don't signal so you don't know which way I'm going. People have cut you off in this situation before, so you make a quick assessment of whether you can trust me. You're also afraid I'll either hit you or make you waste five seconds of your precious time while you watch me so you'll know how to react. My not signaling threatens your safety, diminishes your ability to perform; it undermines your understanding of the traffic pattern. If you make the wrong move once the light turns green, you'll justify it to yourself by blaming me for not signaling—if you're still alive.

Everything, yes, is a metaphor.

We are all connected at those traffic lights.

My business partner, David, and I use an exercise in our workshops that we call Triangle Boid. We've done it with small groups and groups with hundreds of people, with the same result. Each person in the group is asked to secretly identify two others in the room who will serve as two points of a triangle for them, using themselves as the third point. Everyone is someone else's point, though they don't know whose.

As a participant, once those other two points of my triangle are identified, after the word *go,* my job is to maintain a triangle shape using myself and

Things do not change, we change. —**Henry David Thoreau**

those other two points as we move around the room without speaking. Where those two points move, I must move, keeping equidistant from each of them.

An oddly beautiful dance ensues, one that I've seen play out in so many organizations daily: I'm dancing, watching where my boss moves, and moving with him, then seeing him move in a different direction and moving there, too, like seaweed. Everyone in the room becomes hyper-alert to the actions of others around them, maintaining their triangle, basing their own movements on the movements of others, understanding themselves only in relation to others.

> They say that time changes things, but you actually have to change them yourself.
> —Andy Warhol

Before starting, we've told the group that at some point in the exercise, we will tap one of them on the shoulder. If they feel the tap, they should sit down on the floor where they are. Everyone is told that if one of their points goes down, they must also go down.

Once that tap is given—just one tap on one shoulder—even in a room of hundreds of people, every person in the room is down in a short period of time. Like a quiet and odd ballet, people fall. It is a striking image.

We are all interconnected. What I do affects you; what you do affects me. Even the slightest action, just one tap, just one point of the triangle, just one green light.

The Bronco is still going strong-ish, but I fear for its health. I also (not so) secretly desire a Vespa. With working turn signals.

Check your turn signals. Do they work? Signal your intent. Own your triangle. Acknowledge the domino effect. Love your old car. Cherish the history of turns it represents.

✐ Action:

Focused free-write:

- Write for three minutes on this question: Who was I when I was thirteen? Describe yourself in great detail.

- Read what you've written. Now write for three minutes on these questions: Where did that kid go? What turns have I taken away from him or her?

- For two minutes, answer this question: What part of him or her remains and what part would I like to reclaim?

- For the final two minutes, write about the turns you would need to take to get back to that earlier part of yourself you want to reclaim.

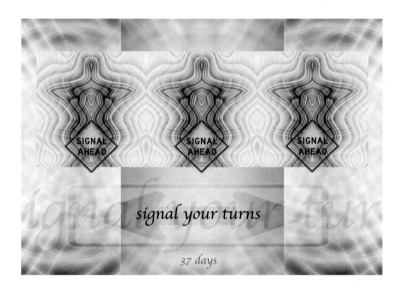

signal your turns

37 days

A hidden connection is stronger than an obvious one. —Heraclitus of Ephesus

✿ Movement:

Mark Twain wrote, "I can teach anybody how to get what they want out of life. The problem is that I can't find anybody who can tell me what they want." Creating a compelling vision of what we want is tough. But doing it means we own it and can start working on strategies to get there. With help from an amazing personal trainer and coach named Michael Scholtz, I recently created a "Wellness Vision." Michael pushed me to make it specific, to identify what is motivating me to achieve it, what the obstacles are, and my strategies for overcoming those obstacles—four crucial pieces of information for any type of vision.

I'll share it as an example. As you read it, think about the kind of vision you'd like to create. Maybe it's not about wellness, but about parenting or relationships or work: "I am energetic and flexible; I can feel the muscles in my body as they flex and move. There is no extra fat on my structure as I move through the world. I am lean and athletic, have redefined myself as an athlete, and have slowed the aging process by being fit. I move quicker and with greater ease and confidence; I am active every day and look for opportunities to play outside with Emma and Tess. I love hiking and biking, and our weekends are mainly spent outdoors. I am strong and sure of my physicality."

My motivators include setting an example for and relating to my daughters, redefining myself as an athlete, and being stronger as I age. My obstacles include setting unrealistic goals, the unpredictability of my schedule, doing for others before myself, and wasting time. My strategies to overcome my obstacles are utilizing "rules" to block out time for work and for exercise, and short-circuiting my all-or-nothing thinking.

- For the next thirty-seven days, devote at least ten minutes a day to creating your own vision, whether for wellness or work or marriage. Make it specific, make it compelling, and make it your own. Then "signal your turns"—tell others about it so they can support you.

No person is your friend who demands your silence, or denies your right to grow. —Alice Walker

PART THREE
Life Is a Verb

Life is a verb.

—Charlotte Perkins Gilman

in what ways am i a stranger
to life?
i am a stranger to . . .
tightropes and chafing dishes and
holding lizards and reading poetry
out loud and rock-climbing and
yodeling and wearing my clothes
backwards and dissecting frogs
and roller coasters and bungee-jumping
and political speeches and
shaving my head and playing
country music and studying for
a degree and hitchhiking and
scuba diving and writing a novel
and giving birth and running a
marathon and getting a
Brazilian wax and eating brains
and driving cross country and
owning my own business and
brandishing a weapon and wearing
contacts and winning a Nobel
prize and traveling to Africa and
going to a prom and baking a
pie and shooting a film
i must remind myself that life
is not a stranger to me . . .
it is i who make myself
a stranger to it

—Marilyn Maciel, "the stranger"

CHAPTER NINE

Become You

As life goes on it becomes tiring to keep up the character you invented for yourself, and so you relapse into individuality and become more like yourself every day. This is sometimes disconcerting for those around you, but a great relief to the person concerned. —**Agatha Christie**

It was a green piece of construction paper with three orange islands pasted on it, creating distinct sections on the page. I'd say the whole page was probably 17 inches long. Maybe, in fact, it was an 11-by-17-inch piece of paper. If I had ever studied the metric system in school, I could provide that data, but I didn't, so let's move on rather than devolve into a full-blown reproach of the American educational system.

At the opening reception, we were asked to create a collage representing our lives, and particularly what was new for us in the two years since we'd last met as a group. We gathered at a reception on the patio, scissors and glue stick in hand, tearing magazines apart and offering images to one another—"This one reminds me of you!," leaving the recipient to wonder why and how—before we invaded the dinner buffet with the same sense of purpose. I wasn't thinking as I tore the paper—or was I? So much of the process was unconscious, and only when I explained my collage to the group the next morning did the truth become clear.

Over the weekend we reintroduced ourselves using our collages. People told of losses in their lives, challenges, new loves, searches for love, successes, priorities.

My collage was a study in minimalism. Others had covered their construction paper with beautiful images; mine held one image and several words. There was a lot of blank space showing through. As I started to talk, I found myself saying something that had never occurred to me until that moment, not even the night before when I had cut out the photograph of a tree blown almost over in half from the force of a wind.

"This," I said, pointing to the tree, "is my life before 2005."

I surprised even myself when I said those words. But, having said them, and with twenty sets of eyes looking at me, expectantly, I felt compelled to continue. And so I did.

As e. e. cummings once wrote, "It takes courage to grow up and become who you really are." After bowing to the wind, being blown into one thing and another—even if they were successful and rewarding—in 2005 I began to right myself, stick my roots deeper into earth, resist the wind, tell my own story, not the one I felt I should tell, not the books others wanted me to write, but my very own.

If I'm honest with myself, I told the group, I have play-acted through my professional life—knowing it wasn't what I truly needed to be doing, sometimes even feeling like I was outside myself watching it. I was successful by anyone's measure, except by my own; I was looking at books I had written as if they were not mine. **And now, ironically, I am the most successful by my own internal measure, and the least successful by anyone else's.** It is a good lesson for me, to be sitting at both the top and bottom of Maslow's hierarchy at the very same time, saying no to financial gain that is at the cost of the Self I have found. There is no other time for me to write but now.

When we lose the right to be different, we lose the privilege to be free. —Charles Evans Hughes

A few years ago I attended a class at Penland School of Crafts. Penland is a magical place for me—I wear my Birkenstocks proudly and throw my makeup to the wind. Studios are open twenty-four hours a day, and you are surrounded by artists making, not surprisingly, art. That year I was enrolled in a two-week class, a plan marred only by the need to leave for two days to don my Power Suit, eyeliner, and briefcase to fly to Dallas and conduct a workshop for the CEO of a big financial institution and his direct reports.

When the wind blows, sand often flies.

It felt like grit in my eyes, the very prospect of leaving this magical place for a corporate gathering of dueling BlackBerrys. I sat at dinner the night before leaving, bemoaning my fate, the injustice of it all, yada, yada, yada. The man I was sitting with was someone I had met the day before, a sculptor taking a blacksmithing course. He listened quietly to my tale of woe, no doubt wishing he had sought out the company of a weaver or a woodworker rather than a whiner. "I feel sometimes like I am speaking, but someone has actually got their hand in my back making my mouth move, like a puppet."

> MOST PEOPLE ARE OTHER PEOPLE. THEIR THOUGHTS ARE SOMEONE ELSE'S OPINIONS, THEIR LIVES A MIMICRY, THEIR PASSIONS A QUOTATION.
>
> —Oscar Wilde

"I'll be right back," he said. "Don't move."

I sat still for ten minutes. He returned with a postcard. "This is from my last show," he said. "I think you'll like the piece on the front of the postcard."

I looked down. On the card was a sculpture he had done of a man in a business suit, a torso. The head was made of recycled farm implements. On the back of the postcard was a view of the back of the torso, in which there was a small door. When it opened, there was a crank that you could turn. And when you turned the crank, the mouth moved. A metaphorical architecture made visible in heavy iron.

When I lived in Sri Lanka in 1976, I was mesmerized by the massive palm trees along the coast, insanely tall and bent over almost double from the force of a wind over time. **We are moving in a direction, it occurs to me, even when we feel like we are not.** Perhaps it isn't apparent today, or tomorrow, or next Thursday, but it will be—the photograph we show the world will clearly delineate what direction that wind was coming from over all those years we lived.

François Duc de La Rochefoucauld once said, "We are so accustomed to disguise ourselves to others that in the end we become disguised to ourselves." The thing about those trees blown by the wind is that pretty soon, they stay that way. It's incremental, but cumulative. It's gradual, but lasting. Intention and direction, intention and direction.

Become you, that You not shaped by outside forces, but the one standing up straight, a perfect balance of wind and still, of solid and sway. I wonder, what wind is blowing you? Is it so gradual that you don't even notice the bend?

Our last day together, you and I, is day thirty-seven: Live an irresistible obituary. The story of our lives is one that we should create, not wait for others to write after we're gone.

Live an Irresistible Obituary

It doesn't matter who my father was; it matters who I remember he was.
—Anne Sexton

My grandmother's house abutted the North Carolina state mental institution's graveyard, a source of rampant and consuming fear when I was a child. Once, on a dare from my brother, I ran into the graveyard, shocked to a standstill at what I found: miles of chain stretched between short white poles, small metal tags hanging at respectable distances. Not names of the insane and discarded dead, just numbers: 12147, 12148, 12149, miles of them.

Are we leaving behind numbers, or stories?

I vote for stories.

I read obituaries. I've read them for years.

Sometimes I'm rewarded with a gem of a life's story, or a spectacular turn of phrase: "He had a God-given talent for operating heavy machinery" was one such jewel, culled from the *Asheville Citizen-Times*.

But it was another obituary from the *Citizen-Times*—regarding Miss Lavern Lorenz—that recently captured my imagination: "Two years prior to her death, Aunty began letting go of parts of her notorious personality. No longer did we hear dirty jokes—the farmer and the visiting minister, the 'pretty little ballerina,' the frog in the pond who said, 'No, I told you, no, no, no!'—and many, many more.

All sorrows can be borne if you put them into a story or tell a story about them. —Isak Dinesen

"Aunty," it continued, "loved to eat. She once topped out at a sturdy 215 pounds, though she would have to strain to make 5'3." Meatloaf, sauerkraut with pork and potatoes, chicken and dumplings, bread pudding, tomatoes and crackers, fried cabbage, creamed corn and always something with gravy. Over time, her food desires haikued to a two-minute egg, soft Italian white bread with black raspberry jam, and lukewarm milk."

Haikued, indeed.

It appears Aunty hated cats, "even on commercials, and would readily scream upon seeing one. Aunty could recite all the presidents in chronological order and give you a short biography of each one."

Years ago the *Washington Post* created a template for obituaries requiring brief descriptors to appear in bold type just under the name of the recently departed, a shorthand of a life, a telegraph of humanity. How to capture a whole lifetime of living in

> The life of every man is a diary in which he means to write one story, and writes another; and his humblest hour is when he compares the volume as it is with what he vowed to make it. —**James M. Barrie**

a snappy subtitle? My personal favorites included "Safecracker" and "Snap, Crackle, Pop Creator." (What would mine be? Yours?)

When I wrote my stepfather's obit, that longish story violated the puritanical staccato of most Southern Baptist death notices (He lived. He tithed. He died. He went Home.) by elaborating just the tiniest bit on how he lived. In the process I started wondering about my own obituary, inevitable as it is. What words would capture me? What kindnesses would stand out? What adventures would define my sense of spirit? What relationships would be mentioned as core to who I am? What about my food preferences, favorite jokes, and capabilities relative to heavy machinery?

So one morning I wrote mine on a Tops Docket Gold legal pad at around 37,000 feet on my way to Seattle. It has become an aspiration statement for me. **If this is what I want people to think and say when I'm gone, what daily decisions must I make to get there?**

Oprah Winfrey once documented the last days of a young mother dying of cancer who used her final months to make videotaped messages for her young children, leaving behind words of wisdom about living—about falling in love, doing laundry, writing thank-you notes, steaming artichokes, creating in the process a primer about how to navigate the big and little things of life—which I came to realize I've been unconsciously doing for my daughters with my blog, 37days, and now this book. She and her husband took their children to Disney World and beyond during those final months, anxious to imprint the experiences in the children's minds for all time, knowing she wouldn't be with them long.

To live in hearts we leave behind is not to die. —**Thomas Campbell**

After the young mother died, Oprah invited her family back to the show. Thinking they would comment on the amazing trips they made together, Oprah asked the children about their best memories of their mother. The little girl quietly responded: "I remember once when my mom asked me to get her a bowl of Cheerios and we ate them together."

It isn't the big things. It's those little ones.

My life was irretrievably altered when my father died on May 12, 1980, too young at fifty-three, an age that seemed old to my teenage self. It is shockingly young, naturally, as I grow nearer to it myself. If my network of friends met the same fate, most of them would already be dead. I now realize how utterly cruel it was for him to leave so early.

I was too young then to honor him as he deserved, so here is just a tiny part of the story I have written to him, too many years later:

> *Melvin Lonnie Digh had deep laugh lines when he died because it seems he was always smiling, a crinkly, crooked smile that turns the eyes down slightly at the outside corners. His funeral was standing-room-only at Calvary Baptist Church because he was a giver, and people came from all around, even from Missouri, to give him something back, a nod, a prayer, a salute, to pay respects.*

LET US ENDEAVOR SO TO LIVE THAT WHEN WE COME TO DIE EVEN THE UNDERTAKER WILL BE SORRY.

—**Mark Twain**

> *Daddy was a barber, a real one— the leather-and-porcelain-chair, hot-lather-machine, straight-razor- that-he-sharpened-on-a-leather- razor-strop kind of barber, not the froufrou beauty salon stylist with fancy-smelling products kind. Modern Barber Shop was my after-school refuge—I could feel those steaming-hot towels, smell blue and green tonics in which black plastic combs stood, and wade in piles of hair on the floor.*

> *He was also a "room mother" when I was in elementary school, an oddity for the time, the only man amid a bevy of women icing orange-and-black cupcakes for Halloween parties, and greasing the pig for Field Day.*

> *As a young girl, I would hold hands with him and gently step up onto his always perfectly shined hard black leather wing tip shoes, one socked foot on each shoe, to twirl a bit. He was particular about those shoes, they slept with wooden forms inside them, so dancing on them was an honor as well as a pleasure. Many afternoons he treated me to a fake shave at the barbershop, lathering up my face, holding me captive under hot towels wrapped efficiently like a white cinnamon roll.*

When Mama wanted to keep me from leaving at sixteen to live in Sri Lanka as an exchange student, it was Daddy who said simply "She's going." An adventurer caught in a small town, he and I plotted to return to Sri Lanka to celebrate my college graduation. He didn't make it to that day, to my wedding, to many moments of my needing him, or to the births of my two girls, for whom he is an abstract, an ancient ancestor, a photograph, a cipher.

A thin rail of a man named Leon used to work in Modern Barber Shop—young, second chair from the door. When Daddy sold the barber shop because of his heart, Leon left to be a policeman. Five years later, as the processional with the last bits of Daddy and over 200 cars made their way to the cemetery, there on a traffic island, alone, standing at attention in full dress uniform, one white-gloved hand over his eye at a full salute, the other holding his hat over his heart, was Leon, a moving tribute to a small-town barber who was so much more than that.

Live an 37 days Irresistible obituary

To live in hearts we

leave behind is not to die.

Daddy died a death that began with his first heart attack at forty-seven and ended when liquid filled his lungs because his heart couldn't pump it out fast enough. His life and his death have made me who I am. To be honest, I would prefer to be less of a person if it kept him here longer.

Decades, Daddy. You've been here all along.

His death at fifty-three in 1980 is the fulcrum around which my life moves. Or perhaps that's not exactly it. Perhaps it is a rivet on which things hinge. No, a grommet through which everything else is laced? Yes, since that would imply a hole, I think that's it. Like Fermat's last theorem, it will take me 357 years to work it through. I suppose we all have something like that to puzzle out, fill up, patch, lace shut.

[It's time to start living the life you've imagined. —**Henry James**]

37 Days: Do It Now Challenge

Life isn't about the big things—the professional achievements, blah, blah, blah—but the little ones, the bowls of Cheerios together, hot-lather shaves, the time in the sandbox, your God-given talent with heavy machinery, the tiny adventures of everyday life. Who are the important people in your life and what do you hope they say about you when you're gone? Live an extraordinary and irresistible life to ensure that when you die, the people who are left have the feeling that with your passing the world has become a duller place.

✐ Action:

Focused free-write:

- Spend ten minutes writing the obituary you want, so you are not just a number or just a name, but a story.

- Write it from three perspectives: As you would like your family to write it, your closest friends, and people in your community or at work.

- What do you want each of those groups to say about you when you're gone? What would they remember most vividly about you? What stories would they tell? What laughs would they recall? Not the big things—the professional achievements—but the little things: the way you smiled at them, that they could always count on you to come to their ballet recitals, the time you offered to babysit so they could go see comedian George Wallace perform. . . .

☼ Movement:

For the next thirty-seven days—and every day—live that obituary.

Epilogue
Every Day Is Day One: Do It for 37 Days

I will not die an unlived life . . . I choose to inhabit my days, to allow my living to open me . . . I choose to risk my significance. —**Dawna Markova**

Every summer I used to disappear from my business life to indulge my secret life as an artist. For most of August, you could find me at the Penland School of Crafts in the mountains of North Carolina, surrounded by people who aren't closet artists like me but bold ones. I studied hand bookbinding, learned to use antique printing presses, and carved woodblock prints.

At Penland I was surrounded by jewelers, blacksmiths, ceramicists, book artists, weavers—passionate people. They knew what they needed to do in life, and they did it with great energy and unique vision. I ventured into that world like a child, ecstatic in the creative sparks from those around me.

But one year I was troubled. At dinner the first night, people described what they do. "I'm a potter," one said. "Sculptor," announced the next. "I'm a management consultant focusing on diversity and structural inequality." Silence.

By breakfast, I had revised my statement. "Writer," I said, and everyone nodded appreciatively. I recognized the moment I said it that it was also a definition that gave me greater clarity, passion, and unique vision.

I always learned a lot about beauty and art at Penland, but I learned much more that year from jeweler Ken Bova, a faculty member. One day he pulled from his wallet a piece of well-folded old paper. On it he had listed goals he developed while considering an earlier career change:

1. Have fun.

2. Make money.

3. Provide for the future.

4. Contribute to the field.

5. Meet new people.

6. Travel.

7. Have leisure time.

8. Learn.

9. Teach what I learn.

"What I've learned is that if some project or opportunity meets four or more of these criteria, it is always successful in some way. Three or less and it's usually a bust," he explained. "For example, if some event allows me to make money, travel, and learn, but that's all, I come home feeling *So what?* I made no new friends, didn't have fun, didn't contribute anything, and just spent four days traveling to someplace I didn't really get to know. I feel my energy was misplaced."

The clarity I had found at Penland made me think about how I was—or wasn't—tying together vision, goals, and action, so once I got home, I created my own criteria for making decisions:

1. **Gut.** Do I feel heaviness or lightness when I think about saying yes?

2. **Fun**. Will doing this help me consciously enjoy life, savor it, and live it fully?

3. **Learn and teach what I learn.** Will I grow intellectually, emotionally, physically, and spiritually, and be able to pass on that learning?

4. **Relationships.** Will I make new friends and be reminded of the value of my current and long-term relationships?

5. **Commitment to family.** Can I minimize time away from home or take my family with me?

6. **Contribute to the field.** Do I believe this project adds to the general knowledge of my art and chosen discipline?

7. **Meaning.** Will doing this make a difference in my life or in the lives of others?

8. **Make money and provide for the future**. Does this allow me to value my work, time, and energy and help me be financially responsible?

9. **Real.** Will I be saying things that need to be said and that I truly believe?

10. **Kindness.** Will doing this truly help someone else?

Now I make sure a potential project meets at least four, hopefully six, of these criteria. You'll have your own criteria. Write them down. If a project, job, or opportunity doesn't meet your criteria, perhaps you should save your energy, vision, and passion for creating another kind of art.

We're all asked to do a lot of things. We probably say yes to things that we wish we hadn't. Here's your four-part challenge: (1) Create your list. (2) Fold it up into a tiny square. (3) Put it in your wallet. (4) When someone calls and asks you to embroider 400 handkerchiefs with a full-color flag of Albania or make 900 brownies in the shape of bookmobiles for a librarian convention, put them on hold, pull out your list to decide if those activities meet your criteria . . . and enjoy having more spare time for the things that do pass the test.

It will free up your thirty-seven days.

What Would You Do with Your 37 Days?

What *are* you doing with your thirty-seven days?

Alfred Adler said we should "trust only movement. Life happens at the level of events, not of words. Trust movement." What, if you did it consistently for thirty-seven days (and perhaps beyond), would create positive vibes, intentional joy, good karma, fantastic direction, and deep expansiveness in your life? What one thing could you do that would start you on the road to greater wholeness, to your real life? Can you do it for just thirty-seven days? Because, as writer Annie Dillard reminds us, "How we spend our days is, of course, how we spend our lives."

The main thing is to keep the main thing the main thing. —**Larry James**

Perhaps it's something simple like cleaning out one drawer every day in your house for thirty-seven days. Perhaps writing one haiku every day for thirty-seven days would break old patterns and help you *see* more. Or eating five fruits and vegetables a day or writing for ten minutes each day or walking for ten minutes a day or writing a postcard to a friend each week. Or pick one of the Do It Now Challenges at the close of each of these stories and do it for thirty-seven days. Whatever it is, however small, do it. Just for thirty-seven days.

That's doable. Decide on It, the Thing You Will Do. And then, do it.

Perhaps it is something you will *stop* doing for thirty-seven days. Stop hiding, stop spending, stop smoking, stop making excuses, stop blaming or judging, stop eating Raspberry Frosted Pop-Tarts with Sprinkles (purely hypothetical example).

Narrow your focus to one thing. One small thing. And just do it for thirty-seven days. Starting today, not next Tuesday, not after you finish off the Honeycrisp apples dipped lovingly in hot caramel sauce, not after that next trip to Bashkortostan or Albuquerque, not after you finish alphabetizing the canned goods in the root cellar or sharpening your grapefruit spoons, but Right Now. Go ahead—deepen, change, inhabit your life fully for the next thirty-seven days. Then start again. Every day *is* day one, a gift.

(While you're at it, answer this question: Why are we so willing to disappoint ourselves by not following through on such an easy commitment?)

As Max Bristol wrote on the back of his jacket in junior high school—a message of great comfort as he ran past me during the mandatory one-mile run in gym class—"a man [and presumably a woman, I must add] can endure anything as long as he knows there is an end to it."

In 2003 the man whose journey sparked this writing was diagnosed with lung cancer. Boyce died thirty-seven days later.

Make use of the next thirty-seven days. It's important. *Every day is day one, a gift.*

Life is a verb:

> Say yes.
>
> Be generous.
>
> Speak up.
>
> Love more.
>
> Trust yourself.
>
> Slow down.

[It's never too late to be what you might have been. **—George Eliot**]

What will you do for the next thirty-seven days?

What will you do with your one wild and precious life?

Risk your significance.

Dive Deeper, Read Further

Reading itself is an intentional practice—it provides solitude, attentiveness, an entrance into someone else's world, and the chance to deepen your own perspective. These are my top choices for good reads to further illuminate each of the six practices for intentional living. You can find additional reading lists as well as a reference list of all those mentioned or quoted in this book on my Web site at www.pattidigh.com.

Intensity: Say Yes

James Carse wrote a small, significant book titled *Finite and Infinite Games* that serves as grounding for much of what I think about. Finite games are games we play to win, while infinite games are those we play to learn. The distinction is an important, life-changing one. Also check out another of his books, *Breakfast at the Victory: The Mysticism of Ordinary Experience.*

In his book *Flow: The Psychology of Optimal Experience,* Mihaly Csikszentmihalyi explores what makes our lives worthwhile, noting the hallmarks of those states of "optimal experience" when we are so engaged that we are out of time, in what he calls "flow." Exploring how we get to those states can help get us back there.

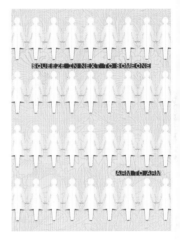

Ellen Langer has spent much of her life examining what it means to escape the banality of mindlessness. In her book *Mindfulness,* she explores how we experience the world (in categories) and how those categories begin to limit what we see and experience. We live mindlessly so much of the time—how would our lives deepen and intensify if we could pay attention instead?

As a redheaded child myself, I could have no greater hero than Pippi. Sweden's Astrid Lindgren brought me Pippi Longstocking, my first strong female role model in the form of a spectacular young girl who says yes to life in a big way.

The Art of Possibility: Transforming Professional and Personal Life is another of those books that came along in my life at the right time. A lively work by Rosamund Stone Zander and Benjamin Zander, it explores cultivating possibility in our lives and provides tools for transformation.

Inclusion: Be Generous

We are tribal beings. We see the world in terms of us and them. We sort people and put them in categories. David Berreby's fascinating look at this phenomenon—and how it helps and hinders us—is called *Us and Them: Understanding Your Tribal Mind.*

If you have children, know children, or were once a child yourself, you will love Todd Parr's brightly colored, simple, fantastic books about difference. My favorites are *The Okay Book* and *It's Okay to Be Different.*

One of the best books ever written about race in America is Richard Powers's extraordinary novel *The Time of Our Singing.* He is brilliant, and the novel is exquisitely written. Read this book.

LET IT BE A BARN

Reading novels and memoirs by a wide variety of writers is a fantastic way to put yourself in someone else's world, to see from their vantage point and not just your own. You can find a long "bridging differences" reading list on my Web site, www.pattidigh.com. Create a book stack that takes you to new places, even uncomfortable ones.

And while you're at it, just go ahead and read everything Pema Chödrön has written.

Poetry: Find and read Philip Larkin's poem "The Mower" and the exquisite poetry of Naomi Shihab Nye.

Integrity: Speak Up

Getting to Maybe: How the World Is Changed by Frances Westley, Brenda Zimmerman, and Michael Patton is one of the best books I've read in a long time. We change the world not by looking at discrete elements, but by understanding the complex relationships among them. This work will change your way of thinking about making changes in communities, businesses, and the world.

Malcolm Gladwell's *The Tipping Point: How Little Things Can Make a Big Difference* was an important book for me. As one reviewer noted, Gladwell gives ideas the quality of action. This is a book that makes you think—and about everything.

Rushworth Kidder knows that ethical dilemmas are not really choices between right and wrong, but between right and right. His work centers on the choices we face daily, as outlined in his book *How Good People Make Tough Choices: Resolving the Dilemmas of Ethical Living*.

Parker Palmer is a favorite of mine. Each of his compelling, soulful books resonates with me, and particularly *The Courage to Teach,* which focuses on the self in teaching. And we are all teachers, aren't we?

Paul Watzlawick's *Change: Principles of Problem Formation and Problem Resolution* is not the kind of book you'd take to the beach with you, but his discussion of first- and second-order change has been vitally important to me. Sometimes the action we need to take is the exact opposite of what we think we need.

Intimacy: Love More

I love writer Natalie Goldberg's spirit. Her *Writing Down the Bones: Freeing the Writer Within* and *Wild Mind: Living the Writer's Life* take the craft and soul of writing straight into Zen. Paying attention to your own story is a way of loving more.

Jack Maguire's *The Power of Personal Storytelling: Spinning Tales to Connect with Others* is a great example of using story to build relationship with others—and with yourself.

I was stuck in an airport one day for eight hours, and in that whole time I didn't look up once from Brian McNaught's book *Sex Camp.* In it, he fictionalizes the experience of the (real) Annual Workshop on Sexuality, posing issues about human sexuality that need to be faced and that we usually avoid.

Parker Palmer's beautiful book *A Hidden Wholeness: The Journey Toward an Undivided Life* shows us how to rejoin soul and role, how to explore our true self, how to be alone together, how to live the questions, and how to weave community in a wounded world.

Personal coach Cheryl Richardson's book *Take Time for Your Life* came into my life at just the right time. Her concept of "extreme self-care," in a world in which self-care can be viewed as selfish, is an important one for all of us—and particularly for women, who are usually seen as caregivers to others and taught not to be selfish from an early age.

Poetry: Derek Wolcott's "Love After Love," Mary Oliver's "Wild Geese," Marianne Williamson's "A Return to Love," and—one of my very favorites (poem *and* poet)—Billy Collins's "Litany." Oh, stop resisting and just go ahead and read everything Billy Collins has ever written.

Intuition: Trust Yourself

My, how I love this book: *Art and Fear: Observations on the Perils (and Rewards) of Artmaking* by David Bayles and Ted Orland. In it they ask us: "What is your art really about? Where is it going? What stands in the way of getting it there?" I'd say we could substitute the word *life* for the word *art* and ask the very same questions.

My friend Jack Condon introduced me to *The Atlas of Experience* by Louise van Swaaij and Jean Klare. It is a lovely, quirky book that taps into my deep love of cartography and mapping, a book in which the authors have created beautiful maps of the human experience. You'll find the Isle of Forgetfulness, the Sea of Possibilities, the Ocean of Peace, the Stream of Inspiration—all in map form. I love this book.

Sogyal Rinpoche's *The Tibetan Book of Living and Dying* has reframed for me what death is—and, by extension, what life is. And what living is.

Dan Pink's *A Whole New Mind: Moving from the Information Age to the Conceptual Age* was a great affirmation of what I felt intuitively: We need different skills to survive in the world of today and tomorrow. All our left-brain skills aren't enough anymore; we need new aptitudes, and this book helps explain what those are. My haiku book review of it:

> Left brain and right brain
> which side is most important?
> the artsy side wins.

The Three Questions and *Zen Shorts* are two children's books that I give to adults. Beautifully illustrated and written by Jon Muth, they get to the heart of what it means to trust, love, and connect.

In her wonderful book *Improv Wisdom: Don't Prepare, Just Show Up,* Patricia Ryan Madson teaches us that to practice the basic rules of improvisational theater is to walk a path toward a spiritually fulfilling life, and that to be completely present and "show up" is the key.

The Zen of Creativity: Cultivating Your Artistic Life by John Daido Loori is very, um, Zen-like. Full of naturalness, spontaneity, and playfulness, it's a beautiful look at what it is to be creative.

And just in case you are one of the eight people on earth who haven't yet read it, Julia Cameron's *The Artist's Way: A Spiritual Path to Higher Creativity* is a classic for good reason.

Intention: Slow Down

In his small book *On Directing Film,* director David Mamet focuses on what it takes to make a movie, but his lessons about intention and the direction of intention struck me as so powerful for living, too. Every action must feed into the spine of the film. So, too, with life.

I read Richard Leider's *Repacking Your Bags: Lighten Your Load for the Rest of Your Life* in its entirety on an airplane flight from Australia. You could probably save the airfare and do it at home. He asks what we have in all the "bags" we carry around—our work bag, our parent bag, our friend bag, and more—and asks us to consider if all those things make us happy. An important book and metaphor for me, particularly when I'm feeling weighed down by responsibilities, missed deadlines, and more. My haiku book review of it:

> *A bag full of stuff*
> *does all this make you happy?*
> *repack and be light.*

Teacher Ron Clark's rules in the classroom, *The Essential 55: An Award-Winning Educator's Rules for Discovering the Successful Student in Every Child,* is a powerful look at setting high expectations and helping children reach them, even those children everyone has written off. There are great implications for this in life beyond school. An engaging, important book.

My older daughter, Emma, first introduced me to Japanese manga and graphic novels. There is something compelling about the art form as a way of exploring our life's stories, slowing them down, frame by frame. Scott McCloud is the man to read on this topic. His *Understanding Comics: The Invisible Art* is a comic book about comic books in which he explains how comics are composed, read, and understood. Teachers, parents—all of us, really—should read this book.

Important concept alert: In *The Path of Least Resistance: Learning to Become the Creative Force in Your Own Life,* Robert Fritz argues that just as water follows the structure of the land, moving around natural obstructions and seeking the path of least resistance, so do we move around the structures of our lives. His advice is to modify the structures themselves, releasing the creative energy inside us to become generative and not simply reactive.

I so love this book that I read it every year. I so love it, in fact, that I've pasted my own photograph on the back cover of my copy of it, as if I actually wrote it myself. Anne Lamott's *Bird by Bird: Some Instructions on Writing and Life* is a must-read.

In *Let Your Life Speak: Listening to the Voice of Vocation,* Parker Palmer quietly challenges us to "live the life that wants to live in us"; to create the quiet, trusting conditions that allow a soul to speak its truth; and to tune out preconceived ideas about vocation so we can hear the call of our wild souls.

Poet Rainer Maria Rilke's *Letters to a Young Poet* was an important book for me: "Go into yourself and test the deeps in which your life takes rise; at its source you will find the answer to the question whether you *must* create." As was James Joyce's *A Portrait of the Artist as a Young Man.*

Poetry: May Sarton's "Now I Become Myself" and Mary Oliver's "When Death Comes."

Artists

The artist is not a special kind of man; every man is a special kind of artist.
—Sri Coomaraswamy [And, one supposes, every woman, too.]

The fantastic art in this book started with an e-mail from a woman named Donna B. Miller. "I made this card to carry with me and remind myself of one of your essays," she explained, "and I thought you might enjoy having a copy, too."

The image she had attached to her e-mail was beautiful. I printed it and dashed out to do errands. Then as I sat in the driveway, it hit me: *Why couldn't this book feature art created by the people who actually read my blog, like Donna?*

I posted a note asking if anyone was interested. Remarkably, over 120 pieces of art came flooding in within two weeks. As my friend, Mike Wagner, put it, this was the literary and artistic equivalent of a community barn-raising. I was—and am—overwhelmed by the art that was created and, even more, by the generosity of spirit that sparked each artists' participation. To each, my deepest thanks.

We told the artists that only 37 pieces of artwork could be used in the book, but once the publisher saw what had been submitted, the decision was made: They would use them all and print the book in four-color to fully showcase what these artists had done. And so, every single contribution is featured on the inside covers of this book, and most are showcased within its pages (see list below). I was so touched by the back-story of the artworks—what the artists saw in the essays they illustrated, how they chose to interpret them, and what process they used. Those back-stories, along with images of the artworks, are online at www.pattidigh.com.

The artists include:

Tamera Abaté: pages 19, 172

Elizabeth Beck (www.ebeckartist.blogspot.com and www.flickr.com/photos/ebeck): page 23

Nancy H. Blackwelder: pages 96, 214

Shawn Borror: pages 26, 165

Dan Bowman (http://thetimesink.net/Blog): page 134

Julia C. Burr (http://jcburrdesigns.com): page 158

Mary Campbell: pages 29, 137, 147, 186, 225 (both)

Kim Cromwell and her brother, **Bob** (www.kimcromwell.com): page 184

Hanz L. Dalken: page 183

Ruth M. Davis: pages xiv, 105

Sarah Davis, painter, Bristol ME: page 148

Sharon L. Delman (http://lifesrandomwalk.blogspot.com): pages 107, 164

Connie Dooley: pages 113, 114 (both)

Denise Doupnik (digital materials courtesy of Maya, Bren Boone, Krista Mettler and On Designs at http://scrapbookgraphics.com): pages 106, 130

Jay Fields (http://jayfieldsandcompany.com): page 162

Lie Fhung, with her original drawing and digital elements from Ztampf.com (http://ztampf.com and http://liefhung.com): pages 50, 120, 181

Aurora Fox (http://foxyartstudio.blogspot.com): pages 22, 49

T. J. Goerlitz, shrine embellished with handmade polymer clay beads by Kelli Schwert (www.studiomailbox.com): pages 115, 136, 221

Katie Green: page 48

Sorrow Grey: page 104

David Guinn: page 133

Guzzisue (http://TravelFibreandThread.blogspot.com): page 156

Rick Hamrick, a Sufi mystic trapped in the body of a corporate IT manager (http://hamguin-nohiding.blogspot.com): page 16

Linda Hanlon, background by Kathryn Balint, edging and overlays by Karen Aicken, font American Writer by Ronna Penner of www.scrapadelic.com (http://lindas-lemonade-stand.blogspot.com): page 175, 223

Rebecca Hansen: pages 36, 86

Thomai Hatsios: page 189

Claire McDonald Herne (http://spygirl.typepad.com): pages 126, 207

Stephanie Hilvitz (http://rodrigvitzstyle.typepad.com): page 188

June Zinn Hobby: page 89

Heather L. Holle, Brooklyn Center, MN (www.alifesosimple.blogspot.com): page 161, 163

Claire Hummel (www.shoomlah.com): page 60

Kate Iredale (http://kateiredale.typepad.com): pages 9, 173

Leah Piken Kolidas, Boston, MA (www.BlueTreeArtGallery.com): pages 103, 150, 185, 190

Shelley Krause (http://butwait.blogspot.com): page 194

Jennifer Krentz (http://sayingyes.typepad.com): page 31, 179, 220

Cindy Jones Lantier (www.lantier.org): pages 33, 57, 178, 215

Callie Leone: page 34

Tami Levin (www.lemontreetales.com and www.101fairylane.com): page 95

Victoria Lipp, using Adobe Photoshop Element 5.0, personal photo, Microsoft Sans Serif font and various definitions for the word 'art' from http://urbandictionary.com (http://mizamigosmumblings.blogspot.com): page 40

Esther Louie, photo by **Nick Beymer:** page 63

Brenda Zimmerman Lux: page 20

Kellee Magee: page 37

Lori Marefka (http://bluegirlredstate.typepad.com): page 143

Kate McGovern: pages 39, 82, 99, 193

Sharon McNeill (www.moonshinecards.com and www.sharonmcneill.com): page 44

Donna B. Miller (http://donnabmiller.typepad.com/my_weblog): pages iii, viii, 209

Nicole Minkin (www.NicoleMinkin.com): pages 55, 222

Tammy Moore (http://digicollage.wordpress.com): pages 119, 213

Liz Gill Neilson (www.lizgillneilson.com): page 85

Nina Newton (www.mamaslittletreasures.com): page 112

Judy Rapp: pages 205, 208

David Robinson, with **Lora Abernathy** (www.davidrobinsoncreative.com): pages 15, 46

Ellouise Schoettler (www.ellouisestory.com and http://ellouisestory.blogspot.com): page 17

Mahima Shrestha (www.meetmahima.wordpress.com): pages 73, 196, 216

Jim Slatton: page 111

Laura Stinson: pages 24, 68, 98, 176

Tony Stowers: page 197

Jan Stovall, with a little help from the late **Peter Alsberg:** page 27

Marisa Taylor: page 121

Wyanne Thompson (www.wyanne.com): page 92

Ann Torrence (www.anntorrence.com): page 146

Ramona Vaughn, using digital art by Christine Borgfeld and Roberta D'Achille: pages 70, 84, 87, 155

Sherri L. Vilov: pages 72, 75, 116

Adele Wayman (http://adelewayman.com): page 66

Trini L. Wenninger (www.PrairieMania.com): page 100

Mat Wojcik and **Megan Lane** (http://amonthoftodays.blogspot.com): page 129

Alice Woodside (www.woodsidecountrystore.com): page 80

Additional artwork on pages 125, 131, 140, 142, and 224 courtesy of the author.

Permissions

With gratitude to these writers who have made their words available for use in this book.

Fidler, Marybeth. "The Bumble Bee," unpublished poem. Used by permission of the poet.

Granfort, Liz. "Elephant Love," unpublished poem. Used by permission of the poet.

Haught, Kaylin. "God Says Yes to Me," from *The Palm of Your Hand*, 1995. Used by permission of the poet.

Hollies, David. "Lost and Found," unpublished poem. Used by permission of the poet.

Huyler, Ann, Obituary of Miss Lavern Lorenz. Used by permission of the author.

Kane, Christine. "The Good You Do," © 2004 Lee Baby Sims Music, ASCAP, from the CD *Right Outta Nowhere*, www.christinekane.com. Used by permission.

Maciel, Marilyn. "clothesline" and "the stranger," unpublished poems. Used by permission of the poet.

Matthews, Sebastian. "Undressing the Muse," first appeared in *We Generous*, Red Hen Press (2007), and is archived at From the Fishouse, an online poetry archive. Used by permission of the poet.

Gratitudes

Many people, other than the author, contribute to the making of a book, from the first person who had the bright idea of alphabetic writing through the inventor of movable type to the lumberjacks who felled the trees that were pulped for its printing. It is not customary to acknowledge the trees themselves, though their commitment is total.

—Richard Forsyth and Roy Rada

Let's imagine that all learning takes place in a dense, primordial forest. Turn off the highway and into the woods and every once in a blue moon, there is a clearing just big enough for a brilliant sky or glowing orb to shine through onto a minuscule circular spot on the forest floor, its translucence revealing flowers working hard to bloom between dark trees. That tiny shot of light has a big job, illuminating the way, one circle at a time. So many people have been that light for me in my life. It would be impossible to list all their names here. I hope they know. I hope I've left no doubt. Yes, you.

A few merit special mention for helping this book take root in that forest.

My father's death at age fifty-three provided my first lessons about how precious life is. It was too high a price to pay for that insight, but I thank Daddy—Melvin Digh—for it, and for so much more. You are missing and forever missed.

To Mama—Frances Digh Hardin—thank you for expanding my world immensely by letting me go to Sri Lanka as an exchange student when I was sixteen, even though it scared you; for always tucking notes into my suitcase so they'd fall out when I unpacked at Girl Scout camp; and much more. To my big brother—Mickey Digh—thanks for putting up with me (and, um, thanks for helping me put out the flames when I set my curtains on fire that time). And to my stepfather—Boyce Hardin—it was your death thirty-seven days after your diagnosis that sparked this writing: My gratitude for revealing the urgency to speak in my own voice, finally.

To Mary and Frank Ptak, my thanks for your ongoing support, and for providing the universe with your little boy, John, so I could find him. To Aunt Joan Fuller, your love and support mean so much to us. And to Victoria "Nana" Ptak, vast memories.

To others whose too-young deaths have framed existence for me—Sheridan Simon, Alan Fuller, Philip Sheremeta, Tara Burgess, and Meta Racine-Bowers—my deepest regrets at your leaving are shot through with my greatest learning from your living.

I'm reminded of what the Quakers call a "clearness committee," a group that helps a person gain clarity of vision. There are three "vice chairs" of my clearness committee, though they don't know they hold that title: My business and creative partner, David Robinson, one of the most incredible people on the planet,who makes me laugh and think so hard my head explodes (and his partner, Lora "S. B." Abernathy, who in her infinite wisdom is responsible for us working together in the first place); Richard Rudman who all the way from New Zealand (with its "extensive roading network") asks me the best questions I've ever been asked—you

> Praise the bridge that carried you over.
> **—George Colman**

are such an amazing treasure to me; and my dear Eliav Zakay from Israel, one of the wisest people I've ever met, even if he can't kayak without falling into the water. Eliav reveals me to myself in ways that make me laugh and think more deeply. To David, Richard, and Eliav, my deepest gratitude and love.

Special thanks also to Rosemary Lauth and Gay Clyburn, my beautiful and mean "Marshall Sisters" who never blink, no matter what I ask or say; Richard and Amanda Ashley, both of whom have everything to do with why I do the work I do; Charles Hampden-Turner, whom I consider my intellectual mentor even when my taking up residence firmly in the quotidian might cause him to disavow that nomenclature; Richard Harris and Dorianne Galarnyk, who open their gorgeous home in New Mexico to me; and Howard Holden, who will chide me if I say something mushy like I love you.

To those associated with the Summer Institute for Intercultural Communication, the women of W2W, my Guilford buddies, the Gubes, Kim Cromwell, Lori Buckwalter, teachers Louise Smith and Mary Rockett, and Mary Castagnoli in Fort Dodge who is literally a gem in a mine, my gratitude.

I feel such support from far-flung friends like Tony Frost (South Africa); Kichom Hayashi (Japan); Hilde "Macht das licht aus" Regnier (Germany); Luiz Ciocchi (Brazil); Johnnie Moore (UK); Ajith Colonne and Nilanthi Jayatilake (Sri Lanka); Dave Pollard (Canada); Yaron Roth (Israel); Meg "M. T. S." Parry (Dubai); Jack Yan (New Zealand); and Andrew Rixon, who all the way from Down Under has a special way of interrogating so you don't feel interrogated but enlightened from the inside out.

To those who have buoyed me by commenting on my blog, my deepest thanks for that engagement. Lines are blurred between real and virtual life as we redefine community together. You may never understand the full impact of your encouragement, but please know it has made big ripples in my pond.

Nikki Hardin, publisher of *Skirt! Magazine,* first approached me about turning the essays on my blog, 37days, into a book—my thanks for that bigger vision. At Globe Pequot Press's skirt! Books division, editor Mary Norris survived my many "requests" with great grace, humoring me when I just needed to put a lid on my inner-control-freak-with-typography-issues. To Imee Curiel, who shepherded the project; Diana Nuhn, the book's designer; Laura Jorstad, copy editor extraordinaire; marketing manager Jaclyn Wilson; and publicist Bob Sembiante— thank you for delivering this book into the world.

Brooks Townes and Pam Ruatto greatly enhanced this manuscript with their wise guidance. Faculty and students from the Great Smokies Writing Program continue to workshop my scribblings with great insight, beginning with Sebastian Matthews who beautifully asked me three questions: "What is your occasion for speech? Where do you stand telling this story? Why are you the one to tell it?"

My thanks also to Nina Graybill; artist Donna B. Miller, who sparked the idea of gathering art from around the world as illustrations; and the artists themselves who contributed such beautiful works as gifts to the universe.

Hannah Kim and Michael Scholtz keep me healthy. I promise I'm taking my Chinese herbs every morning, and doing 419 walking lunges every day. Really.

As readers of my blog know, I would simply be remiss if I didn't thank Johnny Depp and Billy Collins. To each of them, a private message: *Call me.*

Finally, I offer everything and more to my human survival units: John, Emma, and Tess Ptak. I have surely followed my bliss by making this life in the world with them. Amazing Johnny, thanks for always catching me when I'm falling. The greatest thanks go to you—for opening and holding the space for me to write and think, and for keeping me supplied with little tubs of Fage yogurt before I up and went vegan on you.

To my daughters, Emma and Tess: You are my best teachers and the major inhabitants of all the chambers of my heart and the entire solar system of my soul. This book was written just for you.

Lastly, to Sim Sim, who has sat purring in my lap for the writing of three books. May she be there for the next three.

Writing this was harder than writing the book, because there were so many people I wanted to acknowledge by name—and so few trees whose total commitment I wished to require.

Be in touch, OK?

Love,

Patti Digh

Asheville, NC

About the Author

Patti Digh (pronounced *dye*) was born in a small town in North Carolina in the late 1950s; spent the '60s listening to Bobby Sherman, wearing Peter Max hot pants, and campaigning to be class president; the '70s reading *Tiger Beat* magazine, playing Pee Wee football, idolizing Johnny Unitas, and living in Sri Lanka; the '80s at a Quaker college, living in Munich, listening to Joan Armatrading and Jethro Tull, surviving graduate school, and sailing around the world; the '90s filling up a passport, falling deeply in love, having her first child, and writing her first book; and this decade writing more books, having her second child, stalking Billy Collins and Johnny Depp, and finding her voice and passion at long last.

Patti has written two business books and more than a hundred published articles on global leadership and diversity. Her comments have appeared on PBS and in the *Wall Street Journal, Fortune,* the *New York Times, USA Today,* the *Washington Post,* and the *London Financial Times,* among other publications. Patti is a co-founder of The Circle Project (www.thecircleproject.com), an international consulting and training firm that helps organizations and the people in them work more effectively and authentically together across differences. She has dedicated her life to helping people understand the personal and societal costs of racism and other isms that minimize and exclude people.

But no matter what else she is and does, her most important job is being a mother to her two daughters. Patti and her husband, John Ptak (aka Mr. Brilliant), live in the beautiful mountain town of Asheville, North Carolina, with daughters Emma and Tess, their dog Blue, two cats whose furniture-scratching proclivities don't merit their being mentioned by name (oh, alright, all is forgiven—they are Sim Sim and Callie), and, until the recent Unfortunate Incident, a dwarf hamster named Maggie.

Patti continues to write her blog, 37days, from which this book emerged. You can read her essays there at www.pattidigh.com or contact her at patti@pattidigh.com. She'd love to hear from you.

Did You Think You'd Get Out of This Book Without a Final Assignment?

Create a list of twenty people who have helped you in your life and write one or two sentences that capture the gift they have given you, as in "Thank you for teaching me how to whistle,"or "Thank you for asking how you can support me," or "Thank you for separating my frozen foods from the rest of my groceries," or "Thank you for changing how I view turbulence." Then contact them this week by e-mail, a letter, a call, just to say thanks and tell them how they have helped you.

Do it now.

Tomorrow might be too late.